THE COMPLETE
Dictionary
&
Thesaurus

THE COMPLETE
Dictionary
& Thesaurus

CHANCELLOR
PRESS

First published in 2001 by Bounty Books,
a division of Octopus Publishing Group Ltd

This edition published in 2005 by Bounty Books,
a division of Octopus Publishing Group Ltd
Endeavour House,
189 Shaftesbury Avenue,
London WC2H 8JY
www.octopusbooks.co.uk

An Hachette UK Company
www.hachette.co.uk

Reprinted 2014

Copyright © Octopus Publishing Group Ltd

The material in this book has previously appeared in:
First Dictionary (Bounty, Octopus Publishing Group Ltd, 1999)
First Thesaurus (Bounty, Octopus Publishing Group Ltd, 1999)

ISBN: 978-0-753727-12-6

A CIP catalogue record for this book is available from the British Library

Printed and bound in China

CONTENTS

PART 1

DICTIONARY

How to use your dictionary

A dictionary is a book of words

Everyone who has helped to make this book hopes that you will find it clear and useful.

You can use a dictionary to see:

- how words are spelt
- what words mean
- how words are used

Many of the words have pictures that help to show what the words mean.

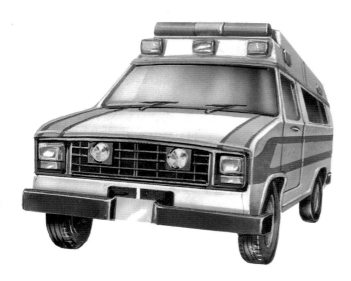

The alphabet

A dictionary is a list of words in alphabetical order. This is the alphabet:

ABCDEFGHIJKLMNOPQRSTUVWXYZ

Words that begin with A come before those beginning with B. Words that begin with B come before those beginning with C, and so on.

In each letter, the words are listed in alphabetical order. For example:

care

careful

careless

carpet

Spelling

Some letters in the spelling of a word are silent. This means that they are used in the spelling but you don't say them. For example:

hour, where we don't say the h

write, where we don't say the w

Grammar

After the main entry word we tell you about the grammar of the word. To make this dictionary easy to use, we only show noun, verb and adjective:

crawl VERB

crayon NOUN

crooked ADJECTIVE

8

If a word can be used in more than one grammatical way, then the main entry word is repeated:

drill NOUN a tool for making holes in things.

drill VERB to make a hole in something.

After the main entry word, for some words we tell you more about their grammar:

calf NOUN (PLURAL calves)

big ADJECTIVE (bigger, biggest)

bite VERB (biting, bit, bitten)

Definitions

The main part of the dictionary entry is the definition. This gives you the meaning of the word. For example:

microscope NOUN an instrument that you look through which makes very small objects appear bigger.

If the word has more than one meaning, then these are separated by numbers:

sponge NOUN **1** something you wash with that soaks up water. **2** a light cake.

Examples

These show you how to use many of the words. They are written in *italic* in the text.

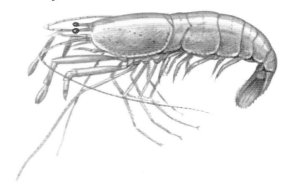

Finding out about words

Some entries have the word *See*.
This tells you to go to a particular word to find out more about it:

bought *See* **buy**. *We bought a new car yesterday.*

This means that you should look at the word **buy** to find out more about the word **bought**.

We have also included many words that we use to talk about language. Examples are:

adjective, adverb, comma, full stop, noun, synonym and verb.

a b c d e f g h i j k l m n o p q r s t u v w x y z

a, an one. *A dog. An egg.*

about on the subject of. *We talked about our holiday.*

above higher than. *The picture is above the television.*

abroad to a foreign country.

absent ADJECTIVE not here, not present. *Jason is absent today because he is ill.*

accident NOUN something, especially something bad, that happens by chance.

accident

ache VERB (aching, ached) to feel a pain for a long time. *My legs ache.*

acorn NOUN the nut that is the fruit of an oak tree. *The huge oak grew from a tiny acorn.*

acrobat NOUN a person who is skilled at walking along high wires or at doing difficult jumps. *The acrobats put on a breathtaking display.*

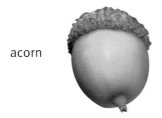

acorn

across from one side of something to the other. *Walk across a road.*

act VERB **1** to play a part in a play or film. **2** to behave.

active ADJECTIVE moving about, busy, energetic.

actor NOUN a person who plays a part in a play or film. *The film we saw on TV had a really good actor in it.*

add VERB to put something together with another thing. *If you add 2 and 3 you get 5.*

address NOUN (plural addresses) the number or name of your house, the name of your road and the town where you live.

address

adult NOUN a person who is grown up, not a child.

adventure NOUN an activity that is unusual and exciting. *Ali's first trip in an aeroplane was quite an adventure.*

advertisement NOUN an announcement telling you about something that people want to sell you. You can see advertisements on television, in newspapers and on big hoardings in the streets.

aeroplane NOUN a vehicle with wings and engines that flies through the air.

aeroplane

afraid ADJECTIVE **1** frightened because you think something bad is going to happen. **2** sorry. *I'm afraid I've broken it.*

after following in time or order. *After lunch.*

afternoon NOUN the part of the day between lunchtime and evening.

again one more time. *You're becoming better at playing that piece of music – but try it again.*

against 1 touching, next to. *Against the wall.* **2** on the opposite side of. *United are playing against Liverpool.*

age NOUN the number of years that you have lived.

ago before now. *Two days ago.*

agree VERB to think in the same way as someone else. *I agree with Lucy.*

ahead in front of you, in a forward position.

air NOUN the mixture of gases that are around the earth and that we breathe. *We went for a walk in the fresh air.*

aircraft NOUN a flying vehicle with wings and engines. Aeroplanes, gliders and helicopters are all different kinds of aircraft.

airport NOUN a place where aircraft take off and land.

ajar ADJECTIVE slightly open. *The door was ajar.*

alarm

alarm NOUN **1** a bell or flashing light that gives a warning of danger. **2** a sudden feeling of fear.

alarm clock NOUN a clock you can set so it rings to wake you up at a certain time.

alike ADJECTIVE similar. *The twins look alike.*

alive ADJECTIVE living.

all the whole of a group or thing.

alley NOUN a narrow path or street.

alligator NOUN a large dangerous animal that is similar to a crocodile.

ajar

alligator

amphibian

allow VERB to let someone do or have something.

almost very nearly. *Emma is almost one metre tall.*

alone ADJECTIVE not with other people.

along from one end of something to the other. *Walk along the road.*

aloud so that people can hear you.

already before now. *I've already eaten my tea.*

also as well, too. *Three hamsters and also two rabbits.*

although even though. *Although it had started to rain, we still went for a picnic.*

altogether 1 completely. *This new music is altogether different.* **2** as a total. *Thirty matches altogether.*

always at all times.

am *See* **be**. *I am six years old.*

amazing ADJECTIVE very surprising and pleasing.

ambulance NOUN a vehicle for carrying people who are ill or injured to and from hospital.

ambulance

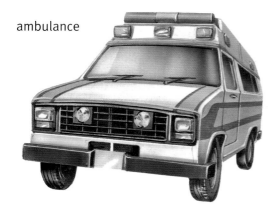

amount NOUN how much there is of something.

amphibian NOUN an animal that can live on land and in water. *Frogs are amphibians.*

an *See* **a**.

and used to join two or more words or groups of words. *Mum and Dad.*

angle NOUN a corner where two lines or surfaces meet.

angry ADJECTIVE (angrier, angriest) having a strong feeling about something that you think is bad or unfair.

animal NOUN a living creature, such as a cat, rabbit or tiger.

ankle NOUN the part of your body where your foot joins your leg.

annoy VERB to make someone feel angry and impatient.

another one more of the same kind. *Another drink.*

answer VERB to say something back to someone who has just asked you something.

answer NOUN **1** what you say or write when you answer a question. **2** something that is given as a result of thinking. *The answer to a maths question.*

ant NOUN a small crawling insect that lives in a large group of similar creatures.

ant

any 1 some of a particular thing. *I don't want to have any chocolate, thanks.* **2** no matter what, who or which kind. *Any size box will do.*

apart at a distance from someone or something. *With his feet apart.*

ape NOUN an animal related to a monkey, with a little or no tail.

appear VERB **1** to come into sight. *Tim suddenly appeared from behind a tree.* **2** to look, to seem.

apple NOUN a round fruit that grows on a tree, with a smooth, red, green or yellow skin. *'Would you like another apple?' asked Miriam.*

April NOUN the fourth month of the year, after March and before May. *Last April it rained almost every day.*

April

apron NOUN a piece of clothing that you wear in front of your normal clothes to stop them from getting dirty. *'Quick, put an apron on before you get paint all over your shirt,' said Carol, crossly.*

aquarium NOUN (plural aquaria or aquariums) a glass or plastic tank that is filled with water and in which you keep fish.

aquarium

are See **be**. *'You are my best friend,' Sally told Sandra.*

aren't = are not. *'You're coming to our home, aren't you?' Callum asked Luke.*

area NOUN **1** a particular part of a city, country, etc. **2** the measure of a surface. *The area of a rectangle is its length multiplied by its width.*

argue VERB (arguing, argued) to disagree with someone, often in an angry way.

arithmetic NOUN adding, subtracting, multiplying and dividing numbers.

arm NOUN one of the two parts of your body that come from your shoulders. *Your hands are at the ends of your arms.*

around situated on every side of something. *A fence around the playground.*

arrive VERB (arriving, arrived) to reach a place, especially at the end of a journey. *Arrive home.*

arrow NOUN a long thin weapon with a sharp point at one end. *Arrows are shot from a bow.*

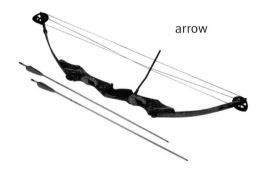

arrow

art NOUN the making of paintings, drawings and sculptures. *My favourite subject at school is art.*

artist NOUN a person who draws, paints or makes other works of art.

as 1 used in comparing things. *As green as grass.* **2** for the reason that, because. *I bought my own diary, as I didn't want to keep borrowing Jack's.*

ask VERB to say something to someone as a question, in order to find out some information. *'What time is the train?' asked Kirsty.*

asleep ADJECTIVE (sleeping).When you are asleep, you are sleeping. *I was asleep in bed when the telephone rang.*

asleep

assembly NOUN (plural assemblies) a group of people who meet together. *School assembly.*

astronaut NOUN a person who travels into space in a spacecraft.

astronaut

at used to show where something is. *At home.*

ate See **eat**. *At lunchtime, I ate my sandwiches and a delicious apple.*

atlas NOUN (plural atlases) a book of maps.

attack VERB to be violent towards someone, to hurt someone.

attention NOUN looking at, listening to or thinking about something carefully. *I gave my homework my full attention.*

attic NOUN a room at the top of a house, just below the roof.

attract VERB **1** to cause to like or admire. **2** to cause to come to something. *Magnets attract iron.*

audience NOUN the people who watch or listen to a play, film or television programme.

August NOUN the eighth month of the year, after July and before September.

August

aunt NOUN the sister of your mother or father.

author NOUN the person who writes a book, play, etc.

automatic ADJECTIVE able to work without human help.

autumn NOUN the season in the year between summer and winter. *In autumn, the leaves fall off the trees.*

awake ADJECTIVE not asleep, not sleeping.

awake

away from one place to another place. *We moved away from Chester to Scotland.*

axe NOUN a tool that has a blade at the end of a long handle and is used for cutting wood.

baby

baby NOUN (PLURAL babies) a very young child that cannot yet talk or walk.

back NOUN **1** the part of your body that is behind you, from your neck to your hips. **2** the part of something that is furthest from the front. *At the back of the room.*

back in the direction that is opposite to the one in which you are facing or where you are. *Mum is driving the car back.*

backwards the direction that is opposite to the one you are facing.

bacon NOUN meat from the back or sides of a pig that is salted or smoked.

bad ADJECTIVE not good, not pleasant. *Bad weather.*

badge NOUN a small piece of metal or cloth you fix to your clothes to show who you are, what you do or what you have done.

badger NOUN a wild animal that lives underground and has a white head and two wide black stripes on it.

bag NOUN a container made of paper, plastic or leather that has an opening at the top and that you use to carry things.

bake VERB (baking, baked) to cook food in an oven.

baked beans PLURAL NOUN beans that are cooked in tomato sauce.

baker NOUN **1** a person whose job is to bake and sell bread and cakes. **2** a shop where you can buy bread and cakes.

baker

balance NOUN steadiness. *Adam lost his balance.*

balance VERB (balancing, balanced) to keep yourself or something steady without falling over.

bald ADJECTIVE having little or no hair on your head. *Graham's father is going bald.*

ball NOUN a round object that is used in games such as football, cricket and tennis.

ballet NOUN a kind of dancing performed by dancers who make carefully planned movements, usually to music.

balloon

balloon NOUN a thin rubber bag which you blow air into so that it becomes larger and goes up in the air. *Coloured balloons at our birthday party.*

banana NOUN a long curved fruit with a yellow skin which you peel off to eat the inside.

band NOUN **1** a group of musicians. **2** a flat narrow strip of cloth that you wear around your head or wrists.

bandage NOUN a long strip of cloth to wrap round a wound.

bang NOUN a sudden loud noise, an explosion.

bananas

bang

bank NOUN **1** a place where your money is kept safely. **2** the raised side along the edge of a river or lake.

bar NOUN **1** a long straight piece of metal. **2** a roughly rectangular piece of solid material. **3** a place where you can buy a drink.

barber NOUN a person who cuts men's hair.

bare ADJECTIVE not covered by clothing.

bark VERB to make a short loud noise.

baseball NOUN a game played with a bat and a ball and two teams of nine players.

basin NOUN **1** a bowl which you use to wash your hands and face. **2** a bowl used for mixing or storing food.

basket NOUN a container made of straw or thin sticks that have been woven together.

basketball NOUN a game in which two teams of five players try to score a goal by throwing a large ball through a circular net at each end of the court.

bat NOUN **1** a specially shaped piece of wood used in some games to hit a ball. **2** a small flying animal which comes out at night and looks like a mouse.

bath NOUN a long large container for water that you sit in to wash your whole body.

bathe VERB (bathing, bathed) to swim.

bathroom NOUN a room in a house with a bath or shower, a basin and often a toilet.

battery NOUN (PLURAL batteries) a container that produces electricity to be used in something such as a clock, torch or radio.

battle NOUN a fight between enemies.

be VERB (am, are, is, being, was, were, been) **1** to exist. **2** to become. **3** to take place.

beach NOUN (PLURAL beaches) an area of land by the sea, covered with sand or small stones. *On sunny days, Mary liked to go to the beach.*

bead NOUN a small piece of coloured glass, wood or plastic used as jewellery or decoration and which has a hole through the middle through which you thread a string or wire.

beak

beak NOUN the hard curved or pointed part of the mouth of a bird. *The bird carried twigs for its nest in its beak.*

bear

bed

bed NOUN the piece of furniture that you lie down to sleep on.

bedroom NOUN the room in your house which is used for sleeping in.

bee NOUN an insect with a yellow and black striped body that makes honey and can sting you painfully.

bee

bean NOUN the seed of a climbing plant that is eaten as a vegetable. *Runner beans are my favourite kind of vegetable.*

bear NOUN a large strong wild animal that is covered with thick rough fur.

beard NOUN the hair that grows on a man's chin and cheeks.

beat VERB (beat, beaten) **1** to hit someone or something very hard. **2** to do better than another person or team in a race or competition. **3** to move regularly. *Can you hear your heart beating?*

beaten See **beat**. *Our team has beaten your team.*

beautiful ADJECTIVE very attractive, very pleasing.

became See **become**. *The smell became stronger.*

because for the reason that. *I can't come to your party because I am ill.*

become VERB (becoming, became, become) to come to be.

beef NOUN the meat of farm cattle such as a cow or bull.

been VERB See **be**. *It has been a lovely day.*

beer NOUN an alcoholic drink made from grain and hops.

beetle NOUN an insect that has hard wing coverings.

before earlier than. *Before eleven o'clock.*

began See **begin**. *Sarah began to laugh loudly.*

begin VERB (beginning, began, begun) to start to do something.

begun See **begin**. *Has school begun yet?*

behave VERB (behaving, behaved) to act. *You should behave nicely.*

behind facing the back of something or someone. *Hide behind the door.*

being See **be**. *You're being silly.*

being NOUN a living thing, especially a person. *A human being.*

believe VERB (believing, believed) to think that something is true.

beside

bell

bell NOUN **1** a hollow metal object that makes a ringing sound when you hit it. **2** a device that makes a ringing sound.

belong VERB to be owned by. *This book belongs to Emma Peters.*

below in a lower position than something else. *Below the ceiling.*

belt NOUN a strip of cloth or leather that you fasten round your waist.

bench NOUN a long seat for two or more people.

bend NOUN the curved part of a road or river.

bend VERB (bent) to make something straight become curved. *Bend your leg.*

bent See **bend**. *He bent the fork.*

berry NOUN (PLURAL berries) a small soft round fruit.

berries

beside at the side of or next to something. *Sit beside me.*

best ADJECTIVE *The best book that I have ever read.*

better ADJECTIVE *Fruit is better for you than crisps.*

between having one person or thing on one side and another person or thing on the other side. *James is sitting between Luke and Tom.*

bicycle NOUN a vehicle which has two wheels and which you pedal with your feet.

bicycle

big ADJECTIVE (bigger, biggest) large in size, importance, etc.

bike See **bicycle**.

bikini NOUN a two-piece swimming costume that women and girls wear.

binoculars PLURAL NOUN a pair of special glasses that you look through to see things that are a long way away.

bird NOUN a creature that has feathers and wings and lays eggs. Most birds can fly.

birthday NOUN the day on which you were born.

biscuit NOUN a small flat cake that is crisp and sweet.

bit NOUN a small piece or amount of something.

bit See **bite**. *I bit into the cake.*

bite VERB (biting, bit, bitten) to use your teeth to cut into something.

bitten See **bite**. *Have you ever been bitten by a dog?*

bitter ADJECTIVE **1** having a sharp and unpleasant taste. **2** feeling angry and sad.

black ADJECTIVE the darkest colour, the colour of coal.

blackbird NOUN a common bird that has black or brown feathers.

blackboard NOUN a dark-coloured board with a smooth surface that teachers write on with chalk.

blame NOUN the responsibility for causing or doing something bad.

blame VERB (blaming, blamed) to think or say that someone is responsible for something.

blanket NOUN a large piece of thick material used as a cover on a bed to keep you warm.

blew See **blow**. *Warm air blew in through the window.*

blind ADJECTIVE not able to see.

blink VERB to shut your eyes and open them again quickly.

block NOUN **1** a large piece of wood, stone, etc. **2** a large building of flats or offices. *We live in a block of flats in the city.*

block VERB to prevent movement.

blood NOUN the red liquid that flows inside the veins in your body. Blood is pumped round the body by the heart.

blouse NOUN a piece of clothing for girls and women that reaches from the neck to the waist.

blow VERB (blew, blown) to make the air move, to move with the air.

blown See **blow**. *The tree was blown down in the storm.*

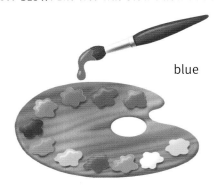
blue

blue ADJECTIVE having the colour of the sky on a sunny day.

blunt ADJECTIVE **1** having a rounded or flat end, not sharp. **2** speaking in a plain way, without wanting to be polite.

board NOUN a flat piece of wood or other material.

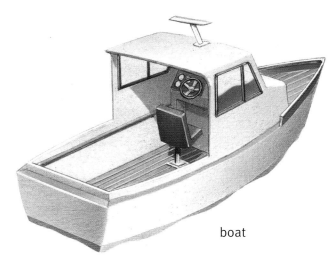
boat

boat NOUN a small ship. There are many different kinds of boat, such as canoes and sailing boats.

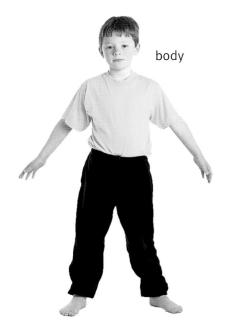

body

body NOUN (PLURAL bodies) **1** all of a person, including their head, arms and legs. **2** the main part of a person, excluding their head, arms and legs. **3** a dead person.

boil VERB **1** to make liquid hot so that bubbles appear on it and it starts to change into steam. **2** to cook food in boiling water.

boiler NOUN a device that burns gas, oil, etc., to produce hot water.

bomb NOUN a device that is filled with materials that will make it explode.

bone NOUN one of the hard white parts under the skin of your body.

bonfire NOUN a large fire outside, often used to burn rubbish.

book NOUN a collection of printed pages fastened together for reading.

bookshop NOUN a shop that sells books.

boot NOUN a shoe that covers your foot and the lower part of your leg.

bored ADJECTIVE not interested, tired of something.

boring ADJECTIVE dull and not interesting.

born VERB (be born) to start your life. *I was born in 1991.*

borrow VERB to take something which belongs to someone else, usually with their permission, and which you are going to give them back later.

both two people or things.

bottle NOUN a container made of plastic or glass that you keep liquids in.

bottom NOUN the lowest part of something.

bought *See* **buy**. *We bought a new car yesterday.*

bounce VERB (bouncing, bounced) to move upwards immediately after hitting a hard surface.

bow (said like **how**) VERB to bend your body or your head to show respect towards someone.

bow (said like **low**) NOUN **1** a knot with two loops. **2** a curved stick that is used for shooting arrows. **3** a long, thin piece of wood with horses' hair stretched on it, used to play a musical instrument such as a violin.

bowl NOUN a deep round container used to mix, store or serve food.

bonfire

box

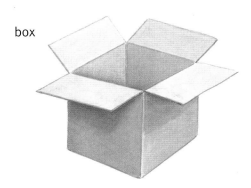

brave ADJECTIVE willing to do things that are dangerous or painful, not showing fear, having courage.

bread NOUN a common food made from mixing and then baking flour, water and yeast.

box NOUN (PLURAL boxes) a container with stiff sides and often a lid. VERB to fight someone by punching with the fists.

boy NOUN a male child.

bra NOUN underwear worn by a woman to support her breasts.

bracelet NOUN a wrist band or ring worn as a decoration.

brackets PLURAL NOUN the marks ( ) that you can put round some words in a sentence. You put them round words that you could leave out and still leave the meaning of the whole sentence clear. For example: *Mrs Green (Samantha's mother) went to see the headteacher.* Brackets are always used as a pair.

brain NOUN the part inside your head that you use to think and feel. The brain sends messages to other parts of your body to control them.

brake NOUN a device that makes a car, bicycle, etc., go slower or stop.

branch NOUN (PLURAL branches) the part of a tree that grows out from the trunk and has leaves, flowers or fruit growing on it.

branch

break

break VERB (broke, broken) **1** to cause to fall into two or more pieces, because it has been hit or dropped. **2** to damage a machine so that it no longer works.

breakfast NOUN the first meal of the day.

breathe VERB (breathing, breathed) to take air into your body and let it out again.

brick NOUN a rectangular piece of baked clay used for building.

bridge NOUN a structure that carries a road or railway over a river, valley, etc.

bright ADJECTIVE having a strong, light colour.

bring VERB (brought) to fetch, carry or take with you.

broke, **broken** See **break**. *Lisa broke her arm yesterday. Paul has just broken a window.*

brother NOUN a boy or man who has the same parents as you.

brought See **bring**. *I've brought an umbrella with me.*

brown ADJECTIVE having the colour of wood or earth.

brush NOUN (PLURAL brushes) tool for sweeping, smoothing or painting, made of stiff hair or nylon.

brush VERB to clean, smooth or tidy using a brush. *I brushed my hair until it was smooth.*

bubble NOUN a ball of air in a liquid.

bucket NOUN a round metal or plastic container that has a handle and is used to hold or carry water.

bud NOUN a small bump on a tree or plant that grows into a leaf or flower.

bug NOUN an insect. Ants and bees are bugs.

build VERB (built, built) to make something by putting pieces together. *We built a sandcastle on the beach.*

building NOUN a structure with a roof and walls, such as a house, shop or factory.

building

built See **build**. *The house that Jack built.*

bulb NOUN **1** the glass part of an electric lamp that gives out light. **2** a round type of root that grows into a plant. *Daffodils grow from bulbs.*

bull NOUN a male form of cattle or certain other animals. A cow is the female.

bump NOUN **1** a minor car accident when cars hit each other. **2** a round swelling.

bump VERB to hit something accidentally.

bunch NOUN (PLURAL bunches) a group of things or people. A bunch of flowers.

bungalow NOUN a house built on one level.

burglar NOUN a thief who breaks into someone's house or office and steals things.

burglar

burn VERB (burnt or burned) **1** to be on fire. **2** to destroy or damage by fire.

burnt or **burned** See **burn**. *The factory was burnt down.*

burst VERB (burst, burst) to split open suddenly because of the pressure from inside. *The balloon burst with a bang.*

bury VERB (burying, buried) to put the body of a dead person into the ground.

bus NOUN (PLURAL buses) a large motor vehicle for carrying passengers. *Karen ran to catch the bus.*

bush NOUN (PLURAL bushes) a small tree that does not grow very high.

busy ADJECTIVE (busier, busiest) working hard, having many things to do, not free to do something.

but 1 used to show a contrast with what has just been said. *I would like to come but I'm on holiday.*
2 except. *She thanked everyone but herself.*

butcher NOUN a shopkeeper who sells meat.

butler NOUN the chief male servant in a grand house.

butt VERB to push or hit with the head or horns like a bull or goat, to ram.

butter NOUN a yellow fat which you spread on bread.

buttercup NOUN a small plant with yellow petals that grows in fields.

butterfly NOUN (PLURAL butterflies) an insect with large colourful wings. Butterflies grow from caterpillars.

butterfly

button NOUN a small round object attached to a piece of clothing and used as a fastener.

buttons

buttress NOUN a support for an outside wall, most common in old buildings.

buy VERB (bought, bought) to get something by paying money for it. *Mum bought me a new shirt and some new shoes for school when we went shopping.*

buzz NOUN (PLURAL buzzes) a low continuous noise like the sound of a bee.

buzz

buzzard NOUN a large bird of prey that hunts other creatures for food.

by 1 used to show the person or thing that has done something. *A play by Shakespeare.* **2** beside. *A seat by the river.* **3** before. *By Thursday.*

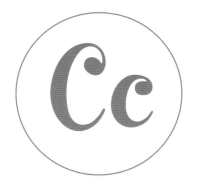

cabbage

cabbage NOUN a green vegetable that can be eaten raw or cooked.

café NOUN a shop with tables and chairs where you can buy and have drinks and snacks.

cage

cage NOUN a structure of bars in which birds or animals are kept.

cake NOUN a mixture of butter, sugar, eggs, flour and other ingredients that is baked before it is eaten.

calculator NOUN an electronic machine that works out mathematical calculations.

calendar NOUN a list of the days, weeks and months of the year.

calf NOUN (PLURAL calves) **1** the young of some animals, especially the cow, elephant or whale. **2** the back of your leg from the ankle to the knee.

call VERB **1** to shout or cry out. *I heard a voice calling in the night.* **2** to visit briefly. *I'll call for you on my way to school.* **3** to telephone. *Call me tomorrow.* **4** to name. *I am called Mark.*

calm ADJECTIVE peaceful, quiet, still.

calves See **calf**.

came See **come**. *We came home late from school.*

camel

camel NOUN an animal with one or two humps that is used for carrying people and goods in the desert.

camera NOUN a piece of equipment used for filming or taking photographs.

camp NOUN a place where people live in tents or huts for a short time, especially on holiday.

camp VERB to live in a tent for a short time.

camp

can NOUN a metal tin or container that is used to keep food or drinks fresh.

can VERB (could) to be able to do something. *I can play the guitar.*

can't = cannot. *I can't read music.*

canal NOUN an artifical waterway made so boats can transport heavy goods. **canary** NOUN (PLURAL

candle

canaries) a small yellow bird.

candle NOUN a wax stick with a string through the middle which burns to give light.

cannot = can not. *I cannot help you any more.*

cap NOUN **1** a soft hat with a peak. **2** a lid or cover for the end of a bottle or tube.

car NOUN a motor vehicle for carrying a few passengers.

car-boot sale NOUN a place where people gather to sell unwanted goods from the backs of their cars.

caravan NOUN a mobile home that can be towed by a car or a horse.

card NOUN **1** stiff paper. **2** a piece of card or plastic made for identification purposes. *Membership card.* **3** a piece of printed card for sending a message to someone. *Birthday card.* **4** a piece of card, part of a pack, with numbers or pictures printed on it for playing a game like snap.

cardboard NOUN thick stiff paper used for making boxes.

cardigan NOUN a knitted woollen garment with sleeves and which fastens down the front.

care NOUN **1** looking after someone. **2** attention.

care VERB (caring, cared) **1** to feel concerned about something. *Joe cares about the environment.* **2** to look after someone. *The children care for their disabled mother.*

careful ADJECTIVE **1** cautious, not taking risks. **2** done with a lot of attention.

careless ADJECTIVE **1** thoughtless, making mistakes because of lack of attention. **2** without any worries.

carpet NOUN a thick covering for a floor or stairs.

carrier bag NOUN a plastic or paper bag used for carrying shopping.

car

carrot NOUN an orange-coloured vegetable that grows under the ground.

carry VERB (carrying, carried) to lift and move something or someone from one place to another.

carry out VERB to fulfil, to do what you have promised or have been told to do.

cart NOUN a vehicle for carrying goods, usually drawn by a horse.

cart VERB to carry something or someone. and find it tiring. *I don't want to cart those bags around town.*

carton NOUN a cardboard box, a container for food or drink. *A carton of juice.*

cartoon

cartoon NOUN **1** a funny drawing. **2** an animated film.

case NOUN **1** a box or bag for moving goods. *A packing case.* **2** an example or occurrence of something. *A bad case of flu.* **3** a question to be decided in a lawcourt, with the facts and arguments put forward by each side.

cash NOUN money in the form of coins and notes rather than cheques.

cassette NOUN a small plastic container of magnetic tape for recording and playing music, stories, etc.

castle NOUN a large building made strong with high walls and towers.

cat NOUN a small furry animal that has whiskers, a tail and sharp claws and is kept as a pet.

catalogue NOUN a list of the things available from a particular company or organization.

catch VERB (caught, caught) **1** to grasp or capture something. *Catch the ball.* **2** to be in time for. *Catch the train.* **3** to get an illness. *You'll catch a cold if you don't wear a coat.*

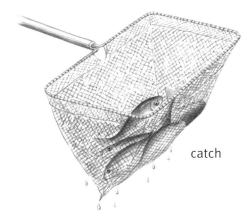

catch

caterpillar NOUN a small worm-like creature that later develops into a butterfly or moth.

cathedral NOUN the main church in an area, a bishop is the church leader in the area.

Catholic NOUN a member of the Roman Catholic Church.

cattle NOUN a collective name for cows, bulls, etc.

cattle

caught See **catch**. *Jake caught the ball.*

cauliflower NOUN a vegetable with a white head of flowers.

cause NOUN **1** the thing that makes something happen. **2** an aim or purpose that a group of people support.

cause VERB (causing, caused) to make something happen.

cave NOUN a hollow place in the side of a hill or cliff or beneath the ground.

CD-ROM NOUN a compact disc containing information which can be displayed on a computer screen.

ceiling NOUN the top part of the inside of a room.

centimetre NOUN a measurement equal to 0.01 metres or 0.4 inches.

centre NOUN **1** the middle of something. **2** a building where people take part in different activities or where they go for help. *A sports centre.*

century NOUN (PLURAL centuries) a period of one hundred years.

cereal NOUN **1** grain produced by plants like wheat, barley, oats, etc. **2** a breakfast food that is made from grain.

cereal

chain NOUN a length of metal rings that are joined together.

chair NOUN a seat for one person that has a back and can be moved around.

chalk NOUN **1** soft white rock. **2** a piece of this used for writing on a blackboard.

change NOUN **1** something that is different. **2** money given back to you when you pay more than a thing costs.

change VERB (changing, changed) **1** to alter or become different. **2** to replace one thing with another. **3** to put on other clothes.

channel NOUN **1** a narrow stretch of water between two countries or seas. *The English Channel.* **2** a wavelength for broadcasting radio or television programmes.

chart NOUN a diagram which presents information in a clear, visual way that is easy to understand.

chase VERB (chasing, chased) to run after someone to try to catch them.

cheap ADJECTIVE **1** not expensive, costing very little. **2** of poor quality.

check VERB to make sure something is correct or safe.

cheek NOUN **1** the round part of your face below your eye. **2** rudeness or lack of respect.

cheerful ADJECTIVE happy.

cheese NOUN a solid food that is made from milk.

chair

cherries

cherry NOUN (PLURAL cherries) a small, round fruit with a stone in the middle.

chest NOUN **1** the front part of your body between the stomach and the neck. **2** a strong box. **3** a piece of furniture with drawers.

chest

chew VERB to break up food with your teeth so that it is easier to swallow. *Chew your food thoroughly.*

chicken NOUN **1** a bird kept for its eggs and meat. **2** someone who is a coward.

chickenpox NOUN a disease which gives you a high temperature and itchy red spots. *There was an outbreak of chickenpox at school.*

child NOUN (PLURAL children) a boy or girl who is not yet an adult, someone's son or daughter.

children *See* **child**.

chimney NOUN a narrow opening above a fire that takes smoke out of a building.

chin NOUN the part of your face below the mouth and above the neck.

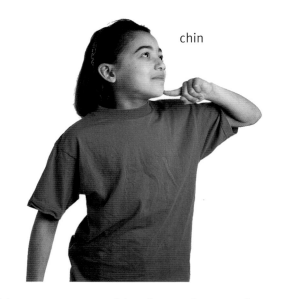

chin

chips PLURAL NOUN thin pieces of potato that are deep-fried in oil.

chocolate NOUN a sweet or drink made from cocoa beans.

choose VERB (choosing, chose, chosen) to select or pick.

chop VERB (chopping, chopped) to cut up into pieces with an axe or a knife.

chose, chosen *See* **choose**. *I chose a pink dress.*

Christmas NOUN the time of year when the birth of Jesus Christ is celebrated.

Christmas tree NOUN a real or artificial fir tree that is decorated with tinsel and ornaments and people put up in their homes at Christmas.

church NOUN (PLURAL churches) a place of Christian worship. *Sally goes to church every Sunday.*

cigarette NOUN tobacco rolled up in a thin paper tube and smoked. *Smoking cigarettes is bad for your health.*

circle

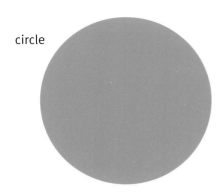

circle NOUN a perfectly round shape, a ring. *We all sat on the floor in a circle.*

circus NOUN (PLURAL circuses) a show, often in a big tent, given by clowns, acrobats, performing animals, etc. *Every year I look forward to going to the circus.*

city NOUN (PLURAL cities) a large and important town.

clap VERB (clapping, clapped) to hit the palms of your hands together to show that you are pleased with something or to get someone's attentio

clarinet

clarinet NOUN a musical instrument with a single reed, played by blowing.

class NOUN (PLURAL classes) a group of children taught together in a school.

claw NOUN one of the sharp nails on an animal's paw or a bird's foot.

clay NOUN soft, sticky earth that hardens when baked. It is used to make pots and bricks.

clean ADJECTIVE not dirty.

clean VERB to remove dirt and dust from something.

clear ADJECTIVE **1** easy to see through. *Clear glass.* **2** easy to understand. *Clear arguments.* **3** with nothing in the way. *A clear road.*

clear VERB **1** to remove unwanted things from a place. **2** to jump over a fence, wall, etc.

clever ADJECTIVE intelligent, able to learn things easily.

cliff NOUN a high steep piece of land next to the sea.

climb VERB to go up towards the top of something.

climb

cloakroom NOUN **1** a room in which you can leave your coat and bags. *I hung my jacket in the cloakroom.* **2** a room with a toilet and washbasin.

claw

clock NOUN a device for showing the time of day. *Look at the clock and tell me the time.*

close (said like **dose**) ADJECTIVE **1** near. **2** careful. *A close look.*

close (said like **rose**) VERB (closing, closed) to shut.

close-up a photograph or film that is taken from very near.

cloth NOUN **1** woven material used especially to make clothes. **2** a piece of cloth used for a particular purpose. *A dishcloth.*

clothes PLURAL NOUN the garments that people wear. *She needs new clothes.*

cloud NOUN a mass of tiny drops of water, dust or smoke, floating in the air.

clown NOUN someone, often a circus performer, who makes people laugh by doing silly things.

clue NOUN something that helps you to find the answer.

coach NOUN (PLURAL coaches) **1** a bus. **2** a four-wheeled vehicle pulled by horses. **3** a trainer, especially for sports.

coal NOUN a hard, black substance that is mined for burning as a fuel.

coast NOUN land by the sea.

coast

coat NOUN **1** a garment with sleeves worn over other clothes to keep you warm outdoors. **2** an animal's fur. **3** a layer of paint.

coconut NOUN large, hollow nut of a palm tree which contains milky juice and a white lining that you can eat.

coconut

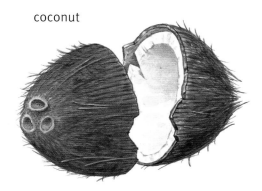

coffee NOUN **1** powder made by roasting and crushing the beans of a plant, used for drinks or as a flavouring. **2** a drink made by mixing boiling water with this powder.

coin NOUN (PLURAL coins) a disc of metal used for money.

coins

cola NOUN fizzy brown drink.

cold ADJECTIVE not warm.

cold NOUN illness that gives you a runny nose and a sore throat.

collar NOUN the part of a shirt or coat that fits round the neck.

collect VERB to gather things together.

comic

college NOUN a place where you can go and do further study after leaving school.

colon The punctuation mark (:) is a colon. It is used to introduce a statement or list. *To bake a cake you will need the following ingredients: flour, sugar, butter, eggs and milk.*

colour NOUN red, blue, green, yellow, etc.

colour VERB to give colour to something with paint, crayons, etc.

colour

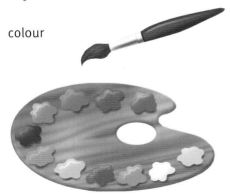

comb NOUN a piece of plastic, metal, etc., with teeth for tidying your hair.

comb VERB to tidy your hair with a comb.

come VERB (coming, came, come) **1** to move towards. **2** to arrive. **3** to go with someone.

comfortable ADJECTIVE **1** making you feel relaxed. **2** not worried, at ease.

comic NOUN **1** a comedian. **2** a children's magazine with cartoon stories.

comment NOUN a remark.

compass

compass NOUN (PLURAL compasses) an instrument used for showing direction that has a magnetic needle which always points to north.

competition NOUN a contest to find a winner.

computer NOUN an electronic machine that stores and processes information when programmed.

concert NOUN a musical performance. *A rock concert.*

conditioner NOUN **1** a liquid that you put on your hair after you have washed it to make it softer. **2** a liquid that you put in your washing machine to make your clothes softer.

container NOUN something that holds something else inside it.

container

continue VERB (continuing, continued) to carry on.

control NOUN **1** power or authority. **2** a switch on a machine. VERB (controlling, controlled) to have the power to make people or things behave exactly as you want them to.

cook NOUN a person who prepares and cooks food. VERB to heat food in some way so it can be eaten.

cooker NOUN something that cooks food, an oven.

cool ADJECTIVE **1** not warm and not cold. **2** calm.

copy NOUN (PLURAL copies) **1** something that is made or done like something else. **2** one example of a book or magazine. VERB (copying, copied) to make or do something exactly the same as something else.

cord NOUN thick string.

corn NOUN a crop such as wheat, barley or maize.

corner NOUN **1** the place where two lines, edges or roads meet. **2** a kick from the corner of the field in football.

correct ADJECTIVE right. VERB to make something right, to mark mistakes in something.

cost NOUN the price of something.

costume

costume NOUN **1** a typical style of clothing worn in the past. **2** clothes worn when acting.

cot NOUN a small bed with sides for a baby or young child.

cottage NOUN a small house in the country.

cotton NOUN **1** a plant which produces soft, white fibre. **2** thread made from the cotton plant. **3** cloth woven from cotton thread.

cotton

cough VERB to push the air noisily from your throat, often because you are ill.

could See **can**. *Could I come in?*

couldn't = could not. *We couldn't go to sleep.*

count VERB **1** to say the numbers one after another. **2** to add up.

country NOUN (PLURAL countries) **1** a land with its own government, people, language, etc. **2** the land outside towns and cities.

cousin NOUN the child of your aunt or uncle.

cover NOUN something put over something else to hide or protect it.

cover VERB to put something over something else to hide or protect it.

cow NOUN the female of cattle, kept on farms for milk.

cowboy NOUN a man who herds cattle in America.

crack NOUN **1** a thin line where something has split but not broken completely. **2** a sudden, sharp noise.

crack

crack VERB to split, but not break completely.

crane NOUN a machine for moving heavy things by lifting them into the air.

crash NOUN (PLURAL crashes) **1** an accident involving vehicles. **2** the noise made by things smashing into one another.

crash VERB to hit another vehicle in an accident.

crawl VERB to move forward on your hands and knees like a baby does before it walks.

crayon NOUN a coloured wax stick or pencil for drawing.

crayon

cream NOUN **1** the thick part at the top of the milk. **2** a pale yellow colour. **3** something you rub into your skin.

creep VERB (crept) to move slowly and quietly.

crept See **creep**. *We crept along the corridor.*

cricket NOUN **1** a team game played with bats, a ball and wickets. **2** an insect.

crocodile NOUN a large reptile that lives in water and on land.

crooked ADJECTIVE not straight. *A crooked path.*

cross ADJECTIVE bad-tempered.

cross NOUN (PLURAL crosses) two lines that go over each other in the shape of + or ×.

cross VERB **1** to go over from one side to another. *Cross the road.* **2** to make a cross shape. *Cross your legs.*

crow NOUN a big, black bird with a loud cry.

crowd NOUN **1** a large gathering of people in a space. **2** the audience at a sporting event or a rock concert.

crown NOUN a circular band, often made of gold and jewels, and worn on the heads of kings and queens.

cruel ADJECTIVE very unkind, deliberately causing pain to others

crumb

crumb NOUN a tiny bit of bread, cake or biscuit.

cry VERB (crying, cried) **1** to let tears fall from your eyes, to weep. **2** to shout out loud.

cub NOUN the young of a wild animal such as a fox, a lion or a wolf.

cuckoo NOUN a bird that lays its eggs in the nests of other birds.

cucumber NOUN a long, thin, round salad vegetable with a green skin.

cuddle VERB (cuddling, cuddled) to show that you love someone by holding them closely in your arms.

cultured ADJECTIVE well educated, with good manners and a knowledge of the arts.

cup NOUN **1** a small, round container with a handle, from which you drink liquids. **2** a prize given to the winner of a competition.

cup

cupboard NOUN a piece of furniture to put things in.

curb VERB to keep something under control. *The government has curbed the powers of the police.*

curl NOUN a piece of hair curved at the end.

curl VERB to twist into a curved shape.

curler NOUN a pin or roller put in hair to make it curly.

curly ADJECTIVE full of curls. *Curly hair.*

currant NOUN **1** a small dried grape used in baking and cooking. **2** a soft, red, black or white berry. *Redcurrant. Blackcurrant. Whitecurrant.*

current NOUN water, air or electricity that moves in a certain direction. *The ocean currents.*

curry NOUN (PLURAL curries) a hot, spicy meal. *John's favourite food is curry.*

curtain NOUN a piece of material hung over a window to keep out light.

curve NOUN a smooth, bending line.

curve VERB (curving, curved) to bend. *The road curves at the top of the hill.*

cushion NOUN a bag filled with soft material to make you more comfortable when you are sitting on something.

customer NOUN a person who buys something.

cut VERB (cutting) to remove a piece of or make an opening in something.

cute ADJECTIVE pretty, attractive. *She's a cute little girl.*

cycle NOUN a bicycle.

cycling VERB riding on a bicycle.

cycling

cymbals PLURAL NOUN a musical instrument made of two round brass plates that are banged together to make a loud, ringing noise.

cymbals

dad, daddy NOUN (PLURAL dads, daddies) a name that children call their father.

daffodil NOUN a yellow flower that grows from a bulb in spring.

daisy NOUN (PLURAL daisies) a wild flower with a yellow centre and white petals.

daisy

damage NOUN harm or injury that is done to something.

damage VERB (damaging, damaged) to harm, injure or spoil something.

damp ADJECTIVE slightly wet, not completely dry.

dance NOUN a series of steps and movements that you make to music.

dance VERB (dancing, danced) to move in time to music.

dandelion NOUN a wild plant with a yellow flower.

danger NOUN something that could bring death or harm.

dangerous ADJECTIVE not safe.

dark ADJECTIVE **1** without much light. *A dark night.* **2** almost black. *Dark hair.*

date NOUN **1** a particular day of the year or the year in which something happened. **2** someone of the opposite sex you arrange to go out with.

daughter NOUN someone's female child.

day NOUN **1** the time from sunrise to sunset. **2** 24 hours.

dead ADJECTIVE not alive.

deaf ADJECTIVE not able to hear.

dear ADJECTIVE **1** much loved. **2** a word that is used to begin a letter. **3** not cheap.

December NOUN the twelfth month of the year.

decide VERB (deciding, decided) to make up your mind about something.

decimal ADJECTIVE counting in tens or tenths.

decorate VERB (decorating, decorated) to add things to make something look better.

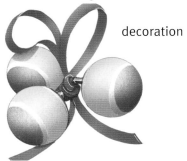

decoration

decoration NOUN something you add to something else to make it look nicer.

deep ADJECTIVE **1** going down or back a long way. **2** the measurement of something from top to bottom or from front to back.

deer NOUN (PLURAL deer) a large wild animal, the male of which usually has branched horns (antlers) on its head.

delicious ADJECTIVE good to eat or smell.

delight NOUN great happiness.

delighted ADJECTIVE very pleased and excited.

desert

deliver VERB **1** to send or take something somewhere. **2** to help at the birth of a baby.

dentist NOUN someone who looks after your teeth.

depth NOUN the measurement of something such as a river between the surface and the bottom.

describe VERB (describing, described) to say what something or someone is like.

desert NOUN a large area of sandy land that does not get a lot of rain and in which very few plants grow.

design VERB to plan or draw something to show how you can make it.

desk NOUN a piece of furniture that you sit at to read or write.

destroy VERB to ruin something so that it can't be mended.

dew NOUN very small drops of water that form on the ground overnight.

diagram NOUN a drawing that shows or explains something.

diamond NOUN **1** a precious jewel. **2** a shape with four equal sides that stands on one of its points.

diary NOUN (PLURAL diaries) a book marked off with the days of the year so that you can write in it the things you have planned to do or have done.

dice NOUN (PLURAL dice) a small cube with spots from one to six on each of its sides, used in playing some games.

did See **do**. *Yesterday I did not have any homework to do.*

didn't = did not. *Yesterday I didn't have any homework.*

die VERB (dying, died) to stop living.

diesel NOUN **1** a vehicle with an oil-burning engine. **2** the kind of fuel used in a diesel engine.

different ADJECTIVE not like another person or thing.

difficult ADJECTIVE hard to do or understand.

dig VERB (dug) to move earth to break it up or to make a hole.

dinner NOUN the main meal of the day that is eaten either in the middle of the day or in the evening.

dig

dinosaur NOUN a large prehistoric animal that is now extinct.

dip NOUN **1** something that is lower. *A dip in the road.* **2** a quick swim. **3** a mixture that you dip other foods into.

dip VERB (dipping, dipped) **1** to put something into a liquid and to take it out again quickly. **2** to make something lower. *Dip your headlights.*

direction NOUN the way in which someone or something is moving, pointing or is aimed at.

dirt NOUN mud, dust or anything that is not clean.

dirty ADJECTIVE (dirtier, dirtiest) not clean.

dirty

disabled ADJECTIVE not able to use a part of your body properly.

disappear VERB to go out of sight.

disappoint VERB to be sad because something you expected or hoped for didn't happen. *We were disappointed that it rained.*

disaster NOUN an unexpected event that causes a lot of damage or suffering.

disco NOUN a place where you can dance to pop music.

discover VERB to find out something, especially for the first time. *I discovered a short-cut to the shops.*

disguise NOUN something you wear so that people will not recognize you.

disguise VERB (disguising, disguised) to change the appearance of something so people will not recognize it.

dinosaur

dish NOUN (PLURAL dishes) a bowl or plate that food is served from.

dishwasher NOUN a machine that cleans the dirty plates, pots and pans that you use when cooking and eating a meal.

disk NOUN a flat piece of plastic with magnetic material that stores information used in a computer.

distance NOUN how far it is between two places.

disturb VERB to interrupt what someone is doing or someone's rest. *Don't disturb him; he's asleep.*

dive VERB (diving, dived) to jump into water head first.

divide VERB (dividing, divided) **1** to share out or separate into smaller parts. **2** to find out how many times one number will go into another. *Ten divided by two is five.*

dizzy ADJECTIVE (dizzier, dizziest) feeling as if you are going to fall over.

do VERB (does, doing, did, done) **1** to perform an action. *Do the dishes.* **2** to be suitable. *That'll do.* **3** used in questions. *Do you like it?* **4** used to form negatives. *Don't throw the ball here.* **5** to cause. *Smoking can do you a lot of harm.* **6** to work at.

doctor NOUN someone who looks after you when you are ill.

does See **do**. *Does your grandma live with you?*

doesn't = does not. *Our grandma doesn't live with us.*

dog NOUN a four-legged animal that barks, usually kept as a pet.

doll NOUN a toy that looks like a person.

doll

dolphin NOUN a large wild animal that lives in the sea.

done See **do**. *I haven't done anything to my model railway for a few days.*

don't = do not. *Don't touch the radiator − it's very hot.*

donkey NOUN an animal that looks like a horse, but is smaller and has longer ears.

door NOUN something on hinges or runners that opens and closes to let you in or out of a building, room or vehicle.

dot NOUN a small, round spot.

double VERB (doubling, doubled) to make two of something, to make twice as much.

down 1 in a direction from a higher to a lower place. **2** along. *Down the road.*

downstairs the ground floor.

dozen NOUN twelve of anything.

drag VERB (dragging, dragged) to pull something heavy along.

drain VERB to let water run out of something.

drank See **drink**. *I drank juice with my lunch.*

draw VERB (drew, drawn) **1** to make a picture. **2** to end a game or a contest without either side winning.

drawer NOUN something you put things in that slides in and out of a piece of furniture.

drawing NOUN a picture made with crayons, pencils, etc.

drawn See **draw**.

donkey

draw

dream

dream NOUN **1** something you seem to see when you sleep. **2** something you think about that you'd like to happen. VERB (dreamt or dreamed) to seem to see when you are sleeping.

dreamt or **dreamed** See **dream**.

dress NOUN (PLURAL dresses) a piece of female clothing with a top and a skirt all in one.

dressing gown NOUN what you wear over your night clothes when you are not quite ready to get into bed.

drew See **draw**.

drill NOUN a tool for making holes in things.

drill VERB to make a hole in something.

drink NOUN a liquid you can drink.

drink VERB (drank, drunk) **1** to swallow any kind of liquid. **2** to swallow a lot of alcohol.

drip VERB (dripping, dripped) to fall in drops.

drive VERB (driving, drove, driven) to be able to control a vehicle.

driven See **drive**.

drizzle NOUN fine rain.

drop NOUN **1** a small amount of liquid. **2** a sweet. *Pear drops.* **3** a fall. *A drop of 100 metres.*

drop VERB (dropping, dropped) to fall straight down.

drove See **drive**.

drown VERB to die because of not being able to breathe underwater.

drum NOUN **1** a musical instrument that you bang with a stick. **2** a large container.

drums PLURAL NOUN lots of different sized drums played by a drummer in a band or orchestra.

drums

drunk See **drink**. *I've drunk too much cola.*

dry ADJECTIVE (drier, driest) not wet.

duck NOUN a water bird with webbed feet.

dug See **dig**. *We dug the garden at the weekend.*

dump VERB to get rid of something that you do not want.

during throughout all the time.

dust NOUN small bits of dirt.

dust VERB **1** to clean dust off something. **2** to sprinkle with powder.

dustbin NOUN a big container that you put your rubbish in outside your house.

duvet NOUN a large material-filled cover for a bed instead of sheets and blankets.

each every one.

eagle NOUN a large bird of prey.

eagle

ear NOUN one of the two openings on the side of your head with which you hear.

early ADJECTIVE (earlier, earliest) **1** near the start of the day. **2** before the normal or right time.

earn VERB to receive money for work that you do.

earth NOUN **1** the planet that we live on. **2** soil, the ground.

earthquake NOUN a sudden and violent movement of the ground, often causing much damage.

east

east NOUN one of the four points of the compass, the direction of the rising sun.

Easter

Easter NOUN the time of year when Christians celebrate the death of Jesus and his coming back to life again.

easy ADJECTIVE (easier, easiest) not difficult to do.

eat VERB (ate, eaten) to put food in your mouth and swallow it.

eaten See **eat**. *We've eaten all the cakes.*

echo NOUN (PLURAL echoes) a sound that bounces off a surface and is heard again.

edge NOUN **1** the sharp, cutting part of a knife, tool, etc. **2** the place or line that marks the beginning or end of something.

eel NOUN a long fish that looks like a snake.

egg NOUN **1** the round shell-covered object laid by birds and some other creatures and from which their babies come. **2** a hen's egg, eaten as food.

egg

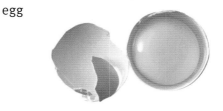

eight the number 8.

eighteen the number 18.

eighty the number 80.

either one or the other of two people or things.

elbow NOUN the part of your arm where it bends.

electric ADJECTIVE worked by electricity.

electricity NOUN the energy that travels along power lines that we use for lighting, heating and making machines work.

elephant NOUN a very big animal with tusks and a trunk.

elephant

eleven the number 11.

emerald NOUN a precious, green jewel.

emerald

empty ADJECTIVE (emptier, emptiest) with nothing inside. *An empty glass.*

end NOUN **1** the point where something stops or finishes. **2** the time when something stops.

end VERB to stop or finish.

enemy NOUN (PLURAL enemies) someone who is against you and wants to harm you.

energy NOUN **1** physical strength to do something. **2** power from electricity, coal, etc., to drive machinery.

engine NOUN **1** a machine that uses fuel to make something work. **2** the front of a train that pulls the rest of it.

enjoy VERB to take pleasure in something.

enormous ADJECTIVE very big.

enough as much or as many as you need.

enter VERB to go into a place.

entrance

enthusiastic ADJECTIVE showing great excitement or approval about something.

entrance NOUN the way in. *The front entrance.*

envelope NOUN a paper cover inside which you put a letter or card.

evergreen

equal ADJECTIVE the same in number, size, value, etc. *All the portions are equal.*

escalator NOUN a moving staircase.

escape VERB (escaping, escaped) to get away or to break free.

especially 1 more than usual. **2** more special.

estate car NOUN a car with a door at the back and extra space behind the back seats.

even still, yet, more than expected. *Today was even hotter than yesterday.*

even ADJECTIVE **1** smooth and flat. **2** equal. **3** that can be divided exactly by two. *2, 4 and 6 are even numbers.*

evening NOUN the time at the end of the day and the beginning of the night.

eventually at the end of a lot of delays, finally.

ever 1 at any time. *No one ever comes to see us.* **2** at all times. *For ever and ever.* **3** said to emphasize something. *I'm ever so tired.*

evergreen NOUN a tree or bush that has green leaves through all the year.

every all, each one.

everybody everyone, every person.

everything all, each thing together.

evil ADJECTIVE very bad or wicked. NOUN a force that causes very bad things to happen.

excellent ADJECTIVE very good indeed.

except apart from.

excited ADJECTIVE very happy and enthusiastic, especially because you are looking forward to something.

excuse NOUN a reason that you give to explain why you have done something or not done something.

excuse VERB (excusing, excused) to say why you did something.

exercise NOUN **1** movements that you do to keep fit. **2** something that you do to train or practise for something.

exercise VERB (exercising, exercised) to do sports, walk, etc., in order to become fit and healthy.

exercise

exhibition

exhibition NOUN a collection of things for people to go to see.

exit NOUN the way out.

expect VERB **1** to suppose that something is going to happen. **2** to wait for.

expensive ADJECTIVE costing a lot of money.

explain VERB to give the meaning of something so that someone else can understand. *I explained how the tourists could get to the museum.*

explode VERB (exploding, exploded) to blow up with a loud bang.

explode

explore VERB (exploring, explored) to go somewhere that you have not been to before to discover what it is like. *We explored the dangerous jungle with excitement.*

explosion NOUN a loud bang made when something explodes. *The noise of the explosion was very loud.*

extra ADJECTIVE another or more besides. *The vitamin tablets give her extra strength.*

extremely very.

eye NOUN one of the two parts of your face with which you see.

eyes

43

face NOUN **1** the front of your head from your hair to your chin. **2** the front of anything. *A clock face.*

face VERB (facing, faced) **1** to be opposite. *Facing the station.* **2** to deal with. *Face a problem.*

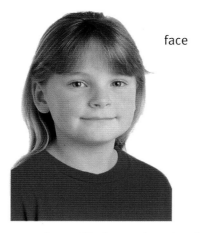

face

fact NOUN a piece of information that is true.

factory NOUN (PLURAL factories) a place where things are made by machines. *A car factory.*

fair ADJECTIVE **1** honest, sticking to the rules. *A fair contest.* **2** light in colour. *Fair skin.* **3** not bad, average. *A fair number of people.*

fair NOUN a show with rides, games, stalls, etc.

fairy NOUN (PLURAL fairies) a tiny, imaginary, winged creature who does magic.

fairy

fairy tale NOUN a children's story about fairies and magic. *The fairy tale had a happy ending.*

fall VERB (fell, fallen) **1** to drop down. *Snow was falling outside.* **2** to get lower. *The ground falls away steeply.*

fallen See **fall**. *Part of the roof has fallen down.*

false ADJECTIVE untrue or incorrect. *The information that I read in yesterday's newspaper turned out to be false.*

family NOUN (PLURAL families) **1** parents together with their children. **2** a group of people who are related. **3** any group of things or creatures that are alike or related.

famous ADJECTIVE well known by lots of people.

fan NOUN **1** something that makes air move to keep you cool. **2** an enthusiastic supporter of something.

fan

far a long way off.

farm NOUN buildings and land used for growing crops or keeping animals.

farmer NOUN someone who owns or looks after a farm. *The farmer kept sheep.*

fast ADJECTIVE **1** quick. **2** firmly fixed. *Stuck fast.* **3** ahead of time. *My watch is ten minutes fast.*

fasten VERB to fix or close.

fat ADJECTIVE (fatter, fattest) **1** having too much flesh on your body, overweight. **2** thick and round.

father NOUN a man who has a child.

fault NOUN a mistake in something.

favourite ADJECTIVE that is liked the best.

fax NOUN (PLURAL faxes) **1** information on paper sent electronically down a telephone line. **2** the machine that sends such information.

fax VERB to send information using a fax machine.

fear NOUN the feeling of being afraid, the feeling that danger is near.

feather NOUN one of the many soft, light coverings on a bird.

feathers

February NOUN the second month of the year after January and before March.

fed See **feed**. *Have you fed the rabbits today?*

feed VERB (fed) to give food to someone. *The mother feeds her children.*

feed

feel VERB (felt) **1** to touch. *Feel the texture.* **2** to experience something. *Feel terrified.* **3** to think. *He feels that eating meat is wrong.*

feet See **foot**.

fell See **fall**. *He tripped and fell.*

felt See **feel**. *After the bumpy ride, I felt ill.*

female NOUN a person or animal that can produce babies or young.

fence NOUN a barrier made of wood or wire that goes round a field or garden.

fence

fetch VERB to go to get something and bring it back.

fever NOUN an illness which gives you a very high temperature.

few not a lot.

field NOUN **1** an area of land surrounded by a fence or hedge, in which crops are grown or animals are kept. **2** any area where sports are played or something else takes place. *A battlefield.*

fierce ADJECTIVE cruel and angry.

fifteen the number 15.

fifty the number 50.

fight VERB (fought) **1** to try to hurt someone. **2** to struggle to get something.

figure NOUN **1** a number. **2** the shape of someone's body, especially a woman's body.

fill VERB to make something full.

film NOUN **1** a movie shown in the cinema. **2** something you put in your camera so that you can take photographs.

finally coming last, at the end. *Finally over.*

find VERB (found) **1** to discover something you have lost. **2** to learn, to work out.

fine

fine ADJECTIVE **1** very thin. *Fine silk.* **2** (of weather) dry, bright. *A fine day.*

fine NOUN money you have to pay if you do something wrong.

finger NOUN one of the four parts of your body at the end of each hand.

finish VERB to stop, to end.

fire NOUN **1** something that burns and gives out heat and light. **2** a gas or electric heater.

fire engine NOUN a large vehicle used to put out fires.

firefighter NOUN someone whose job is to put out fires.

fireworks PLURAL NOUN small chemical devices that burn and make noises to entertain people.

first ADJECTIVE **1** before any others. **2** the most important.

fishes

fish NOUN (PLURAL fishes) a creature that swims and lives in water and breathes through gills.

fishing NOUN the industry or sport of catching fish.

fist NOUN a tightly closed hand. *Clenched fist*

fit ADJECTIVE (fitter, fittest) healthy. *The runner became very fit after training for the New York marathon.*

firefighter

fit VERB (fitting, fitted) to be the right size and shape.

five the number 5.

5

five

fix VERB **1** to fasten something firmly. **2** to decide on something. *We've fixed a date for the wedding.* **3** to mend something.

flag NOUN a piece of cloth used as a sign or signal.

flame NOUN a red or yellow tongue of fire.

flash VERB to shine suddenly and briefly.

flat ADJECTIVE (flatter, flattest) **1** smooth and level. **2** below the right musical note. **3** without any air. *A flat tyre.*

flat NOUN home with the rooms on one floor of a larger building.

flavour NOUN the taste of something.

flew See **fly**. *The birds flew away.*

float VERB to stay on the top of a liquid without sinking, or to be kept up in the air. *My toy boat floated on the pond.*

flood NOUN water that covers what is usually dry land.

floor NOUN **1** the part of a building or room that you stand on. **2** all the rooms on the same level in a building.

flour NOUN a fine, white powder made from grain and used for baking.

flow VERB to run smoothly. *The wine flowed from the bottle.*

flower NOUN the part of a plant with petals and containing the seeds.

flown See **fly**. *Have you ever flown in an aeroplane?*

flu NOUN an illness like a very bad cold that gives you a temperature and makes you ache.

flute NOUN a musical instrument that you blow into.

fly NOUN (PLURAL flies) a flying insect.

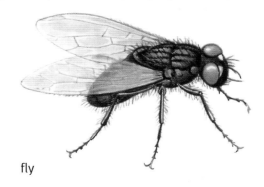

fly

fly VERB (flew, flown) **1** to move through the air like a bird. **2** to go in an aeroplane.

flood

47

fog

fog NOUN thick mist.

fold VERB to bend something over on itself.

follow VERB **1** to go after someone or something. **2** to support. *They follow their local football team.* **3** to understand. *Do you follow my meaning?*

food NOUN something you can eat.

foot NOUN (PLURAL feet) **1** the part of your body that you stand on. **2** a measurement equal to 12 inches or 0.305 metres.

football NOUN a team game in which you kick a ball and try to score goals.

footpath NOUN a path for you to walk on, especially in the countryside.

for 1 to be given to, to be meant for. *This present is for you.* **2** instead of. *New for old.* **3** as long as, as far as. *I ran for two miles.* **4** because of. *We couldn't see you for the crowds.* **5** at a cost of. *You can buy that for £1.*

forehead NOUN the part of your face below your hair and above your eyebrows.

forest NOUN a large area of land thickly covered with trees.

forgave *See* **forgive**. *He said sorry so she forgave him.*

forget VERB (forgot, forgotten) not to remember. *Try not to forget your coat.*

forgive VERB (forgiving, forgave, forgiven) to stop wanting to punish someone who has done something wrong.

forgiven *See* **forgive**. *I've forgiven you for what you did.*

forgot, forgotten *See* **forget**. *They forgot to come to tea. I've forgotten my computer password.*

fork NOUN **1** something with a handle and prongs that you use to eat your food with. *Eat with a knife and fork.* **2** a tool with a handle and prongs for digging the earth. *The fork is kept in the shed.*

fortunate ADJECTIVE lucky.

fortune NOUN **1** good luck. **2** fate, what will happen in the future. *The old woman told him his fortune.*

forty the number 40.

forwards towards the front. *We moved forwards to the front of the crowd.*

fossil NOUN the remains of an animal or plant that have hardened and left a print in rock.

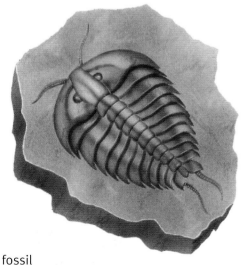

fossil

foster child NOUN a boy or girl who is officially looked after by parents who are not the natural parents.

fought See **fight**. *The soldiers fought in the war.*

found See **find**. *We found the keys down the side of the sofa.*

four the number 4.

four

fourteen the number 14.

fox NOUN (PLURAL foxes) a wild animal like a dog, but with a bushy tail.

fox

frame NOUN the structure surrounding a window, door, picture, etc.

free ADJECTIVE **1** able to do whatever you like. **2** not costing anything. **3** not being used.

freeze VERB (freezing, froze, frozen) to turn something hard and solid by making it very cold.

freezer NOUN a place to keep frozen food.

fresh ADJECTIVE **1** just made. *Fresh bread.* **2** just picked or grown. *Fresh vegetables.* **3** clean and pure. *Fresh air.*

fresh

Friday NOUN the day of the week after Thursday and before Saturday. *I'll see you on Friday.*

friend NOUN someone you know well and like to spend time with. *She has a lot of good friends.*

friendly ADJECTIVE (friendlier, friendliest) behaving in a kind and helpful way. *He is very friendly.*

frighten VERB to make someone afraid. *The dog frightened me when it barked.*

frill NOUN **1** strip of pleated paper or cloth attached to something as a decoration. *A frill on a dress.* **2** an unnecessary extra, a luxury. *No frills.*

frilly ADJECTIVE *He bought a frilly lampshade.*

frog NOUN a small animal that lives on land and in water and has long legs for jumping.

frog

from used to show where something begins. *Smoke comes from a fire.*

front NOUN **1** the position facing forwards. **2** the most important position.

frontier NOUN the border where one country meets another. *Eastern frontier.*

frost NOUN white, powdery ice that forms outdoors in freezing weather.

frown VERB to wrinkle your forehead when you are cross or worried.

frown

froze, frozen *See* **freeze**. *The water froze to form ice. The lake has frozen over.*

fruit NOUN the part of a plant that has the seeds in it and can often be eaten.

fry VERB (frying, fried) to cook in hot oil or fat.

full ADJECTIVE holding as much as is possible.

full

full stop The punctuation mark (.) is called a *full stop*. It is used: **1** at the end of a sentence. *Jo came to our house.* **2** after short forms of a word (abbreviations) and initial letters that stand for a whole word: *'Jan.'* stands for *'January'*.

fun NOUN enjoyment. *We had lots of fun at the fair.*

funny ADJECTIVE (funnier, funniest) **1** something that makes you laugh. **2** odd, strange. *My friend tells funny jokes that make me laugh.*

fur NOUN the soft hair on some animals.

furniture PLURAL NOUN things that you need in a room like chairs, cupboards, tables, etc.

furry ADJECTIVE (furrier, furriest) covered in thick, soft hair. *They had lots of furry kittens in the pet shop.*

furry

future NOUN the period of time after the present.

gale NOUN a very strong wind.

gallop NOUN the fastest speed at which a horse can move.

gallop VERB to move at this speed, to move very fast.

game NOUN something you play, usually with rules.

game

gap NOUN a narrow opening or space.

garage NOUN **1** a place to keep your car. **2** a place where you can take your car to be mended or to get fuel.

garden NOUN land, often by a house, where plants are grown.

gas NOUN **1** something like air that is neither solid nor liquid. **2** fuel used for cooking and heating.

gate NOUN a barrier like a door which opens to let you go through a fence, wall, hedge, etc.

gave See **give**. *We gave Ben his birthday present.*

geese See **goose**.

gel NOUN a smooth, soft substance like jelly which you put on your hair to keep it in a particular style.

gentle ADJECTIVE kind, calm and quiet.

geography NOUN the study of the earth and how people live.

gerbil NOUN a small animal like a large mouse that is kept as a pet.

get VERB (getting, got) **1** to have. **2** to buy. **3** to catch an illness.

ghost

ghost NOUN a spirit that appears and looks like a dead person.

giant NOUN a huge man, often written about in fairy tales.

gift NOUN a present.

geese

giggle VERB (giggling, giggled) to laugh in a nervous or silly way.

giraffe NOUN tall, wild animal with a long neck and legs.

giraffe

girl NOUN a female child.

give VERB (giving, gave, given) **1** to let someone have something to keep. **2** to show or tell. *To give a talk.*

given See **give**. *Have you given her the present?*

glad ADJECTIVE (gladder, gladdest) happy and pleased.

glass NOUN (PLURAL glasses) **1** hard, clear material used in windows. **2** something made of this that you drink out of.

glasses PLURAL NOUN something you wear over your eyes to help you to see better or to protect them, also called spectacles.

glasses

gloves PLURAL NOUN something you wear on your hands to keep them warm or to protect them.

glue NOUN a substance that sticks things together.

go VERB (went, gone) **1** to start or move. *On your marks, get set, go!* **2** to travel. *Go abroad.* **3** to reach. *Does this road go to the beach?* **4** to work.

goal NOUN **1** the posts between which the ball is aimed in football and some other games. **2** the point scored when the ball passes between the posts. **3** something that you aim for or want to achieve.

goat NOUN a hairy animal with horns that looks a bit like a sheep.

gold NOUN **1** a precious yellow metal. **2** the colour of this metal.

goldfish NOUN a small, often golden, fish usually kept indoors in a tank as a pet.

golf NOUN an outdoor game in which a small hard ball is hit with clubs into various holes on a course.

gone See **go**. *Sarah has gone on holiday.*

good ADJECTIVE **1** pleasant, satisfactory. *Have a good time.* **2** kind. *They were good to us.* **3** well-behaved. *Good dog!* **4** used in greeting someone. *Good evening.*

goodbye said when you leave someone.

goose NOUN (PLURAL geese) a big bird with webbed feet.

got See **get**. *Have you got any books on France?*

grab VERB (grabbing, grabbed) to take hold of something suddenly and roughly.

gram NOUN a measurement of weight equal to 0.01kg.

grandfather NOUN the father of your mother or father.

grandmother NOUN the mother of your mother or father.

grapes

grape NOUN a small green or purple fruit that grows in bunches and is used to make wine.

grapefruit NOUN a round yellow fruit with a slightly bitter taste.

grass NOUN a green plant that is food for cows, sheep, horses, etc.

gravy NOUN a brown sauce that you eat with meat.

great ADJECTIVE **1** very big. **2** very good. **3** unusually clever or important.

green NOUN having the colour of grass.

greengrocer NOUN someone who sells fruit and vegetables.

grew See **grow**. *The tree grew very tall.*

grey ADJECTIVE having the colour of ashes or rain clouds.

grill NOUN a metal implement used to cook food over a strong heat.

grill VERB to cook something under a flame or strong heat.

ground NOUN **1** the surface of the earth. **2** soil. **3** a piece of land where you can play a sport.

group NOUN a number of people or things gathered together.

grow VERB (grew, grown) **1** to get bigger. **2** to live and develop. **3** to plant and water flowers, vegetables, etc. **4** to become. *The nights are growing colder.*

grown See **grow**. *I have grown ten centimetres.*

grown-up NOUN a fully grown person, an adult.

guard NOUN **1** someone who watches over something or someone. **2** someone in charge of a train. **3** something that protects you from harm.

guard

guard VERB to protect.

guess VERB to give an answer to something when you are not sure whether it is right or wrong, to estimate. *I guessed the answer to the sum, but I'm not sure that it was right.*

guinea pig NOUN a small, furry animal that can be kept as a pet.

guinea pig

guitar NOUN a stringed musical instrument played with the fingers.

gun NOUN a weapon that fires bullets.

gym NOUN a place where you can go to train and exercise your body.

53

habit NOUN something that you do often or regularly.

had *See* **have**. I had finished.

hadn't = had not. *If they hadn't told us, we wouldn't have heard the news.*

hail NOUN drops of frozen rain.

hair NOUN **1** fine threads that grow on your skin, especially on your head, and also on the skin of animals. **2** a single one of these.

hairdresser NOUN someone who washes, cuts and styles hair.

half NOUN (PLURAL halves) one of the two equal parts that something is divided into, written as 0.5 or $\frac{1}{2}$.

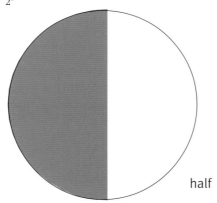

half

half-brother/sister NOUN a brother/sister in your family who has only one of the same parents as you, rather than both.

halves *See* **half**.

hall NOUN **1** the part of a house that is just inside the front door. **2** a big room that can be used for meetings, dances, etc.

ham NOUN meat that comes from a pig's leg.

hamburger

hamburger NOUN a round cake of chopped beef that you eat fried or grilled in a bun.

hammer NOUN a tool used for hitting nails, etc. into things.

hammer

hamster NOUN a little, furry animal kept indoors in a cage as a pet.

hand NOUN **1** the part of your body at the end of your arm. **2** the part of a clock that points to the time.

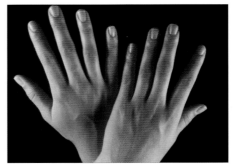

hands

handkerchief NOUN a square piece of material on which you blow your nose.

handle NOUN the part of something you hold it by.

handle VERB (handling, handled) to hold something in your hands.

hang VERB (hung or hanged) **1** to fix something at the top, leaving the lower part free. *I hung the washing on the line and left it to dry.* **2** to kill or die by having a rope tied round your neck.

happen VERB to take place. *Something important is going to happen.*

happy ADJECTIVE pleased or glad.

hard ADJECTIVE **1** solid, not soft. **2** difficult to do.

has See **have**. *It has started to rain.*

hasn't = has not. *It hasn't snowed this year.*

hat NOUN something that you wear on your head.

hat

hatch NOUN an opening in a wall, usually for passing food and dishes through from a kitchen to a dining-room.

hatch VERB to break out of an egg, as a baby bird does.

hatchback NOUN a car with a door at the back that opens upwards.

hate VERB (hating, hated) to dislike someone or something very much.

haunted ADJECTIVE a place said to be visited by a ghost.

have VERB (has, having, had) **1** to own. **2** to receive. **3** to enjoy or experience. **4** to get something done. *I have to do my homework.*

haven't = have not. *I haven't seen David today.*

hay NOUN dried grass used as animal feed.

he (him, himself) a man, boy or male animal.

he'd = he had, he would. *He'd come if he could.*

he'll = he will. *He'll do that.*

he's = he is, he has. *He's on his way.*

head NOUN **1** the part of your body above your neck. **2** the person in charge. **3** the front part or top of something.

headache NOUN a pain in your head.

headteacher NOUN the teacher in charge of a school.

heal VERB to become healthy again.

health NOUN the condition of your body.

healthy ADJECTIVE (healthier, healthiest) well, without any illness.

hear VERB (heard) **1** to receive sounds through your ears. **2** to get news of, to be told.

heard See **hear**. *We heard the news.*

heart NOUN **1** the part of your body that pumps the blood round. **2** a kind of geometric shape. **3** the centre of your feelings. **4** the middle of something.

heart

heat NOUN **1** warmth. **2** a race or competition that comes before the final and decides who will take part in the final.

heat VERB to make something hot.

heavy ADJECTIVE (heavier, heaviest) **1** weighing a lot, difficult to lift. **2** worse or more than usual. *Heavy snow.*

heavy

hedgehog NOUN a small, prickly animal that feeds at night and rolls itself into a ball for protection.

hedgehog

heel NOUN **1** the back part of your foot. **2** the part of your shoe under this.

height NOUN how tall or high something is.

held See **hold**. *He held the baby in his arms.*

helicopter NOUN an aircraft with large blades that go round above it instead of wings.

hello said when you are greeting someone or when you answer the telephone. *I picked up the telephone and said, 'Hello!'.*

helmet NOUN a hard hat worn to protect the head. Workers on building sites wear helmets to protect them from falling objects.

help VERB **1** to do something to make things easier for someone else, to assist. **2** to avoid or stop doing something. **3** to serve food and drink.

hen NOUN a female chicken usually kept for laying eggs.

hen

her, herself See **she**. *I like her.*

herbs

herb NOUN a plant used as a medicine or to make food tastier. *She added some mixed herbs to the stew.*

helicopter

here in, at or to this place. *You are here.*

hers that or those belonging to her. *The football boots over there are hers.*

hiccup VERB to make little choking sounds in your throat.

hid, hidden See **hide**. *Mum has hidden the Easter eggs.*

hide VERB (hiding, hid, hidden) to put out of sight, to keep secret. *'You are hiding something,' she said.*

high ADJECTIVE **1** a long way up from the ground. **2** measuring from top to bottom. **3** very important.

hill NOUN an area of high ground, sloping at the sides. *Climb the hill.*

him, himself See **he**. *I like him.*

hippopotamus NOUN (PLURAL hippopotamuses or hippopotami) a big animal with short legs that lives by rivers in Africa.

his belonging to him, that or those belonging to him. *That book is his.*

history NOUN the study of the past.

hit NOUN **1** a blow. **2** a great success.

hit VERB (hitting, hit) to bang hard against something.

hive NOUN a place where bees live.

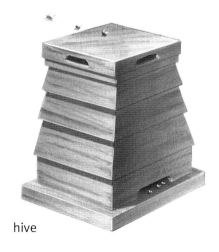

hive

hobby NOUN (PLURAL hobbies) something that you like to do in your spare time.

hold VERB (held) to have or carry something firmly in your hands or arms.

hole NOUN **1** an opening or gap. **2** an animal's home.

holiday NOUN a time of rest when you are not at school or at work.

hollow ADJECTIVE with an empty space inside, not solid all the way through.

home NOUN **1** the place where you live. **2** a place where people or animals live together so that they can be looked after.

honey NOUN the sweet, sticky food that bees make.

hood NOUN **1** something you cover your head with, often part of a coat or jacket. **2** a folding cover, like that on a pram.

hoof NOUN (PLURAL hoofs or hooves) the foot of an animal such as a horse.

hook NOUN a piece of metal or plastic, curved to catch something, or to hang things on.

hook

hoop NOUN a large ring of wood, metal, etc.

hop VERB (hopping, hopped) **1** to jump on one foot. **2** to move by jumping along, as some animals and birds do.

hope VERB (hoping, hoped) to wish for something. *I hoped that I would win the race.*

horn NOUN **1** one of the hard, pointed parts that grow on the heads of animals like cows and goats. **2** a musical instrument that you blow into. **3** something on a vehicle that makes a loud noise as a signal or warning.

horrible ADJECTIVE nasty and unpleasant.

horse NOUN a large animal with a mane and tail that can be ridden or used to pull other vehicles.

horse

hospital NOUN a place where sick people stay for treatment.

hot ADJECTIVE (hotter, hottest) **1** giving off a lot of heat. *Hot sun.* **2** having a burning taste. *The chillies in the soup were extremely hot.*

hotel NOUN a building in which you stay when you are on holiday, where you pay for a room and meals.

hotel

hour NOUN a period of time equal to 60 minutes.

house NOUN a building where usually just one family lives

house

hovercraft NOUN a vehicle that can move over land and water on a cushion of air.

how 1 in what way. **2** by what amount. **3** in what state.

hug VERB (hugging, hugged) to hold tightly in your arms.*I hugged my teddy bear close as I fell asleep.*

huge ADJECTIVE very large.

hum VERB (humming, hummed) **1** to make a sound like a bee buzzing. **2** to sing without opening your lips.

human ADJECTIVE of people. *A human being.*

human NOUN a man, woman or child, a person rather than an animal.

hump NOUN a bump or lump that sticks up.

hundred NOUN the number 100.

hung See **hang**. *I hung my coat on the peg.*

hungry ADJECTIVE (hungrier, hungriest) feeling that you want or need food.

hunt VERB **1** to chase wild animals for food or sport. **2** to search for something.

hurry VERB (hurrying, hurried) to move quickly.

hurt VERB (hurt) to cause pain or harm.

husband NOUN the man that a woman is married to.

I (me, myself) the speaker or writer himself or herself.

I'd = I had, I would. *I'd seen them.*

I'll = I will. *I'll come later.*

I'm = I am. *I'm very happy.*

I've = I have. *I've an idea.*

ice NOUN frozen water.

ice

ice-cream NOUN a sweet, creamy, frozen food, often served in a wafer cone.

ice-cream

ice-skating NOUN moving on ice wearing skates.

iceberg NOUN a large mass of ice that floats in the sea.

icicle NOUN a long pointed piece of ice that hangs down from a roof or other surface.

icing NOUN a mixture made from powdered sugar that is used to cover cakes.

idea NOUN a thought or plan in your mind about what to do, how something can be done, etc.

idea

if 1 supposing that. *I'd buy a new car if I could afford it.* **2** whether or not. *Do you know if it's raining?* **3** whenever. *If I don't keep my room tidy, I can't find anything.*

igloo NOUN an Inuit shelter made with blocks of snow.

igloo

ill ADJECTIVE unwell, sick.

illness NOUN a disease or sickness.

imagine VERB (imagining, imagined) to picture something in your mind.

imitate VERB (imitating, imitated) to copy something or someone.

immediately at once, now.

important ADJECTIVE **1** to be taken seriously. **2** valuable. **3** well known.

impossible ADJECTIVE not possible, cannot be done.

in 1 inside. *Your dinner is in the oven.* **2** at. *They live in Manchester.* **3** into. *He jumped in the pool.* **4** during. *In the school holidays.*

indoors inside a building.

information NOUN knowledge about something.

inhaler NOUN a device you use to breathe in medicines.

initial NOUN the first letter of your name.

injection NOUN medicine put into your body with a needle.

injure VERB (injuring, injured) to harm someone. *To injure your leg.*

ink NOUN a coloured liquid that you use with a pen to write or draw.

insect NOUN a small creature with six legs and a body that is divided into three parts.

insect

inside 1 in or near the inner part of something. **2** indoors. *When it rains outside, I always stay inside.*

instead in place of. *I chose to wear the red dress to the party, instead of the blue.*

instruction NOUN some information that tells you what to do. *The instructions on the map showed the way to the treasure.*

instrument NOUN **1** a tool. **2** something that you play to make music.

instrument

interested ADJECTIVE wanting to know more about something. *Harry was interested in astronomy.*

interesting ADJECTIVE something that keeps your attention.

interfere VERB (interfering, interfered) to get involved in a situation that does not concern you.

Internet NOUN a large number of computers all over the world that are linked together to work as a system.

interrupt VERB to break in when someone else is in the middle of doing or saying something. *James rudely interrupted the conversation.*

into in or to the inside. *I stepped into the room.*

invention NOUN something new that has not been made before. The wheel, the telephone and the television were all inventions.

invisible ADJECTIVE not able to be seen.

invitation NOUN something written or spoken to you, asking you to come to a party, meal, etc.

invitation

invite VERB (inviting, invited) to ask someone to come to a party, meal, etc. *I invited all my friends at school to my birthday party.*

invoice NOUN a document asking for payment for goods that have been sent or work that has been done. *He gave me an invoice for £1500.*

iron NOUN **1** a metal used to make steel. **2** a device for getting creases out of clothes.

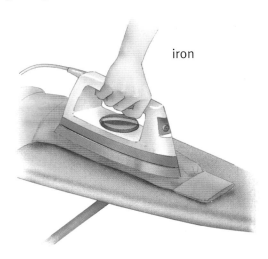

iron

irony NOUN using words to say the very opposite of what they really mean. *'How very clever of you to smash my best dinner plate!'*

irregular ADJECTIVE **1** not regular or usual. *He works irregular hours.* **2** not even or smooth. *The surface of the road was irregular.*

is *See* **be**. *Sally is my best friend.*

island NOUN a piece of land that has water all round it.

island

isn't = is not. *Ray isn't here*

it (itself) that thing, situation, etc.

it's = it is, it has. *It's a very nice present.*

itch NOUN a feeling that makes you want to scratch. *I scratched the itch on my nose.*

item NOUN a single thing on a list or in a group of other things. *An item of news.*

its belonging to it. *Its colour.*

ivy NOUN a climbing evergreen plant with shiny, pointed leaves.

ivy

jacket NOUN a short coat.

jagged ADJECTIVE having sharp, rough edges.

jail NOUN a prison.

jail

jam NOUN **1** a sweet food made by boiling fruit with sugar. **2** a mass of things tightly crowded together. *A traffic jam.*

January NOUN the first month of the year.

jar NOUN a glass container that has a lid and a wider mouth than a bottle.

jazz NOUN a kind of music with a strong rhythm.

jealous ADJECTIVE **1** envious, wanting what someone else has. **2** afraid of losing what you have.

jeans PLURAL NOUN strong, casual trousers, often made out of denim cloth.

jelly NOUN a soft, clear dessert that wobbles when you move it.

jellyfish NOUN (PLURAL jellyfish) a sea creature that looks like a jelly and can sting you.

jersey NOUN a sweater, a jumper.

jet NOUN **1** a powerful stream of liquid, gas, etc., forced through a small opening. **2** a kind of aeroplane with jet engines.

jewel NOUN a precious stone that can be used to decorate valuable ornaments.

jewellery NOUN ornaments like necklaces and rings, made out of precious metals and often decorated with jewels.

jigsaw NOUN a puzzle in which you have to fit together lots of different pieces to make a picture.

jigsaw

jet

job NOUN **1** the regular work that you get paid to do. **2** any piece of work or task.

join VERB **1** to fasten together. **2** to become a member of a group or club.

joke NOUN something funny said to make you laugh.

joke VERB (joking, joked) to say something funny or tell a funny story.

jolly ADJECTIVE happy and cheerful.

journey NOUN the distance you travel to get from one place to another.

jug NOUN a container with a handle and a lip for pouring liquids from.

juice NOUN the liquid in fruit, plants, etc.

July NOUN the seventh month of the year, after June and before August.

July

jump VERB **1** to leap up in the air by pushing off with both your feet. **2** to move suddenly, often because something frightens or surprises you.

jumper NOUN a knitted piece of clothing that you pull over your head to cover the upper part of your body.

June NOUN the sixth month of the year, after May and before July.

jungle

jungle NOUN a thick forest in hot countries.

junk NOUN old things that are not worth very much.

just 1 exactly. *I had just the right money.* **2** almost not. *I just made it in time for lessons.* **3** very recently. *The shop had just closed.* **4** only. *I just wanted to ask you something.*

just ADJECTIVE fair and right. *A just decision.*

justice NOUN **1** treatment that is just, fair and right. **2** a country's system of laws and how they are operated by the law courts. **3** a judge. *A Justice of the Peace.*

justify VERB (justifies, justifying, justified) to defend or to prove that something is just and fair.

jut VERB (juts, jutting, jutted) to stick out farther than other things around it, to project. *The balcony juts out from the side of the house.*

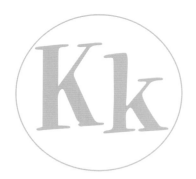

kangaroo NOUN a large Australian animal that has big, strong back legs for jumping and keeps its young in a pouch.

kangaroo

karaoke NOUN entertainment in which people sing along to a backing track while the words appear on a screen.

karate NOUN a Japanese form of self-defence using blows and kicks.

keep VERB (kept) **1** to have something with you that you do not give back. **2** to look after something. **3** to stay or remain. **4** to own.

kennel NOUN a shelter for a dog to live in.

kennel

kept See **keep**. *We kept the video.*

kerb NOUN the raised edge between the pavement and the road.

kettle NOUN a metal or plastic container with a handle and a spout for boiling water in.

key NOUN **1** a shaped piece of metal for opening and closing locks. **2** a part of a typewriter or piano that works when you press it with your finger. **3** a set of musical notes. **4** something that explains symbols or abbreviations on a diagram or map.

keyboard NOUN the set of keys that you press to work an instrument like a piano or computer.

kick VERB to hit with your foot. *I kicked the football and it flew straight into the goal.*

kill VERB to cause someone to die.

kilogram NOUN a measurement of weight equal to 1,000 grams or 2.21 pounds.

kilometre NOUN a measurement of length equal to 1,000 metres or 0.62 miles.

kind ADJECTIVE helpful and friendly, doing good to others. *I always try to be kind to my friends.*

kind NOUN sort, type.

king NOUN **1** the male ruler of a country. **2** a chess piece.

kiss

kiss VERB to touch someone with your lips as a greeting, or because you love them. *When my best friend arrived at the party, I gave her a kiss on the cheek.*

kit NOUN **1** a group of things kept together because they are used for a similar purpose. *A shoe-cleaning kit.* **2** a set of clothing or equipment that you use when you play a sport. *Football kit.* **3** all the bits and pieces that you need to make something. *A model aeroplane kit.*

kitchen NOUN the room where you prepare and cook food.

kite NOUN a light frame covered with paper or material which you hold by a long string and fly in the air on windy days.

kitten NOUN a baby cat.

kittens

knee NOUN the part of your body where your leg bends.

knew See **know**. *We knew the answer.*

knickers PLURAL NOUN pants worn by girls and women.

knife NOUN (PLURAL knives) a device with a blade and handle that cuts things.

knit VERB (knitting, knitted or knit) to make wool into clothes by using special needles or a machine.

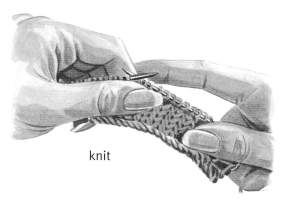
knit

knives See **knife**.

knock VERB to bang against something to make a noise. *I knocked on the door to let them know that I was there.*

knot NOUN **1** the fastening made when you tie two pieces of something together. **2** a hard lump in wood. **3** the way that you measure the speed of a boat.

know VERB (knew, known) **1** to remember or understand something you have learnt. **2** to recognize someone. *I know that I have seen your face before.*

known See **know**. *We have known them for years.*

knowledge NOUN the things that you know and understand, things that you learn by study.

knowledgeable ADJECTIVE clever and well-informed about a subject.

know-all NOUN somebody who thinks they know a great deal about everything.

know-how NOUN practical knowledge and ability.

knuckle NOUN the bones at the joint of a finger.

koala NOUN an Australian animal that looks like a small bear. Koalas live in eucalyptus trees and feed on their leaves.

koala

label NOUN a piece of paper or card which gives you information about the thing that it is attached to.

lace NOUN **1** delicate cloth with a lot of holes in it. **2** a thin piece of cord that you use to tie shoes and boots.

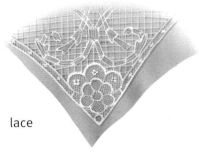

lace

ladder NOUN two long pieces of wood or metal with rungs fixed between them that you use for climbing.

lagoon NOUN a seawater lake separated from the sea by sandbanks or rocks.

laid See **lay**. *The hen laid an egg.*

lain See **lie**. *They have lain in the sun for too long.*

lake NOUN a large area of water with land all round it.

lamb NOUN **1** a young sheep. **2** meat from a young sheep.

lamb

lamp NOUN a device to give light.

land NOUN **1** a country. **2** solid ground, not the sea.

land VERB to come back to solid ground from a ship or an aeroplane.

landing NOUN the floor space at the top of the stairs.

language NOUN the sounds you use to speak or the words you use to write.

lap NOUN **1** the flat area formed by the top of your legs when you sit down. **2** once round a course or track.

lap VERB (lapping, lapped) to drink like a cat does.

large ADJECTIVE big in size or number.

last ADJECTIVE **1** after all the others. *The last train left over an hour ago.* **2** the most recent. *The last time we saw them.*

last VERB to continue for some time.

late ADJECTIVE **1** after the right time. *Late for school.* **2** near the end of a period of time. *Late in the day.*

laugh VERB the sound that you make when you are happy or when you find something funny. *The clowns at the circus always make me laugh.*

laugh

law NOUN a rule that the government makes which everyone has to keep.

lawn NOUN an area of short, mowed grass in a park or garden.

lawn

lawnmower NOUN a machine for cutting grass on lawns.

lay See **lie**. *She lay down on the bed.*

lay VERB (laid) **1** to place or set in a particular position. **2** to produce an egg. *I laid the knives and forks on the table, ready for dinner.*

layer NOUN an amount or level of substance that covers a surface.

lazy ADJECTIVE (lazier, laziest) not wanting to do any work. *Mum says I am lazy because I watch television instead of doing my homework.*

lead (said like **bed**) NOUN **1** a soft, grey metal. **2** the black part in the middle of a pencil.

lead (said like **feed**) NOUN **1** the first position in a race or competition. **2** the main part in a play or film. **3** the strap that you tie to a dog's collar to take it for a walk.

lead (said like **feed**) VERB (led) **1** to go in front to show the way. **2** to be in first place. **3** to be in charge.

leader NOUN **1** someone who goes first. **2** the most important person or the one in charge.

leaf NOUN (PLURAL leaves) the flat, green part of a plant that grows from a stem or branch. Some leaves change colour in autumn.

leaves

lean VERB (leant or leaned) **1** to be in a sloping position. **2** to support yourself by resting against something.

leant or **leaned** See **lean**. *Jo leant against the wall.*

learn VERB (learnt or learned) to study to get knowledge, to find out about things. *I would like to learn to speak French.*

learnt or **learned** See **learn**. *Have you learnt your times tables yet?*

least the smallest in number, amount, etc.

leather NOUN material made from animal skins.

leave VERB (leaving, left) **1** to go away from. **2** to put something in a place where it stays.

leaves See **leaf**.

led VERB *Harry led the way.*

left See **leave**. *Tom left the house very early in the morning.*

left ADJECTIVE to or on the opposite side or direction to right.

leg NOUN **1** the part of your body between your hips and your feet that you use to walk with. **2** the part that supports a piece of furniture.

legend NOUN an old, well-known story that may or may not be true. *The legend of King Arthur.*

leggings PLURAL NOUN tight-fitting, stretchy trousers.

lemon NOUN a sour, yellow fruit.

lemon

lend VERB (lent) to let someone use something for a period of time.

length NOUN the measurement of something from end to end.

lent See **lend**. *I've lent my book.*

leopard NOUN a wild animal of the cat family with yellow fur and black spots.

leotard NOUN a tight-fitting, stretchy body suit that you wear for exercise or dancing.

leotard

less a smaller amount, not so much.

lesson NOUN a period in the school day when a subject is taught.

let's = let us. *Let's go.*

letter NOUN **1** a message written on paper that you send to someone in an envelope, usually through the post. **2** one of the signs you write to make words.

lettuce NOUN a green plant eaten in salads.

lettuce

level ADJECTIVE **1** flat and smooth. **2** even or equal

library NOUN (PLURAL libraries) a building where books are kept for you to borrow and read.

lick VERB to touch something with your tongue.

lick

lid NOUN the cover of a container.

lie NOUN something you say which you know is not the truth.

lie VERB (lying, lied) to tell a lie.

lie VERB (lying, lay, lain) to be in a flat position, as when you are in bed. *We can lie on our backs and look at the stars.*

life NOUN (PLURAL lives) **1** being alive and breathing. **2** the time between birth and death. **3** the way you live or spend your time.

lifeboat NOUN a boat that rescues people who are in danger at sea.

lift NOUN **1** a large metal box on pulleys used to carry people from one floor of a building to another. **2** a free ride in a vehicle.

lift VERB to pick something up and place it in a higher position.

light ADJECTIVE not heavy.

light NOUN **1** brightness from the sun or a lamp that lets you see things. **2** something which gives out light.

light bulb NOUN glass part of an electric light or lamp that gives out light.

lighthouse NOUN tall tower on the coast that flashes a light to warn ships of danger.

lighthouse

lightning NOUN flash of light in the sky in a storm.

lightning

like VERB (liking, liked) **1** to be fond of someone or something. **2** to wish.

like 1 similar to. **2** for example.

likely ADJECTIVE (likelier, likeliest) **1** expected. **2** suitable.

line NOUN **1** long, thin mark. *Draw a line on the blackboard.* **2** a piece of string, wire, etc. *A washing-line.* **3** a row, queue. *A line of cars.*

lion NOUN wild animal of the cat family.

lion

lips PLURAL NOUN the pink edges of your mouth.

liquid NOUN anything that is not solid and flows like water.

list NOUN a number of things written down one below the other.

listen VERB to pay attention to sounds that you hear.

litre NOUN a measurement of liquid equal to 1.759 pints.

litter NOUN **1** rubbish. **2** a family of baby animals all born at the same time.

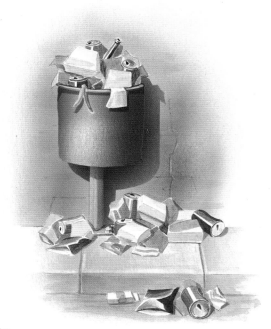

litter

little ADJECTIVE small, not large in size or amount.

live VERB (living, lived) **1** to be alive. **2** to make your home in a particular place. **3** to spend your life in a particular way.

lives See **life**.

living room NOUN room in a home to sit and relax in.

loaf NOUN (PLURAL loaves) bread shaped and baked in one piece.

loaf

loaves See **loaf**

lock NOUN **1** a device that fastens something when you use it with a key. **2** a section of a canal with gates at either end, to move boats between different water levels.

lock VERB to fasten something with a key.

loft NOUN the space in the roof of a house.

log NOUN a thick piece of wood cut from a tree.

lonely ADJECTIVE (lonelier, loneliest) feeling sad because you are on your own or you do not have any friends. *I felt very lonely when we first moved.*

long ADJECTIVE **1** covering a great distance or time. **2** the measurement of something from one end to the other. *The boat is twenty metres long.*

look VERB **1** to see with your eyes. **2** to appear or seem.

loose ADJECTIVE **1** not tight. **2** free.

lorry NOUN (PLURAL lorries) a large vehicle for carrying goods, a truck.

lose VERB (losing, lost) **1** to misplace something. **2** to be beaten in a competition or game.

lost See **lose**. *We lost the football match.*

lot NOUN a large number or amount.

lottery NOUN (PLURAL lotteries) a gambling game in which you buy a ticket with certain numbers in the hope of winning prizes.

loud ADJECTIVE noisy.

loudspeaker NOUN a device that produces the sound in radios, music systems, etc.

lounge NOUN room in a home to sit and relax in.

love NOUN a very strong feeling of liking for someone. *I love you.*

love VERB (loving, loved) to like someone or something very strongly.

lovely ADJECTIVE (lovelier, loveliest) **1** beautiful. *A lovely face.* **2** nice, pleasant. *We had a lovely time on holiday.*

low ADJECTIVE near to the ground, not high.

lucky ADJECTIVE (luckier, luckiest) having good things happening to you by chance.

luggage NOUN the suitcases and bags that you take with you on a journey.

lump NOUN **1** a solid mass of something. **2** a swelling.

lump

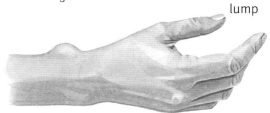

lunch NOUN the meal you eat in the middle of the day. *We went out for lunch and then shopped in the afternoon.*

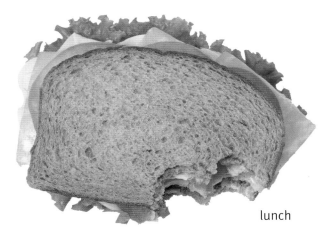

lunch

lung NOUN one of the two organs inside your chest that you use for breathing. The lungs take in oxygen from the air and give out carbon dioxide.

lunge VERB to make a sudden thrust forward. *She lunged at him with a stick.*

lure VERB to attract and tempt, to lead astray. *They were lured by the bright lights of the fair.*

lurk VERB to wait around out of sight with a dishonest purpose, to prowl. *There is somebody lurking under the trees.*

luggage

macaroni NOUN short, thin tubes of pasta.

machine NOUN a piece of equipment that uses power to work.

made *See* **make**. *Made in England.*

magazine NOUN a regular publication in a paper cover that contains stories, pictures, advertisements, etc.

magic NOUN **1** conjuring tricks. **2** using witchcraft to try to control what happens.

magic

magician NOUN a person who does conjuring tricks.

magnet NOUN a piece of metal that draws other metal objects towards it.

main ADJECTIVE most important.

make VERB (making, made) **1** to produce or build something. **2** to cause something to happen. **3** to earn or get.

male NOUN a person or animal belonging to the sex that cannot produce babies or young.

mammal NOUN an animal that drinks milk from its mother's body.

man NOUN (PLURAL men) an adult male.

many (more, most) a large number. *Many schools.*

map NOUN a drawing that shows countries, rivers, towns, roads, etc.

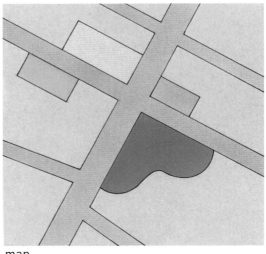

map

marble NOUN **1** a hard stone used for buildings and statues. **2** a small glass ball used to play the game of marbles.

March NOUN the third month of the year, after February and before April.

march VERB to walk with regular strides as soldiers do.

mark NOUN **1** a spot or pattern on something, often spoiling it. **2** a number or letter on a piece of work that shows how good it is.

mark VERB **1** to damage a surface by leaving a stain, etc., on it. **2** to put a number or letter on a piece of work that shows how good it is.

market NOUN a place where people buy and sell things from stalls.

marmalade NOUN jam made with oranges.

marry VERB (marrying, married) **1** to become the husband or wife of someone. **2** to join a man and a woman together as husband and wife.

mascara NOUN make-up that you put on your eyelashes to thicken or colour them.

mask NOUN something that you put over your face as a disguise or to protect it.

matches

match NOUN (PLURAL matches) **1** a short stick with one end coated so that it catches fire when you strike it. **2** a contest between two teams or players.

material NOUN **1** anything that you can make things from. **2** cloth.

mathematics PLURAL NOUN the study of numbers and shapes.

matter NOUN **1** the material from which the universe and everything in it is made. **2** trouble or pain. *What's the matter?*

May NOUN the fifth month of the year, after April and before June.

may VERB (might) **1** to be likely. *I may go out tonight.* **2** to ask if you can do something. *May I leave the room?*

me *See* **I**. *She saw me.*

meal NOUN the food that you eat at a certain time.

mean ADJECTIVE **1** not willing to spend much money. **2** unkind.

mean VERB (meant) **1** to show or indicate. *What does this word mean?* **2** to want or intend to do or say something. *I meant to choose this book, not that one.* **3** designed for a particular use. *This toy isn't meant for babies.*

meant *See* **mean**. *I meant to come earlier, but I forgot about the time.*

measles NOUN an infectious disease that gives you a temperature and red spots on your skin.

measure VERB (measuring, measured) to find out how long something is, how much it weighs, etc.

measurement NOUN the length, width, height, etc., of something.

meat NOUN the food that we eat that comes from an animal's flesh.

medal NOUN a small piece of metal with a special design on it, awarded to winners of sporting events or to people who have been very brave.

medicine NOUN a liquid or pills that you take when you are ill to make you better. *When I have a cold, medicine always makes me feel better.*

May

medicine

medium ADJECTIVE neither large nor small.

meet VERB (met) to come together with someone.

melt VERB to change something from a solid to a liquid.

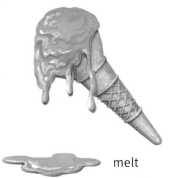

melt

memory NOUN (PLURAL memories) your ability to remember things.

men See **man**.

mend VERB to put something back in its proper condition, so that it works again or is not damaged.

merry-go-round NOUN a fairground ride.

mess NOUN an untidy or dirty condition.

message NOUN written or spoken information sent from one person to another.

met See **meet**. *We met at the station.*

metal NOUN a hard material like copper, tin, iron or gold.

metre NOUN measurement of length equal to 39.37 inches.

miaow VERB to make a noise like a cat.

mice See **mouse**.

microscope NOUN an instrument that you look through which makes very small objects appear bigger.

microwave NOUN **1** a short-length electromagnetic wave. **2** an oven that cooks food quickly by using microwaves instead of heat.

midday NOUN 12 o'clock in the daytime.

middle NOUN the point that is at an equal distance from either of the two ends or edges of something.

midnight NOUN 12 o'clock at night.

might See **may**. *I might have won.*

milk NOUN a white liquid that comes from cows and other female animals, and can be drunk or made into butter and cheese.

millennium NOUN (PLURAL millenniums or millennia) **1** the year 2000. **2** the thousand years beginning in 2000, or more exactly 2001.

million NOUN the number 1,000,000.

mind NOUN your ability to think and feel.

mind VERB to be annoyed or bothered. *I do not mind.*

mine that or those belonging to me. *My sister wanted to keep the trousers, but I told her they were mine.*

minister NOUN **1** someone in charge of a government department. **2** a member of the clergy in the Christian church.

minus NOUN the sign – used when you take away one number from another.

minute NOUN a measurement of time equal to 60 seconds.

mirror NOUN a piece of glass that you can see your reflection in.

mirror

Miss a title that you use before the name of an unmarried woman when you are speaking or writing to or about her.

miss VERB **1** to fail to catch, meet, etc., someone or something. **2** to feel sad because you are apart from someone or something.

mist NOUN thin cloud close to the ground.

mistake NOUN something that you do or think that is wrong.

mix VERB to stir or shake different things together so that they cannot be separated again.

mixture NOUN several different things mixed together.

mobile phone NOUN a telephone without wires that you can carry with you and use wherever you are.

model NOUN **1** a small copy of something. **2** someone whose job is to wear and show off the latest fashions. **3** a particular version of something.

modern ADJECTIVE of the present time, not old. *We live in a modern house.*

moment NOUN a very short period of time. *It will only take a moment.*

Monday NOUN the day of the week after Sunday and before Tuesday.

money NOUN the coins and notes that you use to buy things.

mongoose NOUN (PLURAL mongooses) a small African or Asian animal with a long body known for its ability to kill poisonous snakes.

mongrel NOUN a dog that is a mixture of different breeds.

monitor NOUN the display screen in a computer system.

monk NOUN a member of a religious community of men who live, pray and work together in a building called a monastery.

monkey NOUN an animal with a long tail that climbs trees.

month NOUN one of the twelve periods of time that the year is divided into, about four weeks.

moon NOUN the small planet that goes round the earth and that you can see in the sky at night.

moon

monster NOUN a large ugly creature in stories.

more See **many**, **much**. *More sweets.*

morning NOUN the part of the day between dawn and noon.

mosaic NOUN a picture or design made from pieces of coloured glass or stone.

moss NOUN (PLURAL mosses) a green plant that forms a soft covering on stones in damp places.

most See **many**, **much**. *Most children.*

monkey

moth NOUN an insect that looks like a butterfly and is active at night.

mother NOUN a woman who has a child.

mother

motor NOUN an engine.

motorbike NOUN two-wheeled vehicle with an engine.

motorway NOUN a wide road that is built for fast travel over a long distance.

mountain NOUN a very high hill with steep sides.

mouse NOUN (PLURAL mice) **1** small, furry animal with a long tail and quick movements, often regarded as a pest. **2** device you use with a computer instead of a keyboard.

mouth NOUN the part of your face through which you speak and into which you put food when you eat.

move VERB (moving, moved) **1** to go from place to place. **2** to put something that was in one place or position into a different one.

Mr a title that you use before a man's name when you are speaking or writing to or about him.

Mrs a title that you use before the name of a married woman when you are speaking or writing to or about her.

Ms a title that you use before the name of a woman when you are speaking or writing to or about her.

much (more, most) a large amount. *How much money do you have?*

mud NOUN soil that is wet and sticky.

mug NOUN something that you drink out of that has straight sides and is deeper than a cup.

multiply VERB (multiplying, multiplied) **1** to add a number to itself a certain number of times. **2** to increase.

mum, mummy NOUN (PLURAL mums, mummies) a name that a child calls its mother.

mumps NOUN an infectious disease that makes your neck swollen and sore.

muscle NOUN one of the elastic parts inside your body that work to help you to move.

museum NOUN a building where you can go and see interesting things that are often old and valuable.

mushroom NOUN a plant with a short stem and a round top that you can eat, a fungus.

music NOUN **1** sounds arranged in a pattern for people to sing or play on musical instruments. **2** the sheets of paper that these sounds are written down on.

must VERB **1** to have to do something. *I must be home in time for tea.* **2** to be sure or likely to.

mustard NOUN a hot-tasting yellow paste made from the seeds of the mustard plant.

mute ADJECTIVE not speaking, dumb.

my belonging to me.

myself *See* I. *I can dress myself.*

mystery NOUN (PLURAL mysteries) something not known about or very difficult to understand.

nail NOUN **1** the hard, top part at the end of your finger or toe. **2** short, thin piece of metal, pointed at one end and blunt at the other which is hammered into things to hold them together.

name NOUN the word that someone or something is called by.

narrow

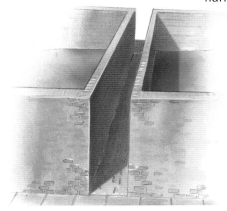

narrow ADJECTIVE not wide, thin.

nasty ADJECTIVE (nastier, nastiest) horrible, unpleasant.

natural ADJECTIVE **1** not man-made. **2** normal.

nature NOUN the things in the world that are not made by people, like plants, the sea, weather, etc.

naughty ADJECTIVE (naughtier, naughtiest) behaving badly.

navy NOUN (PLURAL navies) a country's armed forces that fight at sea.

navy ADJECTIVE a dark blue colour.

near close by, not far away from.

nearly almost, not quite.

neat ADJECTIVE tidy.

neck NOUN the part of your body between your head and your shoulders.

necklace NOUN a piece of jewellery that you wear round your neck.

necklace

need VERB **1** to lack something necessary. *I need a new coat.* **2** to have to do something. *I need to wash my hands.*

needle NOUN a very thin, pointed piece of metal used for injections, sewing, etc.

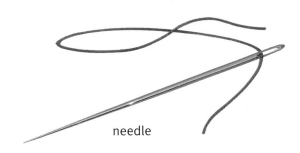

needle

neighbour NOUN someone who lives very near to you.

neither not either of two people or things.

nephew NOUN the son of your brother or sister.

nervous ADJECTIVE worried and frightened about something.

nest NOUN a place where a bird lays its eggs.

nest

net NOUN **1** see-through material made by weaving threads together with equal spaces in between. **2** anything made from this. *A fishing-net.*

netball NOUN a team game in which goals are scored by throwing a large ball through a ring on a high post.

never not ever, at no time.

new ADJECTIVE **1** recently made, not experienced or seen before. **2** not used by anyone before.

news NOUN **1** information about things that are happening. **2** a broadcast of this on the television or radio.

newsagent NOUN someone who sells newspapers and magazines.

newspaper NOUN a daily or weekly publication of news printed on a number of sheets of paper that are folded together.

next ADJECTIVE following straight after, nearest.

nibble VERB (nibbling, nibbled) to eat by taking tiny bites.

nice ADJECTIVE pleasant, attractive or enjoyable.

niece NOUN the daughter of your brother or sister.

night NOUN the time of day when it is dark.

night

nightie NOUN a kind of dress worn by women or girls to go to bed in.

nightmare NOUN a bad and frightening dream.

nine the number 9.

nineteen the number 19.

ninety the number 90.

no 1 a word used when you answer someone to disagree with them, refuse them or to say that something is not true. **2** not any. *The refugees had no food.*

nobody, no one no person.

nod VERB (nodding, nodded) to bow your head as a greeting or as a sign that you agree with something.

noise NOUN a sound, usually loud and unpleasant.

noisy ADJECTIVE (noisier, noisiest) making a loud, unpleasant noise.

none not a single one.

noodles

noodles PLURAL NOUN very thin strips of pasta.

noon NOUN 12 o'clock midday.

normal ADJECTIVE usual, ordinary

north NOUN one of the four points of the compass, the direction that is on your left when you face the rising sun.

north

nose NOUN the part of your face above your mouth through which you breathe and smell.

not a word you use to make something that you say or write have the opposite meaning.

note NOUN **1** a short, written message. **2** a piece of paper money. **3** a single musical sound.

nothing not any thing.

notice VERB (noticing, noticed) to feel or observe something.

nought NOUN nothing, the figure 0 or zero.

November NOUN the eleventh month of the year, after October and before December.

now at this moment, at present.

nugget NOUN **1** a lump of gold, or anything small and valuable. **2** food shaped into small pieces. *Chicken nuggets.*

nuisance NOUN someone or something that annoys you or causes you problems.

number NOUN **1** a word or figure showing an amount. *6 is an even number.* **2** a word or figure used to name a series of things. *House numbers.* **3** the series of digits that you use to telephone someone. *Do you have my number?*

nun NOUN a member of a religious community of women who live, pray and work together in a building called a convent or abbey.

nurse NOUN someone whose job is to look after sick people or young children.

nursery NOUN (PLURAL nurseries) **1** a place where young children are looked after. **2** a place that grows and sells plants.

nursery rhyme NOUN a short, simple poem that children like to recite.

nut NOUN **1** a dry fruit or seed inside a hard shell. **2** a piece of metal with a hole in the middle for screwing onto a bolt.

nuts

nutcracker NOUN an instrument for cracking the shells of nuts.

nutritious ADJECTIVE nourishing and good for you as food. *A nutritious meal.*

nylon NOUN strong, man-made cloth. *Tights and stockings are made from nylon.*

o'clock the way that you say what the hour is when telling the time. *I go to bed at 7 o'clock.*

oak NOUN a large tree that produces acorns.

oar NOUN a long paddle used to row a boat.

obey VERB to do what someone tells you to do. *We have trained our dog to obey us when we tell her to sit.*

object NOUN a thing. Books, chairs, cups and desks are all objects.

ocean NOUN **1** the sea. **2** a very large sea. *The Atlantic Ocean.*

October NOUN the tenth month of the year, after September and before November.

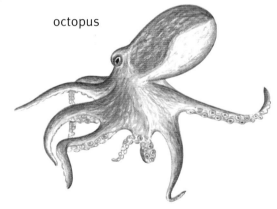

octopus

octopus NOUN (PLURAL octopuses) a sea creature with eight legs.

odd ADJECTIVE **1** strange, weird. **2** not matching, spare. *An odd sock.* **3** of various kinds. *Odd jobs.* **4** that does not divide exactly by two. *1, 3 and 5 are odd numbers.*

of 1 from the whole of a thing. *A piece of bread.* **2** containing. *A collection of books.* **3** belonging to. *The home of the pop star.* **4** about, to do with. *News of the wedding.*

off 1 no longer on. *My button's come off.* **2** away from a place or position. *The thief ran off.* **3** not working or in use. *The lights were off.*

offer VERB **1** to hold out something for someone to take. *He offered me a chocolate.* **2** to be willing to do something for someone. *We offered to wash up.* **3** to suggest a price that you would pay for something. *I'll offer a good price for the car.*

office NOUN **1** a place of business where people work at desks. **2** a government department. *The Office of Fair Trading.*

often many times. *We often go to the park after school, if the weather is warm.*

oil NOUN a thick liquid used as a fuel, to make machines run more easily or for cooking with.

old

old ADJECTIVE **1** not new or young. *My Grandfather says that he is old.* **2** used when referring to the age of someone or something. *The car is three years old.*

on 1 on top of. *The jug is on the shelf.* **2** by or near. *The shop on the corner.* **3** about, to do with. *The lesson on safety in the home.* **4** attached to. *The picture on the wall.* **5** working, in use. *Is the oven on?*

once 1 one time only. *I only ever tried smoking once.* **2** one time in a period of time. *I buy sweets once a week.* **3** some time ago. *Once there were fields where now there are houses.* **4** (at once) immediately.

one 1 the number 1. **2** (oneself) a single person or thing, any person.

oneself See **one**. *To behave oneself.*

onion NOUN a round, white vegetable that has a strong taste and smell and a brown papery skin that you peel off.

onion

only 1 no one or nothing else. *I'm the only one who can control the dog.* **2** no more than. *Only three minutes before the bell.* **3** but. *I want to go, only I can't.*

onto to a position on.

open VERB **1** to remove a cover from something. **2** to be ready for business.

open ADJECTIVE **1** not shut. *An open box.* **2** not closed in. *In the open air.* **3** not covered over. *An open-top car.* **4** spread out. *Open hands.*

operation NOUN treatment for a patient by cutting their body open to take away, replace or mend a damaged or diseased part.

opposite 1 as different as possible, furthest away from. **2** facing.

or used to show that there is a choice between alternatives.

orange NOUN **1** a sweet juicy round fruit that you peel to eat. **2** a drink made from, or tasting like, oranges.

orange ADJECTIVE the colour of oranges, between red and yellow.

orange

orchard

orchard NOUN a field where fruit trees grow.

orchestra NOUN a group of musicians playing different instruments together.

order NOUN **1** a command. *Orders must be obeyed.* **2** the way things are arranged. *The dictionary is in alphabetical order.* **3** tidiness. *Put your desk in order.* **4** a request to provide something. *May I take your order for lunch?* **5** right behaviour. *The police restored law and order.*

order VERB **1** to tell people what to do. **2** to ask to be provided with something.

ordinary ADJECTIVE not unusual, normal. *He wore his ordinary clothes to his brother's party.*

organ NOUN a large musical instrument usually found in churches. Its long metal pipes make different sounds when air passes through them.

oven

ostrich NOUN a large African bird with long legs and a long neck that is unable to fly.

ostrich

other different from the ones that you have just mentioned.

otter NOUN an animal with thick fur that eats fish and is good at swimming.

our belonging to us

ourselves See **we**. *We saw ourselves on the video.*

out 1 away from, not in. *Out of the bath.* **2** not at home. *My parents are out.* **3** no longer in a game. *The captain was out.* **4** not lit. *The fire's out.*

outdoors outside, in the open air.

outside 1 in a position furthest from the middle. **2** not inside a building.

ought VERB to be the right thing to do. *You ought to go to the doctor.*

oval ADJECTIVE egg-shaped.

oven NOUN a cooker that you use to roast or bake food.

over 1 above, covering. *A mist lay over the fields.* **2** on or to the other side of. *Over the road.* **3** finished, at an end. *The holidays are over.* **4** downwards from an upright position. *The toddler fell over.*

owe VERB (owing, owed) **1** to have to pay. *I owe my mum £5.* **2** to be thankful for something someone else has done. *They owed their lives to the courage of the lifeboat crew.*

owl NOUN bird of prey that hunts at night

owl

own 1 belonging to you and to no one else. **2** (on your own) alone, by yourself.

own VERB to have, to possess. *I own a car.*

ox NOUN (PLURAL oxen) a bull that is used in some countries for pulling carts, ploughs, etc.

oxygen NOUN a colourless, tasteless gas that makes up about a fifth of the earth's atmosphere. *All life on Earth needs oxygen to live.*

oyster NOUN an edible sea creature that lives inside two shells. *Some oysters produce a pearl inside their shells.*

ozone NOUN a gas that is a form of oxygen but has three atoms instead of two.

pack VERB **1** to wrap things up or put them into boxes, bags, etc. **2** to crowd tightly together. *Packed into the room.*

package NOUN a small parcel.

packet NOUN a small parcel.

paddle VERB (paddling, paddled) **1** to take your shoes and socks off so that you can walk in shallow water. **2** to move a boat through water with an oar.

page NOUN one side of a piece of paper in a book, magazine, etc.

paid See **pay**. *He paid by cheque.*

pain NOUN the feeling you suffer in your body when you have been hurt or you are ill.

paint NOUN a liquid that you brush onto something to colour it.

paint VERB **1** to colour a wall, ceiling, etc., with paint. **2** to make a picture using paints.

painting NOUN a picture done with paints.

palace NOUN a large and magnificent house where an important person lives, usually a king or queen.

pale ADJECTIVE not having much colour.

palm NOUN **1** the inside of your hand between your wrist and your fingers. **2** a tall tree with no branches but a lot of leaves at the top.

pan NOUN a container with a handle that you use on a stove to cook food in.

pancake NOUN a thin, flat round of batter cooked in a frying-pan.

panda NOUN a large, bear-like animal which comes from China and has black and white fur.

panic NOUN a very strong feeling of fear that makes you lose control of your actions.

panic VERB (panicking, panicked) to have such a feeling.

pant VERB to breathe with short, quick gasps.

pantomime NOUN a funny, musical entertainment for children performed at Christmas.

paper NOUN **1** sheets of material for writing or printing on, or for covering things. **2** a newspaper.

parachute NOUN a device made mostly of a large piece of material that you strap to your body so you can drop safely from an aeroplane.

paint

pair NOUN **1** two similar things that go together. *A pair of shoes.* **2** a single thing made up of two similar parts joined together. *A pair of tights.*

parachute

parcel NOUN something wrapped up in paper.

parent NOUN a mother or father. *He lives with his parents.*

park NOUN a large, public area of grass and trees, usually in a town.

park VERB to drive a vehicle into a position where you are going to leave it for a time.

parrot NOUN a bird with brightly coloured feathers that is often kept as a pet.

part NOUN **1** one of the pieces that something else is made up of. **2** a share in something. *He took no part in the robbery.* **3** the role that an actor has in a play, film, etc.

party NOUN (PLURAL parties) **1** a gathering of people to celebrate an event. **2** a group of people with the same political views.

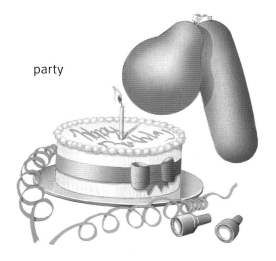

party

pass VERB **1** to go beyond or past. *We passed the station on our left.* **2** to give. *Please pass me the salt.* **3** to succeed in doing something. *Pass the exam.* **4** to go by. *Time passed.*

passenger NOUN someone who travels in a vehicle that is driven by someone else.

past 1 after. *Half past three.* **2** up to and then beyond. *The house is just past the golf course.*

past ADJECTIVE belonging to the past.

past NOUN the time before the present.

pasta

pasta NOUN food that is made from flour, eggs and water and comes in lots of different shapes. *Pasta shells.*

paste NOUN **1** a thin, wet glue for sticking paper. **2** a soft mixture of food, often spread on sandwiches.

pastry NOUN a dough-like mixture of flour and fat used for baking pies, flans, etc.

pat VERB (patting, patted) to tap lightly and repeatedly with the palm of your hand. *John patted the dog.*

patch NOUN (PLURAL patches) **1** a piece of material that you use to cover a hole in something. *Mum sewed a patch over the hole in my jeans.* **2** a small piece of ground. *A vegetable patch.*

path NOUN a track you can walk or ride along. *A cycle path.*

patient ADJECTIVE able to stay calm and wait for something without getting cross.

patient NOUN a sick person who is being treated by a doctor or a nurse.

peacock

pattern NOUN **1** a regular design or arrangement of colours and shapes. **2** something you use as a guide or copy when making something. *A sewing pattern.*

pattern

pause NOUN a short stop.

pause VERB (pausing, paused) to stop for a short time.

pavement NOUN the path for you to walk on beside a road.

paw NOUN an animal's foot that has claws.

pay VERB (paid) to give money to buy something or in return for work done.

pea NOUN a small, round, green seed in a pod that is eaten as a vegetable.

peace NOUN **1** a time when there is no war or fighting between people. **2** calmness and quietness, rest.

peach NOUN (PLURAL peaches) a juicy, round fruit with a large stone in the middle.

peacock NOUN the male of a bird with long blue and green tail feathers that it can spread out like a fan.

peanut NOUN small, oval nut that is often eaten roasted or salted as a snack.

pear NOUN a sweet, juicy fruit which is wider at the bottom and narrower at the stalk.

pebble NOUN a small, smooth, round stone.

pedal NOUN the part of a machine that you push down on with your foot.

pedal VERB (pedalling, pedalled) to push a pedal down to make a bicycle, etc., move.

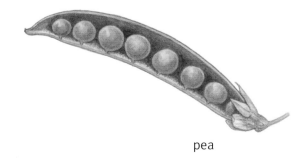

pea

peel VERB to remove the skin from a fruit or vegetable.

peel

pen NOUN an instrument you use with ink to write or draw.

pencil NOUN an instrument with a thin stick of lead through the middle that you write or draw with.

penguin NOUN a black and white Antarctic bird that cannot fly.

penny NOUN (PLURAL pennies or pence) a small coin, a hundredth part of £1.

people *See* **person**.

pepper NOUN **1** a powdered spice used to flavour food. **2** a red or green vegetable that can be eaten raw or cooked.

person NOUN (PLURAL people) a man, woman, or child, a human being.

persuade VERB (persuading, persuaded) to influence someone to do or believe something. *Persuade me to stay*

pet NOUN an animal that you keep for company and enjoyment. *Pet rabbit.*

petal NOUN one of the coloured parts that make up a flower head.

petrol NOUN the fuel used in car engines.

photograph NOUN a picture taken on film with a camera and then developed.

piano NOUN a large, musical instrument with black and white keys which you press to make different notes.

pick VERB **1** to choose. *Pick a card.* **2** to remove something with your fingers. *Pick up a pen.* **3** to collect. *Pick flowers.*

picnic NOUN a meal that you eat outdoors.

picnic

picture NOUN a painting, drawing or photograph.

pie NOUN meat, vegetables or fruit baked in pastry.

piece NOUN **1** a part of something. *A piece of cake.* **2** a single thing. *A piece of work.*

petal

pig NOUN an animal kept on farms for its meat.

pig

pile NOUN a heap of things one on top of the other.

pilgrim NOUN somebody who travels to a holy place for religious reasons.

pill NOUN a small tablet of medicine that you swallow.

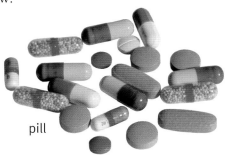
pill

pillow NOUN a cushion to rest your head on in bed.

pilot NOUN the person who flies an aeroplane or who guides a ship into a harbour.

pin NOUN a short, thin, pointed piece of metal that you stick through things to fasten them together.

pink ADJECTIVE pale red in colour.

pink

pipe NOUN **1** a long tube through which liquid or gas flows. **2** something used for smoking tobacco.

pirate NOUN someone who robs ships at sea.

pizza NOUN a flat, round piece of dough covered with tomatoes, cheese, etc., and baked in an oven.

pizza

place NOUN **1** any particular position or area. **2** a position in a competition or race. *We finished in second place.* **3** a seat. *Is this place free?*

plain ADJECTIVE **1** easy to understand or see. **2** not fancy, not decorated, simple.

plan NOUN **1** an arrangement that you make or an idea that you have in advance of doing something. **2** a drawing showing layouts, sizes etc.

plan VERB (planning, planned) to decide or intend to do something.

plane *See* **aeroplane**.

planet NOUN a large body in space that goes round the sun. Earth, Mars and Saturn are planets.

plant NOUN any living thing that grows in the ground and has roots, a stem and leaves.

plant VERB to put a seed, etc., into the ground.

plastic NOUN a man-made material that is light and strong and has many uses.

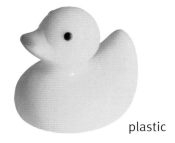
plastic

plate NOUN a flat dish that you eat your food from.

platypus NOUN (PLURAL platypuses) an Australian animal with a beak like a duck.

play NOUN a story performed by actors in a theatre or on television.

play VERB 1 to have fun. 2 to take part in a game. 3 to perform a part in a play or film. 4 to make music on an instrument.

playground NOUN an area where children can run about and have fun on slides, swings, etc.

playschool NOUN a nursery school or playgroup for children who are too young for junior school.

please VERB (pleasing, pleased) to make someone happy.

please said when you want to ask for something politely.

plenty an amount that is more than you need, enough. *I have plenty of money.*

plimsoll NOUN a light, sports shoe with a rubber sole.

plough NOUN a machine that farmers use to turn over and break up the soil.

plug NOUN 1 a device connected to an appliance that you put into an electrical socket. 2 something to block a hole, especially the device that you use to stop the water running out of a bath, washbasin or sink.

plus with the addition of, and, the sign +.

pocket NOUN a small bag sewn into a piece of clothing for you to carry things in.

poem NOUN a piece of writing with the words arranged in short lines which often rhyme.

poet NOUN someone who writes poems.

point NOUN 1 the sharp end of something. 2 the main idea or purpose of something. 3 a mark or position on a compass, dial, etc. 4 a unit used to work out the score in a game, quiz, etc.

point VERB to use your finger to show the direction of something.

poison NOUN substance that could kill you if it gets into your body.

pole NOUN 1 a long, round stick or post. 2 one of the two points at either end of the earth. *The North and South Poles.* 3 one of the two ends of a magnet.

police PLURAL NOUN the men and women whose job is to make sure that people obey the law.

polite ADJECTIVE well-mannered. *A polite child.*

pond NOUN an area of water, smaller than a lake.

pony NOUN (PLURAL ponies) a small horse.

pool NOUN 1 a small area of water or a puddle. 2 a swimming pool.

poor ADJECTIVE 1 owning very little or having very little money. 2 not of a good quality or amount.

pool

poppies

pop NOUN **1** a sudden, sharp sound like that made when you pull a cork out of a bottle. **2** fizzy drink. **3** popular music.

pop VERB (popping, popped) to make a sudden, sound.

pop music NOUN modern music with a strong rhythm.

poppy NOUN (PLURAL poppies) wild plant with a red flower.

porcupine NOUN a small animal with long prickles over its back and sides.

porcupine

pork NOUN meat that comes from a pig.

porridge NOUN soft food made from oats cooked in water and milk.

port NOUN a harbour or a town which has a harbour.

possible ADJECTIVE able to happen or to be done.

post NOUN **1** the way that letters and parcels are collected, sorted and delivered. **2** an upright piece of wood, metal or concrete fixed into the ground.

post VERB to send a letter or parcel through the post.

postcard NOUN a card for sending a message through the postal system without an envelope.

postcode NOUN a group of letters and figures added to an address to help the post office sort mail.

Post Office NOUN the national organization in charge of postal services.

post office a building or a place in a building where you can buy stamps and send letters.

pot NOUN a round container for cooking and keeping things in.

pottery NOUN pots, plates and other objects that are made from clay and then baked hard in an oven.

potato NOUN (PLURAL potatoes) a white vegetable with a brown or red skin that grows under the ground and can be cooked and served in many ways.

pour VERB **1** to make a liquid flow. **2** to rain heavily. *It poured with rain.*

powder NOUN anything that has been crushed or ground into tiny particles.

powder

power NOUN **1** the strength or ability to do something. **2** the legal right to do something. **3** a person or group with a lot of control over other people.

practice NOUN an action that you do regularly.

practise VERB (practising, practised) to keep doing something over and over again to get better at it.

prawn NOUN a shellfish similar to a shrimp.

prepare VERB (preparing, prepared) to get something ready or to make yourself ready for something.

present NOUN **1** a gift. **2** the time that is now here.

present ADJECTIVE **1** in the place spoken of. *Were you present at the prize-giving?* **2** happening or existing now. *The present owner.*

president NOUN the head of government in countries like the United States of America.

press VERB **1** to push firmly. *I pressed the doorbell with my finger.* **2** to make flat or smooth. *We press flowers to make them flat. They can then be placed inside books.*

pretend VERB to act as though things are not as they really are.

pretty ADJECTIVE (prettier, prettiest) very nice to look at. *The shell is very pretty.*

price NOUN the amount of money something costs. *I asked the salesperson what the price of the coat was.*

priceless ADJECTIVE worth a lot of money, very valuable. *The painting in the gallery was priceless.*

priest NOUN a religious leader. *A Catholic priest.*

prim ADJECTIVE very correct and easily shocked by anything rude. *She is very prim. She will never laugh at rude jokes.*

primary colour NOUN red, yellow or blue. All other colours can made by mixing these three colours in different ways.

primary school NOUN a school for children usually between 5 and 11 years old.

prime minister NOUN the head of government in countries like the United Kingdom.

primrose NOUN a wild plant that has pale yellow flowers.

princess NOUN (PLURAL princesses) **1** the daughter of a king or queen. **2** the wife of a prince.

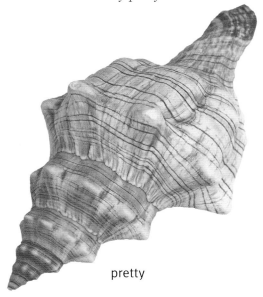

pretty

princess

print VERB **1** to put words and pictures onto paper using a machine. **2** to write without using joined-up letters.

printer NOUN **1** someone whose job is printing. **2** a machine that prints out information from a computer.

prison NOUN a building in which criminals are locked up.

prize NOUN something awarded for good work or for winning a competition or game.

problem NOUN a difficulty, a question that needs answering. *Problem solving.*

program NOUN a set of computer instructions.

programme NOUN **1** a play, show, item, etc., on the radio or television. **2** a leaflet giving details of events that are going to take place in a sporting fixture, during a performance, etc.

project NOUN a subject studied in detail.

promise VERB (promising, promised) to say that you will or will not do something. *I promised that I would take my brother to the sweet shop.*

pronounce VERB (pronouncing, pronounced) to say a word in the way that it is usually said or in a particular way.

protect VERB to guard someone or something from harm. *The guard dog protects the house.*

proud ADJECTIVE feeling that you are better than other people. *I was proud of myself when I won first prize in the school swimming competition.*

prove VERB (proving, proved) to show for certain that something is true. *I proved that I was telling the truth by showing them the letter.*

prowl VERB to move about quietly, trying not to be seen or heard. *The lion is prowling in search of food.*

prune NOUN a dried plum. *Prunes are very good for the digestion.*

prune VERB to cut off or shorten branches of a tree or bush. *I pruned the rose bush in the garden.*

pub NOUN a place where you can buy and drink alcohol. *My uncle owns a pub.*

pudding NOUN **1** a sweet food that is cooked and served hot. *Chocolate pudding.* **2** the dessert course of a meal. *What's for pudding?*

puffin NOUN seabird with a brightly coloured beak. *The puffin perched on the cliff ledge.*

puffin

puddle NOUN a small pool of water, especially one left after it has been raining.

puddle

puff NOUN a small amount of air or smoke blown out of something.

pull VERB to drag something along behind you or move it towards you.

pulp NOUN **1** soft inner part of a fruit or vegetable. **2** a soft mass of other material.

pulpit NOUN a small platform for the preacher in a church.

pulse NOUN **1** the regular beating of blood as it is pumped through the body by the heart. *I can feel my pulse when I touch my wrists.* **2** the regular beat or throbbing of music.

puma NOUN a large wild cat of western America, also called a cougar or mountain lion.

pump NOUN a machine used to force a liquid or gas to flow in a certain direction.

pumpkin NOUN a large, round, deep yellow fruit.

pumpkins

punch VERB to hit with your fist.

puncture NOUN a small hole made by a sharp object, especially in a tyre.

puncture VERB to make or get a puncture. *A nail in the road must have punctured my tyre.*

punish VERB to make someone suffer for something that they have done wrong. *We were punished for making a mess.*

pupil NOUN **1** someone who is being taught. **2** the round, black part in the middle of your eye.

puppet NOUN **1** a toy figure that moves when you pull wires or strings. **2** a cloth figure that you put on your hand like a glove and move with your fingers.

puppet

puppy NOUN (PLURAL puppies) a young dog.

puppy

pyramids

pure ADJECTIVE not mixed with anything else, clean. *The water from the spring was pure enough to drink.*

purple ADJECTIVE of a colour between red and blue.

purr VERB to make a low sound like a cat when it is pleased. *My cat always purrs loudly when I stroke him.*

purse NOUN a small bag for money.

push VERB to press hard against something to try to move it away from you. *I pushed the door hard until it opened.*

pushy ADJECTIVE unpleasantly keen to get things done so as to make yourself noticed. *Amanda is very pushy. She always puts her hand up first when the teacher asks a question.*

pussyfoot VERB to act very cautiously.

put VERB (putting, put) to place something in a particular position. *I put the cup down on the table.*

putty NOUN a soft paste used to fix glass into window frames or fill holes.

puzzle NOUN **1** a difficult problem or question, something that is hard to understand. **2** a game in which things have to be fitted together properly. *A crossword puzzle.*

puzzle

pyjamas PLURAL NOUN a loose jacket and trousers that you wear in bed.

pylon NOUN a tall metal structure used for holding wires that carry electricity over long distances.

pyramid NOUN **1** a shape with a flat base and three or four sloping sides that come to a point at the top. **2** an ancient stone building in the shape of a pyramid constructed over the tombs of the ancient kings and queens of Egypt.

python NOUN a large snake that kills by winding its body round animals and squeezing them.

quack VERB to make a loud harsh noise like that of a duck.

quality NOUN (PLURAL qualities) **1** how good or bad something is. **2** something good in a person's character, what a person or thing is like.

quantity NOUN (PLURAL quantities) the amount of something.

quarrel NOUN an argument. *We had a quarrel.*

quarrel

quarry NOUN a place where people dig stone out of the ground to use for buildings and other things.

quarter NOUN **1** one of the four equal parts that something is divided into. *Kate ate a quarter of the cake.* **2** 15 minutes past or 15 minutes to the hour when telling the time. *At quarter past 11.*

quay NOUN a platform for ships to dock at. *The ships docked at the quay.*

queen

queen NOUN **1** the female ruler of a country. **2** the wife of a king. **3** a chess piece.

question NOUN something that you ask someone.

queue NOUN people or vehicles waiting in a line.

quiche NOUN a tart with a savoury filling.

quick ADJECTIVE fast, not slow.

quiet ADJECTIVE **1** making no noise. **2** still.

quilt NOUN a thick bed-cover.

quilt

quit VERB (quitting, quitted) to leave or stop doing something. *Don't forget to quit the computer program before you turn off the computer.*

quite 1 completely. *I'm not quite sure.* **2** rather. *They took quite a long time.*

quiz NOUN (PLURAL quizzes) a competition or game which tests your knowledge.

quotation NOUN a person's written or spoken words repeated exactly by somebody else.

quotation marks PLURAL NOUN the punctuation marks (' ') or (" ") used before and after words somebody has said.

quote VERB (quoting, quoted) to repeat the exact words that someone else has written or said.

rabbit NOUN a small animal with long ears that lives in burrows or may be kept in a hutch as a pet.

rabbits

race NOUN a competition to see who is the fastest at something. *A cycle race.*

race VERB (racing, raced) to compete in a race.

racket NOUN **1** a light bat with strings across it for hitting the ball in sports such as tennis or squash. **2** a loud and terrible noise.

radiator NOUN **1** a device that heats a room when it is connected to a central heating system. **2** the part of a car engine that keeps it cool.

radio NOUN **1** sounds broadcast over the airwaves. **2** a device for receiving these sounds.

radio

rag NOUN a torn piece of old cloth.

rail NOUN **1** a bar or rod. **2** one of the parallel steel bars that a train runs on.

railway NOUN **1** steel track on which trains run. **2** company that runs this system of tracks and trains.

rain NOUN drops of water that fall from clouds in the sky.

rainbow NOUN an arch of colours that you sometimes see in the sky after it has been raining.

raincoat NOUN a waterproof coat that you wear when it's raining.

raise VERB (raising, raised) to lift up. *I raised my hands in the air.*

ran See **run**. *I ran across the park.*

rang See **ring**. *The telephone rang.*

rare ADJECTIVE not common, unusual. *He was suffering from a rare disease.*

rat NOUN an animal with a long tail that looks like a mouse but is bigger.

rattle NOUN a baby's toy that makes a noise when you shake it.

raw ADJECTIVE not cooked. *The vegetables were raw.*

rat

95

reach

reach VERB **1** to stretch out your arm to touch something. **2** to arrive at.

read VERB to be able to understand words written or printed on a page.

ready ADJECTIVE (readier, readiest) **1** prepared. *Dinner's ready.* **2** willing. *Are you nearly ready to go?*

real ADJECTIVE **1** that actually exists and is not imagined. **2** genuine. *A real diamond.*

realize VERB (realizing, realized) to become aware of something.

really truthfully, in fact.

reason NOUN **1** an excuse, explanation or cause. **2** the ability to think or understand.

record NOUN **1** a written account of something that has been done or has happened. **2** a round piece of plastic onto which music has been recorded. **3** the very best ever achieved.

recorder NOUN a musical instrument which you blow into to play.

red ADJECTIVE (redder, reddest) having the colour of blood.

reflection NOUN an image that you see in a mirror or in water.

refrigerator NOUN a device for keeping food and drink cool.

refuse VERB (refusing, refused) to say 'no'.

register NOUN a list of names.

reindeer NOUN (PLURAL reindeer) a kind of deer that lives in cold places.

remember VERB to keep something in your mind, not to forget.

remind VERB to cause you to remember or think about something or someone.

repair VERB to mend.

repeat VERB to say, do or happen again.

reply VERB (replying, replied) to answer.

report NOUN an account of how well or badly a pupil has done at school.

report VERB to give an account of something that has happened.

rescue VERB (rescuing, rescued) to save someone from danger or captivity.

rescue

rest NOUN **1** a time of not doing anything tiring, sleep. **2** what remains or is left over.

rest VERB not to do anything active, to relax.

restaurant NOUN place where you can buy and eat meals.

result NOUN **1** the effect of certain actions or events. **2** the final score in a game, competition, etc.

return VERB **1** to come or go back. **2** to send or give back.

reward NOUN something that you get for doing something good or helpful.

rhinoceros NOUN (PLURAL rhinoceroses) a large animal with a thick skin and one or two horns on its nose.

rhinoceros

rhyme NOUN **1** a word ending with a similar sound as another. **2** a short poem. *Nursery rhyme.*

rhyme VERB (rhyming, rhymed) to have a similar sound.

ribbon NOUN a narrow length of material for tying or decorating things with. *The dress was covered in clusters of pink ribbons.*

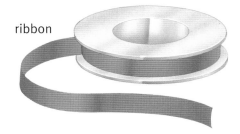
ribbon

rice NOUN a plant that grows in hot, wet places and produces white or brown grains that you cook and eat.

rice

rich ADJECTIVE **1** having a lot of money and goods, wealthy. **2** splendid and valuable. **3** full of goodness or colour.

ridden *See* **ride**. *Have you ever ridden a horse?*

riddle NOUN a puzzling question. *Ask me a riddle.*

ride VERB (riding, rode, ridden) **1** to travel in a vehicle. **2** to travel on a horse or a bicycle.

right 1 on the right. *The right-hand side.* **2** straight. *Right on at the lights.* **3** exactly. *Right on time.*

right ADJECTIVE **1** correct. *Did you get the right answer?* **2** good.

ring NOUN **1** a circle or something in the shape of a circle. **2** a piece of jewellery to wear on your finger. **3** a closed-in space with seats round it where a contest or performance takes place.

ring VERB (rang, rung) **1** to sound a bell. **2** to make a sound like a bell. **3** to make a telephone call.

rinse VERB (rinsing, rinsed) to wash in water without soap.

ripe ADJECTIVE ready to eat.

ripe

rise VERB (rising, rose, risen) **1** to get up. **2** to move upwards. *Steam rising.*

risen See **rise**. *They had risen early.*

river NOUN wide stream of water flowing across land to the sea.

road NOUN track with a hard surface on which vehicles travel.

roar VERB to make a sound like a lion.

roast VERB to cook food in an oven or over an open fire.

rob VERB (robbing, robbed) to steal money or property from someone.

robin NOUN a small garden bird with a red breast.

robot NOUN a machine made to act like a person.

rock NOUN **1** the hard stone that the earth is made of. **2** a large piece of stone. **3** a hard sweet in the shape of a stick.

rocket NOUN **1** a space vehicle or missile. **2** a firework.

rocket

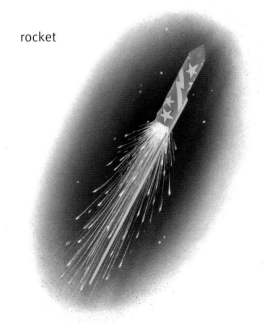

rod NOUN a long, straight stick or bar.

rode See **ride**. *She rode the bicycle along the street.*

roll NOUN **1** a long piece of something wound around itself into a tube shape. **2** a small loaf of bread for one person.

roll VERB **1** to turn over and over, like a ball. **2** to make something into a round shape. **3** to make something flat and smooth by passing a rounded object over it.

roller skates PLURAL NOUN wheels fitted to the soles of shoes for skating over flat surfaces.

roof NOUN the outside covering of the top part of a building, vehicle, etc.

room NOUN **1** one of the areas into which a building is divided, with its own walls, ceiling and floor. **2** enough space for something.

root NOUN the part of a plant that grows underground.

rope NOUN strong, thick cord made of separate threads twisted together.

rose

rose NOUN a beautiful flower that grows on a stem with thorns.

rose See **rise**. *The sun rose.*

rotten ADJECTIVE gone bad and not fit to eat or use. *The apple was too rotten to eat.*

rough ADJECTIVE **1** not smooth or even. *A rough edge.* **2** stormy. *A rough sea.* **3** done quickly, not accurate. *A rough drawing.*

round **1** spinning or moving in circles. *The wheels went round.* **2** surrounding. *The path goes round the lake.* **3** in or into all parts. *They showed us round the house.*

round ADJECTIVE shaped like a ball.

round NOUN **1** one stage in a competition or sporting event. **2** one of a series of regular visits that people make during their work. *A paper round.* **3** a whole slice of bread.

roundabout NOUN **1** a place where several roads meet and cars drive in a circle. **2** a merry-go-round.

rounders NOUN a team game played with a bat and ball.

route NOUN the way you take to get to a place. *I took my usual route to work.*

routine ADJECTIVE with little variety. *I have a routine job.*

routine NOUN the usual way of doing things. *Getting up late upsets my routine.*

row (said like **no**) NOUN people or things in a neat and tidy line.

row VERB to move a boat through water using oars. *I rowed the boat along the river*

row (said like **how**) NOUN **1** an argument, a quarrel. **2** a loud noise.

royal ADJECTIVE belonging to or connected with a king or queen.

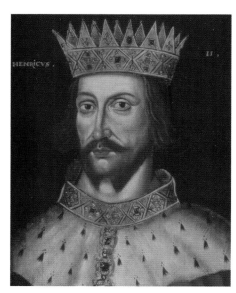

royal

rub VERB (rubbing, rubbed) to move something backwards and forwards against something else. *I used a tissue to rub the mark off my jacket.*

rubber NOUN **1** the strong, elastic material from which Wellingtons, tyres etc., are made. **2** a piece of this used to remove pencil marks.

rubbish NOUN **1** waste material. *A pile of rubbish.* **2** silly nonsense. *Everything he said was a load of rubbish!*

rude ADJECTIVE **1** not polite. *He was very rude to me.* **2** not decent. *A rude joke. The joke that she told was very rude.*

rug NOUN **1** a mat for the floor. **2** a thick blanket.

rugby NOUN a team game played with an oval ball.

ruin VERB to completely spoil or damage something. *The stain on my dress has completely ruined it.*

rule VERB (ruling, ruled) **1** to govern. *The king ruled wisely throughout his reign.* **2** to make a decision. *The ball was ruled out of play.* **3** to draw a straight line.

ruler NOUN **1** someone who governs a country. *He was the ruler of the kingdom.* **2** a long, straight-edged piece of wood, plastic, etc., used to draw straight lines or to measure things with.

run VERB (running, ran, run) **1** to move on your legs at the fastest pace. **2** to work. *The car costs a lot to run.* **3** to flow or drip down. *The paint ran.* **4** to go or continue. *The motorway runs for miles.* **5** to be in charge of something. *He runs his father's business.*

rung NOUN a bar in a ladder. *My foot was on the bottom rung when I fell off the ladder and broke my arm.*

rung See **ring**. *Have you rung the bell?*

runner NOUN **1** a person who runs, especially in a race. **2** a thin wooden or metal strip on which something slides or moves.

rush VERB to hurry.

rust NOUN the brown substance that forms on iron that has come into contact with water.

sack NOUN **1** a large bag made out of a rough material. **2** the loss of your job. *My boss said my work was poor, so I got the sack.*

sad ADJECTIVE (sadder, saddest) feeling unhappy.

safe ADJECTIVE not in danger.

safe NOUN a strong locked box for keeping valuable things secure.

said See **say**. *I said 'Go.'*

sail NOUN piece of cloth fixed to the mast of a boat so that it catches the wind and moves the boat through the water.

sail VERB **1** to travel on water. **2** to control a boat on water.

sail

sailor NOUN someone who works on a boat as a member of the crew.

salad NOUN raw vegetables or fruit mixed together and eaten with other foods as part of a meal.

salt NOUN tiny, white grains that you put on your food to flavour it.

same 1 exactly like something else. *The twins wore the same clothes.* **2** not changed. *She was just the same as I remembered her.* **3** always only one thing or person. *We go to the same school.*

sand NOUN tiny grains of stone, such as you find on the beach or in the desert.

sandals PLURAL NOUN open shoes for wearing in the summer, with straps that go over the top of your feet.

sandwich NOUN two slices 0f bread with a filling in between them.

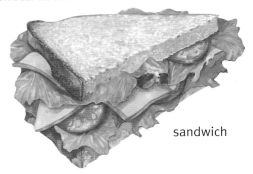

sandwich

sang See **sing**. *We sang carols.*

sank See **sink**. *The ship sank.*

sat See **sit**. *The children sat still.*

satchel NOUN a bag with a shoulder strap that you carry your school books in.

satellite NOUN **1** a man-made device sent into space to collect signals which it sends back to earth.

satellite

satellite dish NOUN large round metal object fixed to buildings to collect television signals which are sent using satellites in space.

Saturday NOUN the day of the week that comes after Friday and before Sunday.

sauce NOUN a thick liquid that you put on your food to flavour it.

saucepan NOUN a pan with a lid and a handle, that you use to cook food in.

saucepan

saucer NOUN a small dish on which you put a cup.

sausage NOUN a thin tube of skin filled with a mixture of meat, cereal, spices, etc.

save VERB (saving, saved) **1** to rescue from danger. **2** to keep something so that you can use it later. **3** to stop wasting something. **4** to stop a ball from going into a goal.

saw NOUN a tool with a zigzag blade that you use to cut things like wood.

saw

saw See **see**. *Laura saw her sister coming towards her.*

say VERB (said) **1** to speak. **2** to give your opinion.

scales PLURAL NOUN a weighing machine.

scare VERB (scaring, scared) to frighten.

scarf NOUN (PLURAL scarves or scarfs) a length of cloth you wear round your neck, usually to keep warm.

school NOUN a place where children go to learn.

science NOUN the study of how natural things behave and the knowledge that we have about them.

science

scissors PLURAL NOUN a pair of hinged blades that you use to cut things with.

scissors

scooter NOUN **1** a child's toy with a handle, two wheels and a platform for the feet. **2** a kind of motorcycle.

score NOUN the number of points, goals, etc., made in a game.

scratch NOUN a mark or wound made by scratching.

scratch VERB **1** to damage a surface with something sharp and rough. *Our cat is always scratching furniture with his claws.* **2** to rub your skin to stop it itching. *Jamie scratched his arm.*

scream VERB to give a loud, high-pitched cry.

screen NOUN **1** a flat surface on which films are shown. **2** the front surface of a television, computer monitor, etc. **3** a frame which protects people from heat and cold or hides something from view.

screw NOUN piece of metal like a nail but with a thread around it. It is put into hard surfaces with a screwdriver.

screwdriver NOUN a tool used for turning screws.

screwdriver

sea NOUN the salt water that covers most of the earth's surface. *A calm sea.*

seal NOUN **1** a sea creature that eats fish and swims by using flippers. **2** a mark, often made from wax, that is fixed to important things to show that they are genuine.

seal VERB **1** to put a seal on something.**2** to fasten something firmly. **3** to make something airtight.

search VERB to look for, to try to find. *Search party.*

seaside NOUN the place next to the sea, especially where people go for their holidays.

season NOUN **1** one of the four parts into which the year is divided: spring, summer, autumn and winter. **2** a time in the year for a particular activity. *The football season.*

seat NOUN something on which you sit.

second ADJECTIVE being the one after the first, 2nd.

second NOUN **1** a length of time. *There are 60 seconds in one minute.* **2** a brief moment.

secret NOUN something that only a few people know.

see VERB (saw, seen) **1** to look at something through your eyes. *I could see the hills in the distance.* **2** to understand. *I see what you mean.* **3** to meet or visit. *I went to see my friend.*

seed NOUN the part of a plant from which a new one grows.

seed

seem VERB to appear to be.

seen *See* **see**. *Have you seen this video?*

seesaw NOUN a plank, balanced so that when children sit on either end, one end goes up as the other comes down.

seesaw

selfish ADJECTIVE not caring about others, thinking only of yourself.

sell VERB (sold) to part with things in return for money. *She sold her house.*

Sellotape NOUN (trademark) sticky tape on a roll.

semi-circle NOUN a half circle. *We stood in a semi-circle.*

semi-colon NOUN The punctuation mark (;) is called a *semi-colon*. It is used to join two parts of a sentence and is used instead of 'and', 'but' or another conjunction. For example, in the sentence, '*I am very tired; I am also hungry.*' the semi-colon is used instead of '*and*'.

send VERB (sent) to cause or order someone or something to go or be taken somewhere. *James was sent to the headteacher's office.*

sensible ADJECTIVE having the ability to make good decisions.

sent See **send**. *I've sent her a birthday card.*

September NOUN the ninth month of the year, after August and before October.

September

set NOUN a collection of things. *A set of encyclopedias.*

set VERB (setting, set) **1** to put into a position. **2** to give someone work to do. *What homework has been set?* **3** to become hard. *The concrete set quickly in the warm sun.* **4** to go down below the horizon. *The sun sets earlier in the winter.* **5** to prepare a table for a meal.

seven

seven the number 7.

seventeen the number 17.

seventy the number 70.

sew VERB (sewed, sewn or sewed) to stitch material together with a needle and thread. *Sew a dress.*

sewn See **sew**. *I've sewn on a new button.*

shade NOUN **1** area sheltered from the sun or strong light. *Stand in the shade.* **2** something that keeps out light or makes it less bright. *A lampshade.* **3** a slightly different depth of colour. *A lighter shade of blue.*

shadow NOUN **1** an area of shade. **2** the dark shape cast by an object where it blocks out the light.

shake VERB (shaking, shook, shaken) **1** to move something up and down and from side to side very quickly. **2** to take someone by the right hand as a sign of greeting or agreement. **3** to shiver.

shaken See **shake**. *After you've shaken the bottle, pour the milk.*

shall to intend to happen, to happen in the future. *I shall be on holiday next week.*

shallow ADJECTIVE not deep.

shampoo NOUN special soap to wash your hair with.

shampoo

shan't = shall not. *We shan't be coming to the party.*

shape NOUN the form that something has, an outline.

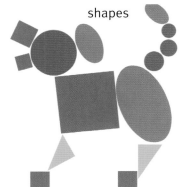

shapes

share NOUN a part or portion of something. *There were many guests at the birthday party, but we all had a share of the cake.*

share VERB (sharing, shared) **1** to use or do something with others. *The friends shared a flat.* **2** to divide. *She shared her sandwiches with her friend.*

shark NOUN a dangerous fish with sharp teeth.

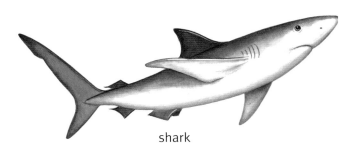

shark

sharp ADJECTIVE **1** having a fine point or a thin cutting edge. **2** thinking quickly.

shave VERB (shaving, shaved) to make your skin smooth by cutting off the hairs with a razor.

she (her, herself) that woman, girl or female animal.

she'd = she had, she would. *She'd have come if she could.*

she'll = she will. *She'll be here soon.*

she's = she is, she has. *She's a very nice girl.*

shed NOUN a small, wooden building for storing things in.

sheep NOUN (PLURAL sheep) a farm animal kept for its wool and meat.

sheep

sheet NOUN **1** large piece of cloth for covering a bed. **2** a single piece of paper.

shelf NOUN (PLURAL shelves) a length of board fixed to a wall or fitted in a cupboard on which you put things.

shell NOUN the hard, outside part of an egg, nut, snail, etc.

shells

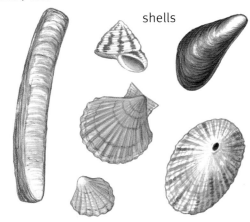

shelves See **shelf**.

shine VERB (shining, shone or shined) to give a bright light.

shiny ADJECTIVE (shinier, shiniest) giving a bright light.

ship NOUN a large boat.

shirt NOUN a piece of light clothing worn on the upper part of the body that has sleeves and a collar. *A red cotton shirt.*

shiver VERB to shake, often from fear or the cold.

shoe NOUN something that you wear over socks or tights to cover your foot.

shone See **shine**. *The sun shone brightly yesterday.*

shook See **shake**. *The wind shook the windows.*

shoot VERB (shot) **1** to fire a weapon at and hit a target. **2** to kick or throw a ball to score in a game. **3** to take a photograph or make a film.

shop NOUN somewhere goods are sold.

shore NOUN the land by the edge of the sea or a lake.

short ADJECTIVE **1** not long. *A short distance.* **2** not tall. *A short man.* **3** lasting only a little time. *A short break.*

shorts PLURAL NOUN short trousers. *Running shorts.*

shot See **shoot**. *The president was shot.*

should ought to. *You should be more polite.*

shoulder NOUN the part of your body at either side of your neck where your arms join it.

shouldn't = should not. *You shouldn't have been so naughty.*

shout VERB to call out loudly. *The player shouted at the referee.*

shout

show NOUN **1** a performance or entertainment. **2** a collection of things for people to look at. *A fine show of roses.*

show VERB (showed, shown) **1** to cause something to be seen. **2** to go with to guide. *Show me the way.* **3** to explain. *I'll show you how to do it.*

shower NOUN **1** a brief fall of rain. **2** a water-spraying device that you stand under to wash your body.

shower

shown See **show**. *I was shown how to work out the sums.*

shrank See **shrink**. *The clothes shrank in the rain.*

shrimp NOUN a small sea creature.

shrink VERB (shrank, shrunk) to get smaller.

shrunk See **shrink**. *My favourite jumper has shrunk in the washing machine.*

shut VERB (shutting, shut) to close.

shy ADJECTIVE nervous and uncomfortable in the company of others.

sick ADJECTIVE poorly, not well.

side NOUN **1** one of the flat surfaces of something such as a box. **2** not the front or the back. **3** a sports team.

sight NOUN **1** the ability to see. **2** something that is seen. **3** a place or view that is worth seeing, especially for tourists.

sign NOUN **1** an object or symbol that conveys a meaning. **2** a notice, giving information, directions, etc. *Follow the signs.*

sign

silence NOUN quietness, the absence of sound.

silk NOUN a very fine thread used to make a soft, delicate cloth.

silly ADJECTIVE (sillier, silliest) foolish, not sensible.

silver NOUN **1** a precious metal. **2** the colour of this.

since 1 after the time when. *We haven't seen them since they moved.* **2** because. *I must go since it's so late.*

sing VERB (sang, sung) to make music with your voice. *She sings tunefully.*

sink NOUN a basin with taps and a plug-hole, for washing dishes, clothes, etc.

sink VERB (sank, sunk) to go down below a surface. *The boat sank without trace.*

sip VERB (sipping, sipped) to drink by taking only tiny amounts into your mouth at a time.

sister NOUN a girl or woman who has the same parents as you.

skateboard

sink

sit VERB (sitting, sat) to be in a position where your bottom is on a seat.

sitting-room NOUN room in a home to sit and relax in.

six the number 6.

sixteen the number 16.

sixty the number 60.

size NOUN **1** how big something is. **2** a particular measurement. *She asked for a dress in size 12.*

skate NOUN **1** a boot or shoe with a blade fitted to the underneath so that you can move on ice. **2** a roller skate.

skate VERB (skating, skated) to move on ice with skates.

skateboard NOUN a board with roller-skate wheels fitted to the underneath.

skeleton NOUN the framework of bones in your body.

ski VERB to move on snow.

ski

skin NOUN **1** the outer layer of your body. **2** outer covering of a fruit or vegetable.

skip VERB (skipping, skipped) **1** to jump with light, quick steps. **2** to jump over a rope which swings over your head and under your feet.

skirt NOUN a piece of women's clothing that hangs down from the waist.

sky NOUN (PLURAL skies) the space around the earth.

skyscraper NOUN a very tall building in a city.

sledge NOUN a vehicle for moving over snow and ice.

sleep VERB (slept) to rest in bed with your eyes closed and your mind and body in an unconscious state, not to be awake.

sleep

sleet NOUN partly-frozen rain.

sleeve NOUN the part of a garment covering the arm.

slept See **sleep**. *I slept for seven hours last night.*

slice NOUN thin piece of food cut from something larger.

slid See **slide**. *They slid on the ice.*

slide NOUN **1** something with a slippery surface down which you can slide. **2** a picture that can be projected onto a screen. **3** a clip girls wear to keep their hair tidy.

slide VERB (sliding, slid) to move smoothly over a surface.

slip VERB (slipping, slipped) **1** to slide and lose your balance. **2** to make a mistake.

slipper NOUN a light shoe to wear indoors.

slippery ADJECTIVE smooth, wet or greasy and difficult to hold or walk on.

slow ADJECTIVE **1** taking a long time, not fast. **2** behind the right time. *My watch is slow.* **3** not quick to understand.

slug NOUN a creature like a snail, but with no shell.

small ADJECTIVE little, not big.

smash VERB to break into pieces.

smell NOUN the effect of something on your nose.

smell VERB (smelt or smelled) to have a particular smell that you can sense.

smelt or **smelled** *See* **smell**. *I smelt something burning.*

smile VERB (smiling, smiled) to look pleased and happy, often with your mouth turned up at the corners.

smile

smoke NOUN the cloudy gas that is produced when something burns.

smoke VERB (smoking, smoked) to suck tobacco smoke from a cigarette, cigar or pipe into your mouth and let it out again.

smooth ADJECTIVE having an even surface, not rough.

snack NOUN a light meal.

snail NOUN a small creature with a shell on its back.

snail

snake

snake NOUN a long creature with no legs.

sneeze VERB (sneezing, sneezed) to suddenly and noisily let air out of your nose and mouth, as when you have a cold.

snooker NOUN game in which you use a long stick to hit coloured balls into pockets at the sides of a large table.

snore VERB (snoring, snored) to breathe noisily through your nose and mouth when you are asleep.

snow NOUN flakes of frozen water that fall from the sky in cold weather.

snowflake NOUN one of the soft, white bits of frozen water that fall as snow.

so 1 in the way described. *The house was empty and stayed so for some years.* **2** therefore, in order that. *It was cold, so I lit the fire.*

soap NOUN a substance that is used with water for washing.

sock NOUN a piece of clothing that covers your foot and the bottom of your leg and is worn inside shoes.

socket NOUN a hole into which something else fits.

sofa NOUN a comfortable seat for two or more people with a back and arms, a settee.

soft ADJECTIVE **1** not hard. **2** smooth and nice to touch. **3** gentle.

soil NOUN the top layer of the ground in which plants grow.

sold See **sell**. *We sold the car for £500.*

soldier NOUN someone whose job is to fight in an army.

solid ADJECTIVE **1** having a firm shape, not liquid or gas. **2** not hollow inside. **3** of the same material all the way through. *Solid gold.*

some 1 a few, but not all. **2** used when you are not being exact about what you are referring to. *At some point we will have to talk about this.*

something a thing that is not named, any thing.

sometimes now and then.

son NOUN someone's male child.

song NOUN words sung to music.

soon in a short time.

sore ADJECTIVE painful, aching. *Sore feet.*

sorry ADJECTIVE (sorrier, sorriest) feeling sad, wanting to apologize for something you have said or done. *I'm so sorry.*

sort NOUN a group of things or people of a particular type.

sort VERB to arrange things in order.

sound NOUN anything that you hear.

sofa

soup

soup NOUN a liquid food made by boiling meat, vegetables, etc., in water.

sour ADJECTIVE having a sharp taste, not sweet.

south NOUN one of the four points of the compass, the direction that is on your right when you face the rising Sun.

south

space NOUN **1** the universe beyond the Earth's atmosphere. **2** an empty or open area.

spaceship NOUN a vehicle that can travel in space.

spade NOUN a tool for digging with, a kind of shovel.

spaghetti NOUN long strings of pasta.

sparrow NOUN a very common, small brown bird.

speak VERB (spoke, spoken) to talk, to say things.

special ADJECTIVE not ordinary. *She is special.*

speed NOUN how quickly something moves.

spell VERB (spelt or spelled) to put the letters in a word in the right order.

spelt or **spelled** See **spell**. *I spelt the words correctly.*

spend VERB (spent) **1** to pay out money. **2** to pass the time. *He liked to spend his time reading.*

spent See **spend**. *They spent all the money.*

spice NOUN a powder or seeds of a plant used to flavour food.

spider NOUN a small creature with eight legs that usually spins a web.

spider

spill VERB (spilt or spilled) to pour something out or over something else without meaning to.

spilt or **spilled** See **spill**. *Jo spilt the milk.*

spill

spin VERB (spinning, spun) **1** to twist something into a thread. **2** to make something by forming threads. **3** to go round and round very fast.

splash VERB to make a liquid scatter in drops, especially so that it makes someone or something wet.

splash

spoil VERB (spoilt or spoiled) **1** to ruin. **2** to make a child selfish. *You spoil him.*

spoilt or **spoiled** See **spoil**. *The bad weather spoilt our holiday.*

spoke, spoken See **speak**. *Angela spoke to the man in German.*

spooky ADJECTIVE (spookier, spookiest) something that is strange and frightening.

sponge NOUN **1** something you wash with that soaks up water. **2** a light cake.

spoon NOUN a tool you use to stir, serve and eat food.

sport NOUN games, activities, etc., that you do for pleasure.

spot NOUN **1** a small, round mark, a dot. **2** a pimple. **3** a particular place.

spray VERB to scatter liquid in lots of small drops. *We used the hose to spray water all over the garden.*

spread VERB (spread) **1** to lay something out flat. *We spread the blanket on the ground.* **2** to thinly cover a surface with something. *Spread butter on your toast.* **3** to move out over a wider area. *News of the disaster spread very quickly.*

spring NOUN the season of the year that comes after winter and before summer.

spring

spun See **spin**. *The wheels spun fast.*

square NOUN **1** a shape with four equal sides. **2** an open space in a town or city, surrounded by buildings.

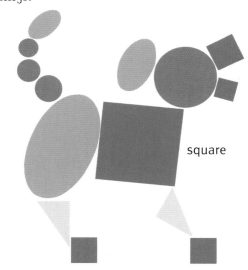

square

squash NOUN **1** lots of people crowded into a small space. **2** a fruit drink. **3** a racket game for two or four players.

squash VERB to crush or squeeze.

squeak VERB to make a short, high-pitched noise.

squeeze VERB (squeezing, squeezed) to press the sides of something together, usually to get liquid out of it or to force it into a smaller space.

squirrel NOUN a small animal that has a bushy tail and which climbs trees.

stable NOUN a building in which horses are kept.

stage NOUN **1** raised platform on which actors perform. **2** a point in the development of someone or something.

stage

stairs PLURAL NOUN a series of steps in a building that lead from one floor to the next.

stamp

stamp NOUN **1** a small piece of paper that you must stick onto a letter before you post it. **2** a small device that prints words or signs on paper.

stamp VERB **1** to hit the ground with your foot. **2** to print a mark with a stamp. **3** to put a postage stamp on an envelope.

stand VERB (stood) to be upright on your feet.

star NOUN **1** one of the small, bright points of light you can see in the sky at night. **2** a shape with five or six points. **3** a famous entertainer.

stare VERB (staring, stared) to look at someone or something for a long time without blinking.

start VERB to begin. **station** NOUN **1** a building on a railway or bus route where you begin or end a journey. **2** a building that is a centre for a particular service. *A fire station.*

stay VERB **1** to stop and remain. **2** to be a guest. *We stayed in a hotel for the weekend.*

steal VERB (stole, stolen) to take something that belongs to someone else without their permission.

steam NOUN the gas produced when water boils.

steep ADJECTIVE rising or falling sharply.

steep

stem NOUN the part of a plant above the ground on which the leaves and flowers grow.

stem

step NOUN **1** the act of putting one foot in front of the other when you are walking. **2** a flat surface that you put your foot on to go up or down to a different level. **3** one of a series of actions you take when making or doing something. **4** (steps) a stepladder, one that is hinged so that it stands up by itself.

step-mother/father NOUN the person who your father/ mother has remarried.

stick NOUN **1** a long, thin piece of wood. **2** a thin piece of anything. *A stick of rock.*

stick VERB (stuck) to fix together with glue.

still ADJECTIVE not moving.

sting NOUN **1** the part of an insect's body that it uses as a weapon. **2** the painful wound caused by the poison from an insect's sting.

sting VERB (stung) to cause a painful wound and swelling in a part of your body.

stir VERB (stirring, stirred) to mix something by moving it round with something such as a spoon.

stocking NOUN a piece of women's clothing that fits over the foot and leg.

stole, stolen See **steal**. *The thief stole the jewels.*

stomach NOUN the part inside your body where your food is digested.

stone NOUN **1** a piece of rock. **2** the hard seed inside some fruits such as cherries or peaches. **3** a measurement of weight equal to 14 pounds or 6.35 kilograms.

stood See **stand**. *The children stood up.*

stool NOUN seat with three or four legs but no back or arms.

stool

stop VERB (stopping, stopped) **1** to come to a standstill. **2** to prevent.

store NOUN **1** a collection of things for future use. **2** a place to keep things. **3** a large shop.

store VERB (storing, stored) to put something away for future use.

storm NOUN bad weather, usually with thunder, lightning and heavy rain.

storm

story NOUN (PLURAL stories) an account of something real or imaginary.

straight 1 in a straight line. **2** directly. *Go straight there.*

straight ADJECTIVE not bent. *Straight hair.*

strange ADJECTIVE unusual, odd. *A strange taste.*

straw NOUN **1** the dried stems of plants like wheat that are used for animal bedding, or for making mats and baskets. **2** a thin tube that you suck a drink through.

strawberry NOUN (PLURAL strawberries) a soft, juicy, red fruit.

stream NOUN a small, narrow river. *There are tadpoles in the stream.*

street NOUN road in a town or village with houses along it. *High Street.*

strength NOUN power, energy. *Superhuman strength.*

stretch VERB **1** to make something bigger by pulling it. **2** to reach out. **3** to hold your arms and legs out straight and tighten your muscles.

strict ADJECTIVE severe in matters of discipline and rules of behaviour.

string NOUN **1** strong thread used for tying things. **2** one of the wires or threads stretched over a musical instrument, tennis racket, etc.

string

strip NOUN a long, narrow piece of land, cloth, etc.

stripe NOUN one band of colour in between others.

strong ADJECTIVE powerful, not easy to break.

stuck See **stick**. *The pieces of the aircraft kit were stuck together.*

study VERB (studying, studied) to spend your time learning about a subject.

stung See **sting**. *I was stung by a wasp.*

submarine NOUN a type of ship that can travel underwater.

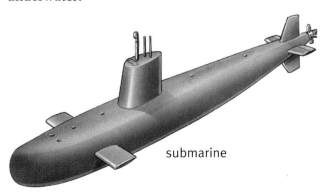

submarine

subtract VERB to take away a number or amount from a larger number or amount.

subway NOUN a path for you to walk on that goes underneath a busy road.

such **1** so much. *We're such good friends.* **2** like. *People such as you and me.*

suck VERB **1** to draw in liquid or air. **2** to eat something by melting it in your mouth as you move it round with your tongue. *Suck an ice lolly.*

suddenly happening very quickly and unexpectedly.

sugar NOUN a sweetener for food and drinks.

sugar cane

suit NOUN a set of matching clothes. *Trouser suit.*

suitcase NOUN a case for carrying your belongings in when you are travelling.

sum NOUN an exercise in simple arithmetic.

summer NOUN the season of the year that comes after spring and before autumn.

summer

sun NOUN the bright star that gives heat and light during the day. *The earth goes round the Sun and that gives us heat and light.*

Sunday NOUN the day of the week before Monday.

sunflower NOUN a plant that can grow to be very tall. It has a very large flower with yellow petals.

sung See **sing**. *The songs were sung well by the children.*

sunk See **sink**. *The 'Titanic' was sunk by an iceberg.*

sunny ADJECTIVE (sunnier, sunniest) brightly lit by the sun. *It was a sunny day.*

sunrise NOUN the rising of the sun at the beginning of the day, dawn.

sunrise

sunset NOUN the going down of the Sun at the end of the day.

supermarket NOUN a large, self-service shop which sells lots of different foods and other goods.

supper NOUN the last meal of the day.

sure ADJECTIVE without doubt, certain.

surface NOUN the outside or top of something.

surgery NOUN (PLURAL surgeries) the place where doctors or dentists see their patients.

surprise NOUN an unexpected event. *Surprise party.*

swallow NOUN an insect-eating bird with a forked tail. *Swallows on the telegraph wires.*

swallow VERB to make food pass from your mouth down your throat.

swam See **swim**. *I swam three lengths.*

swamp NOUN waterlogged land, a bog or marsh.

swamp VERB to overwhelm, flood. *The radio station was swamped with complaints.*

swan NOUN a large, usually white bird with a long neck that lives on rivers and lakes.

swap NOUN something given in exchange for something else. *This stamp is a swap.*

swap VERB (swapping, swapped) to exchange one thing for another. *He swapped his football for a cricket bat.*

swat VERB (swatting, swatted) to hit with a sharp blow. *He swatted the fly with a newspaper, but missed.*

sway VERB **1** to lean in one direction and then another. *He swayed from side to side.* **2** to be uncertain.

sweater NOUN a woollen garment for the top part of your body, a pullover.

sweep VERB (swept) to brush clean. *Dan swept the leaves from the path.*

sweet ADJECTIVE **1** sugary to the taste. *The tea tasted sweet.* **2** kind and pleasant. *She is very sweet.*

sweet NOUN a small, sweet, sugary item to eat, such as a toffee, chocolate or mint.

sweet pea NOUN a climbing plant which often has sweet-smelling flowers.

swallow

swan

swell VERB (swells, swelled, swollen) to grow larger, to expand. *He swelled with pride.*

swell NOUN **1** the process of swelling. **2** the rise and fall of the sea's surface.

swelling NOUN a part of the body that has swollen. *There was a swelling on his neck.*

swept See **sweep**. *I swept the floor.*

sweep

swim VERB (swimming, swam, swum) to travel through water by moving your arms and legs. *I go swimming every Monday evening.*

swim

swimming costume NOUN a tight-fitting garment that women and girls wear when they go swimming.

swimming pool NOUN a pool made for people to swim in.

swimming trunks NOUN the shorts that men and boys wear when they swim.

swing NOUN a seat hanging from ropes or chains that you can sit on and swing.

swing VERB (swung) to repeatedly move backwards and forwards or from side to side from a fixed point.

switch NOUN a control for turning electricity on and off.

swivel (swivels, swivelling, swivelled) VERB to turn round. *I swivelled in amazement.*

swoop VERB to come down with a rush.

sword NOUN weapon with a handle and long, sharp blade.

sword

swordfish NOUN a large seafish with a long upper jaw that looks like a sword.

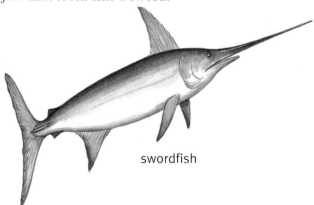
swordfish

swum See **swim**. *Three people have swum the Channel.*

swung See **swing**. *The soldiers swung their arms as they marched.*

syringe NOUN instrument for injecting liquids into the body.

syringe VERB to clean with a syringe. *I had my ears syringed.*

syrup NOUN a thick sweet liquid. *Golden syrup.*

syrupy ADJECTIVE very sweet, like syrup.

table NOUN **1** a piece of furniture with legs that support a flat top. **2** a set of figures arranged in order. *Times tables.*

table tennis NOUN an indoor game in which two or four players hit a light ball backwards and forwards across a low net on a table, ping pong.

tablet NOUN a small piece of solid medicine, a pill.

tadpole NOUN the young of a frog or toad.

tail NOUN the part at the back of an animal, bird or fish.

take VERB (taking, took, taken) **1** to get hold of something. *Take my hand.* **2** to carry or remove. *Let me take your coat.* **3** to have or use. *Do you take sugar in your tea?* **4** to travel in a vehicle. *Take a taxi.* **5** to need. *How long will it take to do your homework?* **6** to steal. *Someone has taken my money.*

take-away NOUN food bought to eat at home.

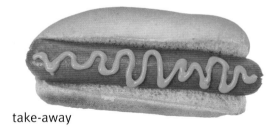

take-away

taken See **take**. *Who has taken my bag?*

tale NOUN a story.

talk VERB to speak, to have a conversation.

tall ADJECTIVE **1** higher than average. *A tall glass.* **2** having a particular height. *The tree was 20 metres tall.*

tambourine NOUN a small drum with metal discs round the edge.

tame ADJECTIVE not fierce or wild.

tank NOUN **1** a large metal container for holding liquids or gas. **2** an armoured vehicle.

tap NOUN a device that you turn to control the flow of liquid, gas, etc., from a pipe or container.

tape NOUN **1** a narrow strip of ribbon, paper, etc. **2** a strip of plastic covered with a magnetic material and used to record sound, pictures, computer data, etc.

tape VERB (taping, taped) to record sound, pictures, computer data, etc., on magnetic tape.

tart NOUN pastry case with a sweet or savoury filling.

taste VERB (tasting, tasted) to use your tongue to feel the flavour of something.

tasty ADJECTIVE having a pleasant taste.

taught See **teach**.

taxi

taxi NOUN a car with a driver who you pay to take you somewhere. *Call a taxi.*

tambourine

tea NOUN **1** a hot drink. *Make a cup of tea.* **2** a meal that you eat in the afternoon or early evening.

teabag NOUN a small bag filled with tea leaves that you pour boiling water on to make a drink of tea.

teach VERB (taught) to train someone in the knowledge of a subject or skill, to give lessons. *I teach Sophie how to play tennis.*

teacher NOUN a person whose job is to teach. *My maths teacher gave me good marks.*

team NOUN a group of people who play on the same side in a game or who work on something together. *The netball team.*

teapot

teapot NOUN a container with a lid, handle and spout, that you use for making and pouring tea.

tear (said like **beer**) NOUN a drop of salty water that comes from your eyes when you cry. *Helena burst into tears.*

tear (said like **bare**) VERB (tore, torn) to pull to pieces. *Tear the paper into strips.*

tear

tease VERB (teasing, teased) to make fun of someone.

teaspoon NOUN a small spoon that you use to stir tea or coffee.

teeth *See* **tooth**.

telephone NOUN the electrical system or the piece of equipment that you use to dial a number and talk to someone in another place.

telescope NOUN instrument that helps you to see objects that are far away more clearly.

television NOUN **1** the sending of sound and pictures over radio waves. **2** the piece of electrical equipment that receives these.

tell VERB (told) **1** to make something known by speaking about it, to pass on information. **2** to decide or find out.

temperature NOUN how hot or cold something is.

ten the number 10.

ten

tennis NOUN a game for two or four people in which a ball is hit with rackets over a net on a court.

tent NOUN a movable shelter for camping out in, made of canvas or nylon stretched over a framework of poles and fixed down with ropes.

term NOUN **1** one of the periods of time that the school year is divided into. **2** a condition of an agreement.

terrible ADJECTIVE very bad or frightening. *Rachel had a terrible experience.*

test NOUN a set of questions to measure your knowledge, an examination.

than used when you compare two things or people. *I like this dress better than that one.*

thank VERB to tell someone that you are grateful for something they have done, said, or given to you. *I thanked my parents for the presents. My sister always thanks the vet for his help.*

that 1 used in joining a sentence. **2** who or which. *The house that Jack built.* **3** (PLURAL those) the one there, the one described. *That dog bit me.* **4** to such an amount. *His jokes weren't that funny.*

the 1 used to refer to that particular thing or person. *The queen.* **2** used to refer to the only people or things of that type. *The media. The poor.*

theatre NOUN **1** a building with a stage where plays, etc., are performed. **2** a room in a hospital where operations are carried out.

their belonging to them.

theirs that or those belonging to them.

them See **they**. *I like them.*

themselves See **they**. *They helped themselves to sweets.*

theme park NOUN an amusement park where the rides and activities are based round a single theme.

then 1 at that time. *There were no motorways then.* **2** next, afterwards. *We had dinner and then went for a drink.* **3** if that is the case. *If you know the answer, then put your hand up.*

there 1 in or at that place. *We're nearly there.* **2** used at the beginning of a sentence with a verb like 'be'. *There is no hope.*

there's = there is, there has. *There's been an accident.*

thermometer NOUN an instrument for measuring temperature.

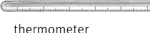

thermometer

Thermos NOUN (trademark) a container to keep drinks hot.

these See **this**. *These books.*

they (them, themselves) **1** the ones described. **2** used instead of 'he' or 'she'.

they'd = they had, they would. *They'd forgotten her birthday present.*

they'll = they will. *They'll be here soon.*

they're = they are. *They're back!*

they've = they have. *They've gone.*

thick ADJECTIVE **1** not thin. **2** measuring a particular amount. *The castle walls were a metre thick.* **3** not watery. *Thick gravy.* **4** difficult to see through. *Thick fog.*

thief NOUN (PLURAL thieves) someone who steals.

thieves See **thief**.

thin ADJECTIVE (thinner, thinnest) **1** narrow, not thick. **2** not fat. *A thin girl.* **3** watery. *Thin soup.*

think VERB (thought) to use your mind, to have an idea or opinion.

third ADJECTIVE the one after the second, 3rd.

thirsty ADJECTIVE (thirstier, thirstiest) wanting or needing a drink.

thirteen the number 13. *Unlucky thirteen.*

thirty the number 30.

this (PLURAL these) the one here. *This is a good book.*

thorn NOUN sharp prickle growing on a plant like a rose. *Gareth pricked his finger on a thorn.*

thorn

those See **that**. *Those animals.*

thought NOUN an idea or opinion.

thought See **think**. *I thought about our holiday last year.*

thousand NOUN the number 1,000.

thread NOUN **1** a long, thin piece of cotton or nylon used with a needle when sewing. **2** a long, thin length of any other material. **3** a raised line that winds round the outside of a screw.

three the number **3**.

threw See **throw**. *Jack threw the ball.*

throat NOUN **1** the part of your body at the front of your neck. **2** the tube in your neck that takes air to your lungs and food to your stomach.

through 1 from one end or side to the other. *We drove through the village.* **2** from beginning to end. *All through the winter.* **3** by means of. *We got in through the window.* **4** because of. *I dropped the jug through carelessness.*

throw VERB (threw, thrown) to send something through the air by a movement of your arm.

thrown See **throw**. *How far have you thrown the ball?*

thumb NOUN the short, thick finger on the side of your hand.

thunder NOUN the loud noise that follows lightning.

Thursday NOUN the day of the week after Wednesday and before Friday.

ticket NOUN a piece of paper or card to show that you have paid to go on or into something.

ticket

tickle VERB (tickling, tickled) to touch someone lightly to make them laugh.

tide NOUN the regular rising and falling of the sea.

tie NOUN **1** a piece of clothing worn under the collar of a shirt and knotted at the front. **2** an equal score in a game or competition.

tie VERB (tying, tied) **1** to fasten or knot with string, rope, etc. **2** to finish a game or competition with equal points.

tiger NOUN a large animal of the cat family that is yellow-brown with black stripes.

tight ADJECTIVE **1** fastened very firmly. **2** fitting very close to the body, not loose.

tights PLURAL NOUN a close-fitting garment that covers all the lower half of the body.

tiger

till until. *I can play till tea.*

till NOUN a machine that has a drawer for money and adds up the prices in a shop.

time NOUN **1** the passing of hours, days, weeks, years, etc. **2** a particular moment in the day. *Teatime.* **3** a period or occasion. *We had a good time.* **4** the speed and beat of a piece of music.

tin NOUN **1** a soft metal. **2** a metal box or container.

tiny ADJECTIVE (tinier, tiniest) very small.

tip NOUN **1** the end of something. **2** a small amount of money that you give to someone who does you a service. **3** a helpful piece of advice. **4** a place where rubbish is dumped.

tip VERB (tipping, tipped) **1** to put something onto one edge so that it overturns. **2** to give someone a tip.

tiptoe VERB to move on your toes, especially when you are trying not to make a noise.

tiptoe

tired ADJECTIVE feeling that you need to rest or sleep.

tissue NOUN a paper handkerchief.

to **1** in the direction of, towards. *A train to Manchester.* **2** as far as. *We came to the end of the road.* **3** against. *Back to back.* **4** compared with. *I prefer drawing to painting.*

toad NOUN animal like a frog.

toast NOUN bread browned in a toaster or under a grill.

toaster NOUN a machine that heats bread so that it goes crisp and brown.

toboggan NOUN a light sledge.

toboggan

today this present day.

toddler NOUN a child who has just learnt to walk.

toe NOUN one of the five parts of your body at the end of your foot.

toffee NOUN a hard, sticky sweet.

together **1** joined into one piece, group, etc. **2** all at the same time.

toilet NOUN a lavatory.

told See **tell**. *The teacher told us a story.*

tomato NOUN (PLURAL tomatoes) a round, juicy, red fruit eaten raw or cooked.

tomorrow the day after today.

tongue NOUN the part in your mouth with which you taste things.

too 1 also, as well. *I went on holiday to France and my parents came too.* **2** more than you need or want. *The food looked so delicious that we all ate far too much at Christmas.*

took See **take**. *Jo took Sam's favourite book.*

tool NOUN an instrument that you use to do a job.

tooth NOUN (PLURAL teeth) **1** one of a row of white, bony parts in your mouth that you use to bite your food. **2** one of a row of pointed bits on things such as a comb, zip, saw, etc.

toothbrush NOUN a small brush for cleaning your teeth.

top NOUN **1** the highest point or position. **2** the highest part of something. **3** a spinning toy. **4** a piece of clothing that you wear on the upper part of your body.

torch NOUN battery-operated light that you carry in your hand.

tore, torn See **tear**. *Someone has torn my coat.*

tortoise NOUN a slow-moving animal with a hard shell covering its body.

tortoise

total NOUN the complete amount when everything is added up together.

touch VERB **1** to feel with your hands. **2** to be against something. **3** to be moved in your feelings.

towel NOUN a piece of paper or cloth used for drying things.

tower NOUN a tall building or a tall part of a building.

town NOUN a place with a large number of houses, shops, etc.

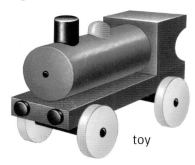

toy

toy NOUN something that a child plays with.

track NOUN **1** a rough path. **2** the mark left by tyres, footprints, etc. **3** a railway line. **4** a single piece of music on a tape or disc.

tractor NOUN a vehicle used on farms.

traffic NOUN the moving vehicles on roads, motorways, etc.

train NOUN a line of railway carriages pulled by an engine.

trainers PLURAL NOUN sports shoes.

trampoline NOUN a large piece of canvas held by springs in a frame for jumping on.

travel VERB (travelling, travelled) to go from one place to another, to go on a journey.

tray NOUN a flat board with raised edges that you can carry things on.

tread VERB (trod, trodden) to put your foot on the ground, as when you walk.

treasure NOUN a store of valuable and precious things.

tree NOUN a tall plant with a trunk and branches.

triangle NOUN **1** a shape with three sides. **2** a musical instrument in this shape.

trick NOUN **1** something done to deceive you. **2** a clever action done to amuse you.

trick VERB to make someone believe something that is not true.

tricycle NOUN a vehicle with three wheels, especially a child's toy.

trip VERB (tripping, tripped) to stumble and lose your balance.

trod, trodden See **tread**. *He trod on the beetle.*

trousers PLURAL NOUN a piece of clothing that fastens at the waist and covers each leg separately.

truck NOUN a lorry or heavy goods vehicle.

true ADJECTIVE correct, real, not false.

trumpet NOUN a musical instrument that you blow into.

trunk NOUN **1** the main stem of a tree. **2** the main part of your body. **3** the long nose of an elephant. **4** a large box to put your things in when you are travelling.

trust VERB to believe in and depend on the goodness of someone.

truth NOUN whatever is true.

try VERB (trying, tried) **1** to make an effort to do something. **2** to test something out. **3** to examine someone in a court of law.

tube NOUN **1** a round, hollow length of metal, plastic, rubber, etc. **2** a small, soft container that holds things like toothpaste, cream or paint.

Tuesday NOUN the day of the week after Monday and before Wednesday.

tulip NOUN a spring flower that grows from a bulb.

tumble VERB (tumbling, tumbled) to take a sudden fall.

tumble dryer NOUN a machine to dry wet clothes.

tuna NOUN a large fish used as food.

tunnel NOUN a long passage under the ground or under water.

tunnel

turkey NOUN a large bird kept on farms for its meat.

turn VERB **1** to move round, like a wheel. **2** to change direction. **3** to become. **4** to use a control to do something.

turquoise NOUN a bluish-green colour.

twelve the number 12.

twenty the number 20.

twig NOUN a thin stem on a branch.

twin NOUN **1** either of two children born to the same mother at the same time. **2** one of two things exactly the same. *Twin beds.*

twist VERB **1** to wind threads together. **2** to turn and pull a part of your body so that it hurts. *Twist your ankle.* **3** to curve.

two the number 2.

typewriter NOUN a machine with a keyboard for printing letters onto paper.

tyre NOUN a rubber tube filled with air that fits round the outside of a wheel.

tulip

ugly ADJECTIVE (uglier, ugliest) not attractive to look at.

umbrella NOUN a piece of nylon stretched over a folding frame that keeps the rain off you when you put it up.

umbrella

uncle NOUN 1 the brother of your mother or father. 2 the husband of your aunt.

under 1 below, lower than. *Under the bed.* 2 less than. *Reductions for children under 16.* 3 in the process of. *New ideas under discussion.* 4 subject to, obeying. *Under starter's orders.*

underground ADJECTIVE below the ground. Rabbits live underground in burrows.

underground NOUN an underground railway. *The London Underground.*

underneath under something else. *I looked underneath the bed for my slippers.*

understand VERB (understood) to know what someone is saying or what they mean.

understood See understand. *I understood what I had to do.*

underwear NOUN clothes that you wear next to your skin, but underneath other clothes.

undress VERB to take your clothes off.

unhappy

unhappy ADJECTIVE (unhappier, unhappiest) sad.

uniform NOUN the special clothing worn by a particular group of people, such as police officers, nurses or schoolchildren.

universe NOUN all of space and everything that exists.

untidy ADJECTIVE (untidier, untidiest) not neat and tidy.

unusual ADJECTIVE strange, not normal or usual.

up 1 to an upright position. *Stand up.* 2 to a higher place. *Climb up the ladder.* 3 at an end. *Your time is up.* 4 along. *Up the road.*

upon on.

upset VERB (upsetting, upset) 1 to tip over, to spill. 2 to make someone unhappy.

upside-down 1 in a position where the top is at the bottom and the bottom is at the top. 2 in an untidy mess.

upside-down

us See we. *Come and visit us.*

use VERB (using, used) 1 to do something with a thing. *I shall use the saw to cut wood.* 2 to have done something often in the past. *We used to sit over there.*

vacuum cleaner NOUN a machine that sucks up dust and dirt from carpets.

valley NOUN a lower area of land between mountains or hills, especially with a river running through it.

valley

valuable ADJECTIVE worth a lot of money.

van NOUN a vehicle for carrying goods.

vase NOUN a container to put flowers in or use as an ornament.

vegetable NOUN a plant used for food.

Velcro NOUN (trademark) a fastening for clothes, shoes, etc., in which two nylon strips stick together when you press them against each another.

very especially, most.

vest NOUN a piece of underwear worn on the upper part of your body, usually for extra warmth.

vet NOUN an animal doctor.

vicar NOUN a priest in the Anglican church.

video NOUN **1** a film or other recording that you watch by playing it through your television set. **2** a machine for recording television programmes and playing videos.

video VERB to make a video recording of something.

video camera NOUN a camera that records film onto video tape.

video game NOUN an electronic game played on a computer.

view NOUN **1** something that you see, a scene. *A view of the sea.* **2** an opinion or attitude.

village NOUN a small group of houses and other buildings, but not as big as a town.

vinegar NOUN a sour liquid used to flavour food, especially chips.

violent ADJECTIVE behaving in a way that causes great harm.

violet NOUN **1** a bluish-purple colour. **2** a small purple or white spring flower.

violin NOUN a musical instrument with four strings that is played with a bow.

violin

visit VERB to go to see a person or place and stay there for a time.

visitor NOUN someone who visits a person or place.

voice NOUN the sound that you make when you speak or sing.

volcano NOUN (PLURAL volcanoes) a mountain that sprays out lava and steam through an opening at the top or in the sides.

vote VERB (voting, voted) to choose what you prefer by putting a mark on a piece of paper, raising your hand, etc.

wagon NOUN a truck for heavy loads that is pulled by horses, railway engines, etc.

wait VERB to stay in a place until an expected event happens.

wake VERB (waking, woke or waked, woken or waked) to make or become conscious again after being asleep.

walk VERB to move by putting one foot in front of the other.

wall NOUN **1** a barrier of brick or stone. **2** the side of a room or building.

wallet NOUN a small, flat case for keeping paper money in.

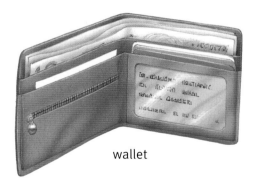

wallet

wand NOUN a thin rod, especially one that you do magic tricks with.

want VERB to need or wish for something. *I want a bicycle for my birthday.*

war NOUN a period of fighting between countries or peoples.

ward NOUN a room in a hospital which has beds for patients.

wardrobe NOUN a cupboard for hanging your clothes in.

warm ADJECTIVE **1** quite hot. *A warm day.* **2** able to keep in the heat. *A warm coat.*

warn VERB to tell someone in advance about a possible danger, result, etc.

was See **be**. *The party was good.*

wasn't = was not. *I wasn't sure.*

wash VERB to clean with water.

washing machine NOUN a machine for washing clothes.

wasp NOUN a stinging insect like a bee.

wasp

waste NOUN things that are used, damaged, etc., rubbish.

waste VERB (wasting, wasted) to use too much of something when it is not needed. *To waste time.*

watch NOUN a small clock to wear on your wrist.

watch VERB **1** to look at carefully. **2** to take care of.

water NOUN the clear liquid found in rivers and seas that is needed for people and animals to live.

waterfall NOUN a flow of water where a river falls straight over the edge of a cliff or a big rock.

waterfall

wave NOUN **1** a ridge on the surface of the sea caused by the tide or by the wind. **2** a movement of your hand. **3** the way in which some forms of energy move.

wave VERB (waving, waved) to move your hand to greet someone or to attract their attention.

way NOUN **1** a road, path, lane, etc. *The Fosse Way.* **2** the right direction to follow. *The way out.* **3** how something is done. *The way to make tea.*

we (us, ourselves) the people speaking.

we'd = we had, we would. *We'd better go.*

we'll = we will. *We'll come again.*

we're = we are. *We're very happy.*

we've = we have. *We've had a nice time.*

weak ADJECTIVE not strong.

wear VERB (wore, worn) **1** to dress in something. **2** to damage something because it is always being used. *Wear a hole in the carpet.* **3** to last. *These shoes have worn well.*

weather NOUN the conditions of sun, rain, temperature, etc., at a particular time.

web

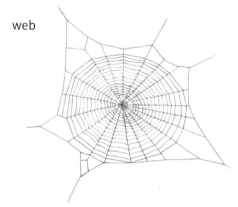

web NOUN **1** the network of threads that spiders spin. **2** the piece of skin between the toes of water birds, like ducks. **3** a computer information system on the Internet. *The World Wide Web.*

wedding NOUN a marriage service and the celebrations that follow it.

Wednesday NOUN the day of the week after Tuesday and before Thursday.

weed NOUN a wild plant growing where it is not wanted.

week NOUN a period of time equal to seven days and nights.

weep VERB (wept) to cry.

weigh VERB **1** to measure how heavy something or someone is. **2** to have a particular weight.

weight NOUN a measure of how heavy something or someone is.

well 1 in good health. **2** in a good or right way. *He did his job well.*

well NOUN a deep hole dug in the ground to reach water or oil.

went See **go**. *Chris went home.*

wept See **weep**. *They wept at the sad news.*

were See **be**. *They were happy.*

weren't = were not. *You weren't here.*

west NOUN one of the four points of the compass, the direction of the setting Sun.

wet ADJECTIVE (wetter, wettest) not dry. *I always get wet when it rains.*

whale NOUN the largest animal that lives in the sea.

whale

what 1 which thing or person? **2** to what extent? **3** that which. *I did exactly what he said.*

wheat NOUN a plant producing grains that are made into flour.

wheel NOUN **1** a round object that turns on an axle to move a vehicle, work a machine, etc. **2** a steering wheel.

wheelbarrow NOUN a small cart that has one wheel at the front and two legs and handles at the back which is used for carrying things.

wheelchair NOUN a chair on wheels so that people who cannot walk are able to move.

when 1 at what time? *When are you going shopping?* **2** at the time at which. *It was late when we went to bed.*

where 1 at or in what place? *Where are my gloves?* **2** at, in or to which. *I'm going where the Sun is shining.*

which 1 what person or thing? *Which boy do you mean?* **2** the one or ones that. *The game which we are playing.*

while during the time that. *I went to work while you were still asleep.*

whisker NOUN one of the hairs growing on both sides of a cat's mouth.

whisper VERB to speak to someone so quietly that other people cannot hear.

whisper

whistle NOUN **1** a small, metal tube that gives a loud, shrill sound when you blow into it. **2** a sound that you make when you force your breath out from between your lips.

white ADJECTIVE having the colour of snow.

who (whom, whose) **1** which person? **2** the person that. *The boy who shouts the loudest.*

whole ADJECTIVE **1** the complete thing or amount. **2** in one piece.

whom, whose See **who**. *Whose shoe is this?*

why for what reason? *Why are you late?*

wide ADJECTIVE **1** large from side to side, not narrow. **2** completely. *She left the window wide open.*

width NOUN the measurement of something from side to side.

wife NOUN (PLURAL wives) the woman a man is married to.

wild ADJECTIVE living in a free and natural way, not tame.

will NOUN **1** the power that you have in your mind to decide what you do. **2** a desire. *The will to win.* **3** a piece of paper that says what you want to do with your possessions when you die.

will used when referring to the future. *I hope you will come to my party.*

win VERB (winning, won) to be the first or best in a competition, game, etc.

wind NOUN a current of air blowing across the surface of the earth.

wind

windmill NOUN **1** a tall building with sails on the outside that turn in the wind to work the machines inside so that grain is crushed into flour. **2** a toy on a stick that blows round in the wind.

window NOUN an opening in a building with glass over it that lets in light and air.

wine NOUN an alcoholic drink made from grapes.

wing NOUN **1** one of the two parts on the sides of a bird's body that it uses to fly. **2** one of the two parts on the sides of an aeroplane that help it to fly. **3** one of the parts of a car covering the wheels. **4** the position of a player in games like football.

winter NOUN the season of the year that comes after autumn and before spring.

wipe VERB (wiping, wiped) to clean or dry the surface of something by lightly rubbing it.

wire NOUN a thin thread of metal.

wish NOUN a desire or longing for something.

wish VERB to want something to be true, to want to do something.

with 1 having. *A girl with blue eyes.* **2** in the company of, including. *They came with us.* **3** using. *He walked with a stick.* **4** because of. *The chimney was black with soot.*

without not having.

wives See **wife**.

woke, woken See **wake**. *I woke up late.*

wolf NOUN (PLURAL wolves) a wild animal like a large dog.

wolves See **wolf**.

woman NOUN (PLURAL women) an adult female.

women See **woman**.

won See **win**. *Our team won the game.*

won't = will not. *I won't go.*

wonder NOUN a feeling of surprise and amazement or the cause of this feeling.

wonder VERB **1** to be surprised and amazed. **2** to want to know or understand.

wonderful ADJECTIVE very good and pleasing.

wood NOUN **1** the material that tree trunks and branches are made of. **2** a place where trees grow together.

woodpecker NOUN a bird with a long, sharp beak for boring holes in tree trunks to eat insects.

wool NOUN **1** the soft, thick hair that grows on sheep, goats, etc. **2** the thread or material made from this hair.

word NOUN the letters and sounds that together make up a single unit of language.

wore See **wear**. *Sarah wore a new dress.*

work VERB **1** to do a task, especially as a job. **2** to move or go properly.

work NOUN a job, a task.

worm NOUN a long, thin creature without legs that lives in the soil.

worn See **wear**.

worse ADJECTIVE See **bad**. *Even worse news.*

worst ADJECTIVE See **bad**. *The worst winter for years.*

would used in reported speech or writing, to express a condition, etc. *You said you would come.*

wouldn't = would not. *I wouldn't say that.*

wrinkle NOUN a line in your skin, especially when you grow old.

wolf

Xmas NOUN a short way of writing 'Christmas'.

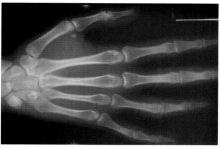
X-ray

X-ray NOUN **1** a beam of radiation that takes pictures of the inside of your body. **2** the picture made by sending X-rays through your body.

xylophone NOUN a musical instrument that you play by hitting flat bars with a hammer.

yacht NOUN a sailing boat.

yarn NOUN thread.

yawn VERB to open your mouth wide, as when you are tired or bored.

year NOUN a period of time equal to 365 days, 52 weeks or 12 months.

yell VERB to shout out.

yellow ADJECTIVE having the colour of egg yolks.

yes used to answer someone to agree with them, or to say that something is true.

yesterday the day before today.

yet up to this time.

yo-yo NOUN a toy made of a round piece of wood or plastic on a string that you make go up and down.

yogurt NOUN food made from milk.

yolk NOUN the yellow part in the middle of an egg.

you (yourself, yourselves) the person or people being spoken to. *Would you like to come with me?*

you'd = you had, you would. *You'd know them.*

you'll = you will. *You'll be sorry.*

you're = you are. *You're lucky.*

you've = you have. *You've been told.*

young ADJECTIVE not old.

your belonging to you.

yours that or those belonging to you.

yourself, yourselves See **you**. *Did you enjoy yourself last night?*

zebra

zebra NOUN wild animal like a horse, with black and white stripes.

zero NOUN the figure 0, nothing.

zig-zag NOUN a line shaped like a row of Ws.

zip NOUN a fastener with two rows of teeth which you pull together to fasten things.

zoo NOUN a park where wild animals are kept in cages for people to look at.

yo-yo

Aa Bb Cc Dd

Zz Yy Xx Ww Vv

Adjectives, nouns and verbs

Adjectives

An **adjective** is a word that tells us about a noun. *In 'a small car' 'small' is an adjective that describes 'car'.*

When we compare two people or things, we add *–er* to the adjective or put *more* in front of the adjective: *rich, richer; small, smaller; more dangerous.*

When we compare three or more people or things we add *–est* to the adjective or put *most* in front of the adjective: *rich, richest; small, smallest; most dangerous.*

Nouns

The name of a thing is called a **noun**. There are different kinds of noun.

A **proper noun** is the name of a particular person or thing. Your name is a proper noun. The names of places are also proper nouns. Examples of proper nouns are: *William Shakespeare, France, London, Queen Elizabeth.* Proper nouns start with a capital letter. All other nouns are called *common nouns*, for example: *book, child, rice.*

Concrete nouns are the names given to things that you can see or touch, for example: *book, child, dog.*

Uu Tt Ss Rr

Ee Ff Gg Hh Ii Jj Kk Ll Mm

Abstract nouns are the names given to feelings, qualities or ideas, for example: *surprise, happiness, beauty.*

Collective nouns are the names of a group of people or things. For example: 'flock' in 'a flock of sheep'; 'crowd' in 'a crowd of people'.

The **singular** is the form of a noun that we use when we talk about one person or thing. This is in contrast to the **plural**, the form of a noun that we use when we talk about two or more people or things. For example, the plural of 'dog' is 'dogs'. The most common way to make a word into the plural is to add 's': *book, books.*

Verbs

A **verb** is a 'doing' word. It tells us what is happening or being. Examples of verbs are: *go, think, play.*

A verb shows us when an action takes place. For example with the verb 'help':

present I help; I am helping
past   I helped; I have helped
future I will help

The spelling of the verb changes when the word is used to show different times. For example, 'ed' is usually added when the verb is used in the past: *help, helped (I helped Dad yesterday).*

Qq Pp Oo Nn

PART 2

THESAURUS

INTRODUCTION

A **thesaurus is a collection** of lists of words with similar meanings. It is a kind of word finder that should help you find the exact word you are looking for by giving other words that have similar meanings to the one you are thinking of. So listed under 'funny' you will find: amusing, comic, humorous, ridiculous, witty, laughable, droll; and also strange, weird, peculiar, odd, curious.

There are also lists of words associated in meaning with a particular word (the headword). They cannot replace that word but nevertheless belong to the same group.

So, under 'mathematics' are listed the following associated words:

- add up
- subtract
- take away
- divide
- multiply
- count
- measure
- calculate
- work out

This is not a comprehensive thesaurus. We have mainly chosen words that younger readers will be familiar with, particularly such overworked words as get, good and nice. So, for example, you could say: 'I had a nice time at the party. The people were nice. The food was nice and we played lots of nice games.'

But instead, you might say:
'I had a wonderful time at the party and I met several interesting people. The food was delicious and we played some amusing games.' Do you think that's nicer?!

It's not quite true to say that a synonym is a word with exactly the same meaning as another word. More often synonyms are words with perhaps very

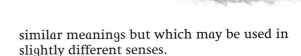
writer

similar meanings but which may be used in slightly different senses.

We talk about a tall man, tall trees and a tall building but we say a high mountain (and also a high building), but never a high man (or woman) or high trees.

You may get on your 'high horse' but the horse you ride is a tall horse. You might also think that fast and quick are interchangeable, but some people drive fast cars and so make quick journeys.

It is important to look up in a dictionary any word you do not understand or are not sure about. A thesaurus does not give definitions.

The word 'thesaurus' comes from the Greek word for 'treasury' and, indeed, this is what it is – a treasury of words. By helping you to find the exact word you are looking for, we hope that we will help you to write in a more interesting and vivid way.

Enjoy our rich language!

THE STORY OF ENGLISH

During the 100 or so years after the Roman armies left Britain in 408 AD to defend Rome against invaders, tribes from northern Germany and Scandinavia (the Anglo-Saxons) conquered Britain and drove the native Celtic British people into Wales and Cornwall. There they continued to speak their own language. (Welsh survives but the Cornish language died out in the 18th century).

We now call the language of the invaders Anglo-Saxon or Old English. Here is a clear example of Old English, from the Anglo-Saxon Chronicle of the 800s:

Breten iegland is eahta hund míla lang, and twa hund míla brad; and here sind...

Britain island is eight hundred miles long and two hundred miles broad; and here are...

...on thaem ieglande fíf getheodu: Englisc, Brettisc, Scyttisc, Pihtisc and Boc-laeden.

...on this island five languages: English, British, Scottish, Pictish and Book Latin.

This language is the basis of modern English and provides us with most of our very basic vocabulary and grammar, parts of the body, relationships, names of animals, geographic features and so on. The Vikings from Scandinavia, who later plundered and settled in parts of the country, introduced new words. Many of our words beginning with sk– (such as sky, skill and skirt) are Viking words. And they gave names to the places where they settled: the 'dale' in Grimsdale means 'valley', the 'by' in Rugby means 'village' and 'wick' in Blowick means 'bay' or 'inlet'. And their pronouns: 'they, them, their' etc. replaced Anglo-Saxon ones.

The enrichment of English with the introduction of new words from different languages has led to some duplication of words which allows for subtle and delicately different shades of meaning. We can have an English wedding or a French marriage, we can be brotherly or fraternal and we can forgive or pardon folk or people. This huge range of choice can be seen in this thesaurus with its variety of synonyms.

When English, once regarded as a 'rough, uncouth tongue', returned as the language of the ruling classes in the 14th century it had changed greatly and had absorbed thousands of French words. Norman French provided English with new ways of expressing more abstract ideas and emotions such as charity and passion; or words to do with administration and justice such as jury, felony, govern, prince, duke. And Norman cooks served pork, mutton and beef rather than English pig, sheep and cow.

ski

sky

Viking

135

OLD ENGLISH

On the following pages you can find out where words that we use today came from originally, and how the English language has changed over time. You can see the beginnings of the language in the examples from Old English shown on this page. There is a section which shows some of the main differences between American English and British English, including lists of things which are called by completely different names, as well as points about the major spelling differences between the two branches of the language. Also included are lists of words which have been taken into the English language from other languages, and a collection of common idioms. Finally, a map demonstrates how widely used the English Language is, as an official language or as a second language, in many countries around the world.

OLD WORDS WITH NEW MEANINGS:

Acre: this was once a field but now means a measure of land.
Fond once meant foolish but now means loving.
A **knave** was once a servant but is now a rascal.
Nice once meant fussy and hard to please.
Silly once meant blessed but now means stupid.
A **villain** was once a peasant but has now become a rogue.

moon

A simple Old English vocabulary:

English	Old English
cold	cald
cow	cu
day	daege
green	grene
hill	hill
king	cynning
land	land
man	mann
milk	milc
moon	mona
mouse	mus
night	niht
street	straet
sun	sunne

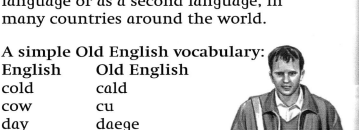

man

land

AMERICAN ENGLISH

American English is different from British English. Some words have different spellings, and some words that are used to describe the same thing are completely different. Today these differences do not seem so noticeable, as British and American people are both exposed to each other's cultures through films, television and books, and so tend to be able to understand each other. This was not always the case. Even up until the Second World War, the situation was quite different. For example, a book published in America might have needed a glossary to explain certain words in the British edition.

ball park/playing field
bill/banknote
candy/sweets
checkers/draughts

HERE WE SHOW SOME OF THE COMMONEST DIFFERENCES BETWEEN THE TWO VARIATIONS OF THE ENGLISH LANGUAGE.

Some common differences between British and American spelling:
British **re** (centre, fibre, theatre) usually becomes **er** (center, fiber, theater.)
British **our** (colour, harbour, honour) becomes **or**, (color, harbor, honor.)

WHERE THE BRITISH HAVE LL THE AMERICANS HAVE L TO INFLECT WORDS LIKE TRAVEL (TRAVELLING, TRAVELLED – BRITISH), TRAVEL (TRAVELING, TRAVELED – AMERICAN).
Here are some common examples of differences between British and American English spellings: (American spelling appears first.)

aluminum/aluminium
defense/defence
gray/grey
check/cheque
plow/plough
skillful/skilful
color/colour

theater/theatre
molt/moult
mold/mould
labor/labour
fiber/fibre
woolen/woollen

American English also has over 4000 entirely separate words. Here are just a few: (American words appear first)

cookie/biscuit
fall/autumn
first floor/ground floor
gas/petrol
homely/ugly
hood/car bonnet
trunk/car boot
jelly/jam
ladybug/ladybird
antsy/fidgety
drapes/curtains
cotton candy/candyfloss
crosswalk/pedestrian crossing

downspout/drainpipe
duplex/semi-detached house
ground round/best mince
lightning bug/glow-worm
pacifier/baby's dummy
diaper/baby's nappy
realtor/estate agent
station wagon/estate car
teeter-totter/see-saw
yard/garden
zucchini/courgette
eggplant/aubergine
sidewalk/pavement

gasoline/petrol
pants/trousers
airplane/aeroplane
trash/rubbish
mad/angry
movie/film
chips/crisps
french fries/chips

ladybug/ladybird

teeter-totter/see-saw

drapes/curtains

trunk/car boot

hood/car bonnet

BORROWED WORDS

Some words from other languages have become part of the English language. Here are some examples.

Arabic

cotton, algebra, sofa, sugar, chemistry, cipher, genie, yashmak, wadi, mohair

Greek

alphabet, geology, philosophy, chemist, character, oxygen, angel, coriander, symphony, rhinoceros, crocus, pylon, chaos

pylon

Latin

dental, focus, exit, circus, rostrum, ibex, pavement, juniper, damson

circus

Dutch

boom, skipper, landscape, yacht, gas, coffee, tea, cork

Turkish

divan, kiosk, yoghurt

Spanish

patio, zero

yacht

divan

Hindi and Urdu

bandana, bangle, dinghy, loot, shampoo, cowry, thug, sari, dungarees, guru, kedgeree, mynah

Polynesian

tattoo

loot

Italian

piano, pizza, ballot, bandit, opera, crescendo, pantaloon, porcelain, confetti

piano

Native American

canoe, moose, tomahawk

Afrikaans

springbok, aardvark, apartheid, kraal, veld

springbok

French

gateau, chamois, grill, beef, picnic, flute, giblets, fort, fortress, fairy

Icelandic

fairy, saga, geyser

Inuit

kayak, anorak, igloo

Norwegian

lemming

flute

Persian

shah, bazaar, paradise, shawl, cushy

Portugese

palaver, verandah, monsoon, albino, macaw

macaw

Sanskrit

juggernaut, jungle, jute, pundit, nirvana

IDIOMS

An idiom is a group of words used together to mean something different from the same words when they are used on their own. Here are some common examples:

To beat about the bush. To avoid something or to approach it in a roundabout way.

On cloud nine. Very happy.

Fifty-fifty. Shared equally.

On the other hand. Alternatively.

To keep something under one's hat. To keep something secret.

For the high jump. In serious trouble.

Keen as mustard. Enthusiastic.

To turn over a new leaf. To change.

One in a million. Special.

Hit the nail on the head. To be exactly right about something.

Nose to the grindstone. Working incessantly.

Flat out. At top speed.

Pour oil on troubled waters. To calm or soothe a difficult situation.

Finger on the pulse. Well informed about what is happening.

Raining cats and dogs. Raining very heavily.

Rub up the wrong way. To irritate or annoy.

Scatter-brained. Unable to concentrate on one thing.

Thick as thieves. Very friendly.

Quick on the uptake. Quick to understand.

To wash one's hands of. To refuse to take responsibility.

Take the bull by the horns. To tackle a problem boldly.

Vanish into thin air. To disappear completely.

Throw down the gauntlet. To set a challenge.

Come a cropper. To fail.

The green-eyed monster. Jealousy.

Kill two birds with one stone. To get two good results from a single action.

Baker's dozen. Thirteen.

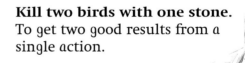

THE SPREAD OF ENGLISH

Up to about 400 years ago English was spoken only in a tiny part of the world now called the British Isles. Today the language is spoken in nearly every part of the world. It is now the native language of Great Britain, Ireland, Australia, Canada, New Zealand and the United States. It is widely spoken in South Africa and other parts of Africa as well as in India, Pakistan, Sri Lanka and the West Indies. English is now also accepted as the international language of commerce, science, technology and diplomacy.

English is spoken by at least 400 million people, and is spoken as a first language by 330 million people.

English is used as an official language in the following countries, accounting for a total population of 1.6 billion. In many other countries it is also used as the common second language, or the main

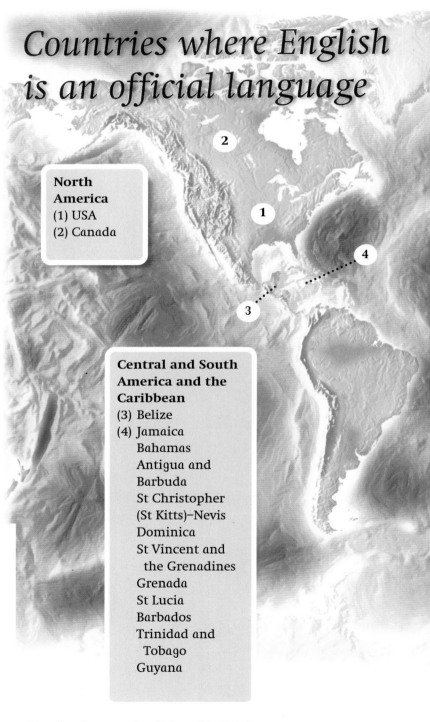

Countries where English is an official language

North America
(1) USA
(2) Canada

Central and South America and the Caribbean
(3) Belize
(4) Jamaica
    Bahamas
    Antigua and
    Barbuda
    St Christopher
    (St Kitts)–Nevis
    Dominica
    St Vincent and
      the Grenadines
    Grenada
    St Lucia
    Barbados
    Trinidad and
      Tobago
    Guyana

Most Jamaicans speak a dialect of English that sounds quite different to standard British or American English. A dialect might use different words and expressions.

Introduction

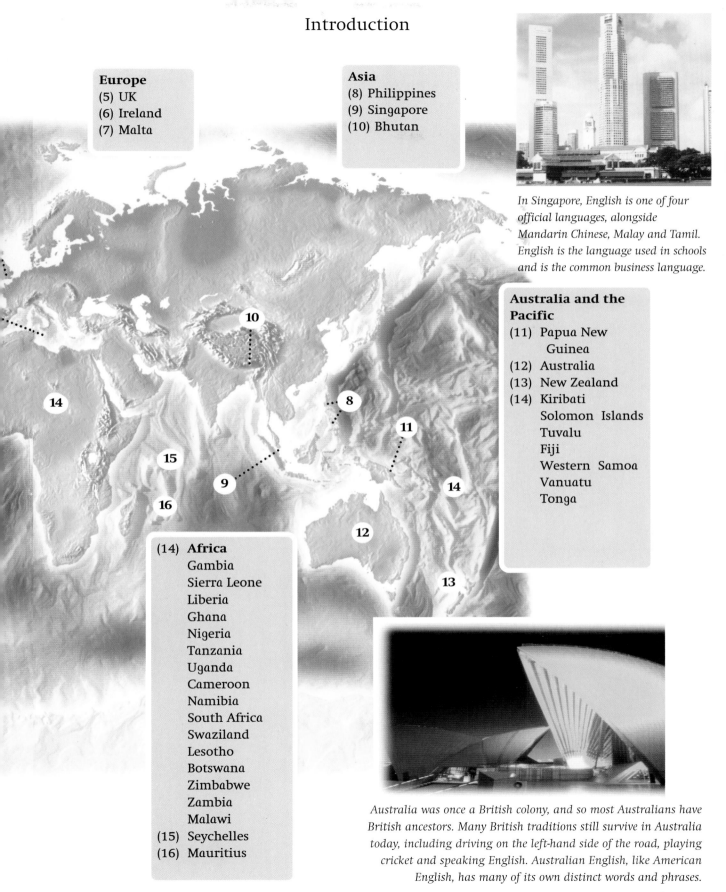

Europe
(5) UK
(6) Ireland
(7) Malta

Asia
(8) Philippines
(9) Singapore
(10) Bhutan

In Singapore, English is one of four official languages, alongside Mandarin Chinese, Malay and Tamil. English is the language used in schools and is the common business language.

Australia and the Pacific
(11) Papua New Guinea
(12) Australia
(13) New Zealand
(14) Kiribati
Solomon Islands
Tuvalu
Fiji
Western Samoa
Vanuatu
Tonga

(14) **Africa**
Gambia
Sierra Leone
Liberia
Ghana
Nigeria
Tanzania
Uganda
Cameroon
Namibia
South Africa
Swaziland
Lesotho
Botswana
Zimbabwe
Zambia
Malawi
(15) Seychelles
(16) Mauritius

Australia was once a British colony, and so most Australians have British ancestors. Many British traditions still survive in Australia today, including driving on the left-hand side of the road, playing cricket and speaking English. Australian English, like American English, has many of its own distinct words and phrases.

141

HOW TO USE THIS THESAURUS

Headwords

The headword or entry word is the word you look up to find other words with similar meanings (synonyms). These headwords are arranged alphabetically.

Parts of speech

After the headword is the part of speech – noun, verb, adverb, adjective, or preposition.

Synonyms

Synonyms (words with similar meanings) follow the part of speech. They are listed in the order of common usage, rather than alphabetically.

nag VERB pester, annoy, badger, go on about, henpeck.

nail VERB fix, peg, fasten, hammer in.

naive ADJECTIVE innocent, simple, unsophisticated, gullible.

naked ADJECTIVE nude, bare, unclothed.

name NOUN **1** title, label, designation. **2** reputation, character, fame. *He's making a name for himself.*

name VERB call, christen, term, entitle, dub. **2** indicate, specify. *He named the culprit.*

nap VERB sleep, doze, snooze, rest.

narrate VERB tell, describe, recount, relate.

narrow ADJECTIVE fine, thin, slender, limited, tight, cramped. An *opposite word* is wide.

narrow-minded ADJECTIVE biased, bigoted, intolerant. An *opposite word* is broad-minded.

nasty ADJECTIVE **1** bad, dreadful, horrible, offensive, unpleasant, offensive. **2** dirty, filthy, foul. **3** unfriendly, unkind rude, mean, vicious. An *opposite word* is nice.

natter VERB chatter, gossip.

natural ADJECTIVE **1** normal, usual, common. **2** inborn, instinctive, hereditary. **3** frank, open, genuine, unsophisticated, artless. *Opposite words* are **1** unnatural, **2** learned, **3** artificial.

naughty ADJECTIVE bad, unruly, disobedient, mischievous. *Opposite words* are well-behaved, good.

nausea NOUN sickness, queasiness, squeamishness.

nautical ADJECTIVE *See* **naval**.

naval ADJECTIVE maritime, nautical, marine, seafaring.

navigate VERB sail, pilot, steer, guide, direct.

nearly ADVERB almost, not quite, practically, roughly.

neat ADJECTIVE smart, tidy, orderly, spruce. *Opposite words* are untidy, sloppy.

need NOUN necessity, shortage.

need VERB **1** want, require, call for. **2** rely on, depend on, count on.

needy ADJECTIVE poor, needful, penniless, destitute. An *opposite word* is rich.

neglect VERB ignore, overlook, forget. An *opposite word* is look after.

negotiate VERB bargain, haggle, mediate, deal, talk about, discuss.

neighbourhood/neighborhood (US) NOUN district, area, locality, surroundings.

nervous ADJECTIVE anxious, fidgety, edgy. An *opposite word* is calm.

nest NOUN burrow, den, lair.

net NOUN mesh, net, trap, snare.

neutral ADJECTIVE **1** impartial, unbiased, fair, even-minded. **2** dull, mediocre.

never ADVERB not ever, at no time, under no circumstances. An *opposite word* is always.

new ADJECTIVE **1** unused, fresh. **2** novel, original, unfamiliar. **3** modern, recent, just out, up-to-date, latest. *Opposite words* are second-hand, old-fashioned, out of date, stale, old.

news NOUN information, report, bulletin, account.

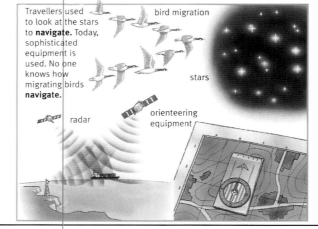

Travellers used to look at the stars to **navigate.** Today, sophisticated equipment is used. No one knows how migrating birds **navigate.**

bird migration

stars

orienteering equipment

radar

Examples

Example sentences are given to show how some words should be used in context.

Opposite words
(antonyms)

appear at the end of an entry, after the synonyms, for example *never/always.*

Numbers
Numbers distinguish different meanings of one word. For example, *note* can mean either *letter, message* or *signal, symbol.*

nibble VERB bite, peck, gnaw. *See also* **eat.**

nice ADJECTIVE **1** beautiful, fine, lovely, attractive, pretty, pleasant, good. **2** delicious, tasty, scrumptious **3** friendly, warm, kind, likeable, considerate, good-natured. **4** comfortable, cosy. *A nice, warm bed.* **5** smart (UK), stylish. *A nice new dress.*

nimble ADJECTIVE spry, agile, nippy, lively, swift. *Opposite words are slow, clumsy.*

nip VERB cut, bite, pinch.

nobility NOUN **1** aristocracy, gentry, nobles. **2** dignity, majesty, eminence, worthiness. *Opposite words are* **1** *hoi polloi, common people.* **2** *meanness.*

nod VERB **1** beckon, signal, indicate, gesture, agree. **2** doze, sleep.

noisy ADJECTIVE loud, rowdy, deafening, boisterous. *Opposite words are quiet, silent.*

nomadic ADJECTIVE wandering, roving, migratory, itinerant. *The travellers led a nomadic lifestyle.*

none PRONOUN not one, not any, nobody. A word that sounds similar is nun.

nonsense NOUN rubbish, drivel, rot, trash, gobbledegook.

nook NOUN corner, alcove, niche, recess.

normal ADJECTIVE common, ordinary, usual, natural, average. *An opposite word is abnormal.*

nostalgic ADJECTIVE longing, yearning, homesick, wistful, sentimental.

notable ADJECTIVE remarkable, outstanding, famous, notable, momentous. *An opposite word is commonplace.*

note NOUN **1** letter, message. **2** signal, symbol. *A musical note.*

note VERB **1** remark, notice, observe. **2** record, write down.

notice VERB see, note, perceive, detect, observe. *An opposite word is overlook.*

notify VERB inform, tell, announce, declare, advise.

notion NOUN idea, thought, whim. *I had a notion you might think that.*

nought NOUN zero, nil, nothing, naught.

nourish VERB feed, support, sustain. *An opposite word is starve.*

novel ADJECTIVE new, fresh, original, innovative, uncommon, unusual. *Opposite words are trite, familiar, hackneyed.*

novice NOUN beginner, learner, pupil, tyro, apprentice.

now ADVERB **1** instantly, at this moment, immediately. **2** at this time, at present.

nude ADJECTIVE naked, bare, undressed, unclothed, stripped.

nudge VERB elbow, prod, poke, push.

nuisance NOUN bother, pest, trouble, worry, plague.

numb ADJECTIVE insensible, dead, frozen, unfeeling.

number NOUN figure, amount, quantity, total.

numerous ADJECTIVE many, several, abundant. *Opposite words are few, scant.*

nurse VERB care for, mind, tend, look after, nourish.

nut NOUN Some different kinds of nut: almond, brazil, cashew, chestnut, cobnut, coconut, hazelnut, peanut, pecan, pistachio, walnut.

nutty ADJECTIVE foolish. *See also* **mad.**

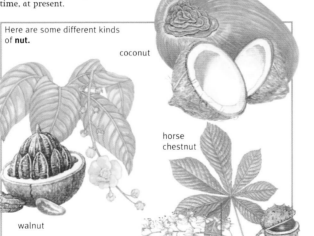

Here are some different kinds of **nut.**

coconut

horse chestnut

walnut

Associated words
These appear either in an illustrated panel or are listed after a headword. For example, under accommodation are listed all the different kinds of dwelling people live in, from bedsits to mansions.

Words that sound the same (homonyms)
also appear at the end of entries, where appropriate.

Illustrations
On every page, one of the headwords is illustrated, to demonstrate its different meanings.

abandon VERB **1** leave, forsake, desert, quit. *They abandoned the sinking boat.* **2** give up, cancel, forgo.

abbreviate VERB shorten, reduce, condense, contract, abridge. *Opposite words are extend, lengthen.*

ability NOUN **1** skill, knack, gift, flair, know-how. **2** capability, facility.

able ADJECTIVE skilful/skillfull(US), clever, talented, capable, gifted.

abolish VERB do away with, cancel, destroy, get rid of, erase. *Opposite words are keep, retain.*

about ADVERB around, close to, nearly, almost. *It's about one o'clock.*

about PREPOSITION **1** relating to, concerning, regarding. **2** nearby, surrounding.

absent ADJECTIVE not present, missing, gone away. *An opposite word is present.*

absolute ADJECTIVE complete, total, perfect, certain.

abundant ADJECTIVE plentiful, full, ample, overflowing. *An opposite word is scarce.*

accelerate VERB speed up, quicken, go quicker, hurry, hasten.

accent NOUN **1** stress, emphasis. **2** pronunciation, tone of voice, brogue. *A Welsh accent.*

accept VERB **1** receive, take. *Accept a present.* **2** admit, acknowledge, tolerate, believe. *I accept that you are right. Opposite words are refuse and reject.*

accident NOUN **1** mishap, disaster. **2** crash, collision.

accommodation NOUN *See below and also* **house.**

accompany VERB go with, escort, follow.

account NOUN **1** report, description, story, tale, record. *An account of the accident.* **2** invoice, bill.

accurate ADJECTIVE precise, correct, right, true.

ache NOUN pain, suffering. VERB hurt, throb.

achievement NOUN accomplishment, attainment, success, exploit, feat. *An opposite word is failure.*

acquaintance NOUN **1** associate, colleague, friend. *An opposite word is stranger.* **2** knowledge, understanding. *A slight acquaintance with Russian.*

act NOUN **1** deed, action, achievement, feat. **2** a decree, statute. *An Act of Parliament.* VERB **1** work, behave, carry out. *He's acting very strangely today.* **2** perform, imitate, mimic, pretent.

action NOUN **1** deed, act, feat. **2** mechanism, motion, functioning. **3** battle, conflict. *He was killed in action. An opposite word is rest.*

active ADJECTIVE busy, alert, agile, on the go, brisk. *Opposite words are idle, lazy.*

activity NOUN **1** work, job, occupation, hobby, pastime. **2** liveliness, movement, bustle, business.

actual ADJECTIVE real, genuine, correct, certain.

adapt VERB **1** alter, modify, fit, suit. **2** get used to, adjust, acclimatize.

add VERB **1** attach, join, affix, connect. **2** combine, mix. *Add the ingredients together.* **3** (add up) total, come to.

Here are some different kinds of **accommodation.**

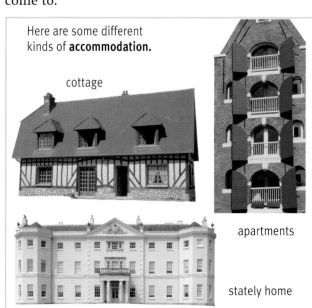

cottage

apartments

stately home

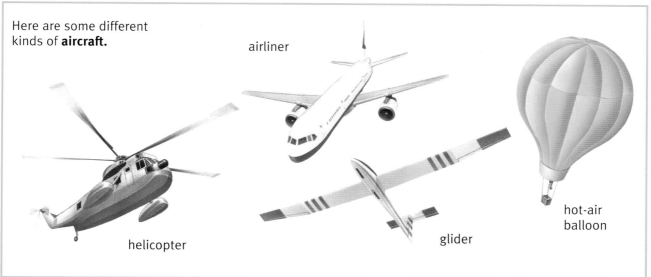

Here are some different kinds of **aircraft.**

airliner

helicopter

glider

hot-air balloon

additional ADJECTIVE extra, more. *Additional help.*

adequate ADJECTIVE enough, sufficient, ample. An *opposite word* is inadequate.

adjacent ADJECTIVE near, next to.

admire VERB respect, esteem, approve, like, prize, appreciate, value, look at with pleasure. *Opposite words* are despise, dislike.

adopt VERB take care of, choose, follow, select.

adore VERB worship, love, idolize, honour/honor (US), revere. *Opposite words* are hate, loathe.

adult NOUN and ADJECTIVE grown-up, mature. An *opposite word* is immature.

advance VERB **1** progress, move forward, further, go on, proceed. An *opposite word* is retreat. **2** lend, give. *Advance some money.*

advantage NOUN help, benefit, asset, gain. *Opposite words* are drawback, handicap.

adventure NOUN exploit, undertaking, venture. *The camping trip was an adventure.*

advertise VERB publicize, promote, plug, make known, hype.

affect VERB **1** influence, change, alter, involve, disturb, upset. *The whole village was affected by the floods.* **2** pretend, assume, put on, feign.

affection NOUN liking, fondness, warmth, love. *Opposite words* are coldness, indifference. *A great show of affection.*

afraid ADJECTIVE frightened, alarmed, scared, timid, nervous.

after PREPOSITION following, behind, later. An *opposite word* is before.

again ADVERB once more, another time, often.

age NOUN **1** period of time, date, span, epoch, years. **2** elderliness, senility, maturity.

aggressive ADJECTIVE hostile, violent, forceful. *An aggressive sales promotion.*

agile ADJECTIVE nimble, active, lively, sprightly.

agree VERB **1** see eye to eye, accept, harmonize, match. **2** consent, be willing, decide. *They agreed to meet the next day.*

aid VERB help, assist, back, support. *Opposite words* are hinder, obstruct.

aim NOUN purpose, ambition, hope, intention, goal. VERB point, direct at, target.

aircraft NOUN Different kinds of aircraft: airliner, airship, balloon, biplane, bomber, fighter, glider, helicopter, jet, microlight, seaplane, Zeppelin.

aisle NOUN corridor, gangway, passageway, path.

alarm NOUN warning signal, siren. VERB scare, frighten, startle, terrify, distress.

alert ADJECTIVE **1** ready, awake, attentive, on the look out, watchful. **2** active, bright, nimble. *An alert mind. Opposite words* are unprepared, stupid. VERB warn, tell.

alike ADJECTIVE similar, same, resembling, identical. *Opposite words* are unlike and different.

alive ADJECTIVE living, active, in existence, lively, alert. *Opposite words* are dead, lifeless, dull.

all ADJECTIVE every, whole, entire, complete, total. *Opposite words* are nothing, none, some.

allow VERB permit, let, tolerate, authorize. *Dogs are not allowed in the store.* An *opposite word* is forbid.

ally NOUN see **friend**.

alone ADJECTIVE and ADVERB solitary, lonesome, friendless, on one's own, single-handed. An *opposite word* is together.

aloud ADVERB loudly, clearly, audibly, noisily. An *opposite word* is silently.

alphabet NOUN Different kinds of alphabet: Braille, Cyrillic, Devanagari (Hindi), Greek, hieroglyphs.

alter VERB **1** change, vary, revise, amend, adjust, modify, adapt. **2** switch, transfer, exchange, swap, replace. *Opposite words* are keep, retain, conserve.

amaze VERB surprise, astound, astonish.

amazing ADJECTIVE surprising, astounding, extraordinary, incredible, strange, unusual, odd.

ambition NOUN aim, goal, target, aspiration, objective, wish, eagerness, drive, enthusiasm. *Opposite words* are indifference, diffidence.

ammunition NOUN Some different kinds of ammunition: arrow, bomb, bullet, cannonball, hand grenade, mine, rocket, shell, torpedo.

amount NOUN quantity, sum, total, whole, measure, volume.

amphibian NOUN Different kinds of amphibian: caecilians, frogs, newts, salamanders, toads.

amuse VERB cheer up, entertain, make laugh, divert, interest, please. An *opposite word* is bore.

amusing ADJECTIVE funny, humorous, comical, witty, enjoyable. *Opposite words* are dull, boring.

ancestor NOUN forebears, predecessors, forefathers. An *opposite word* is descendant.

ancient ADJECTIVE old, aged, antique, prehistoric, primeval. *Opposite words* are modern, recent.

anger NOUN fury, indignation, annoyance, ire, rage.

angry ADJECTIVE cross, furious, mad, annoyed, irate, upset, indignant. An *opposite word* is pleased.

A frog is an **amphibian.**
Here is its lifecycle.

eggs

tadpoles

frog

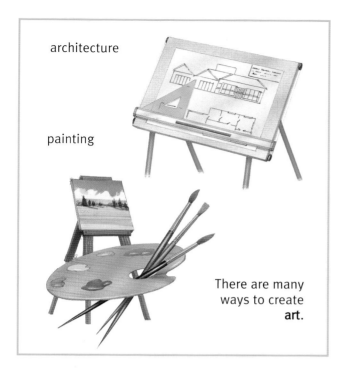

architecture

painting

There are many ways to create **art.**

announce VERB declare, reveal, proclaim, state, make known, report, publish, reveal.

announcement NOUN statement, notification, proclamation, publication, advertisement.

annoy VERB irritate, bother, upset, make angry, trouble, harass.

answer NOUN **1** reply, response. **2** solution, explanation. *What is the answer to the problem?*

anxious ADJECTIVE nervous, worried, afraid, uneasy, concerned, jittery.

apart ADVERB separately, away from, singly, independently, cut off from. An *opposite word* is together

apologize VERB say sorry, express regret.

appeal NOUN attraction, allure, fascination, charm. VERB ask, beg, urge, implore, request, entreat.

appear VERB **1** become visible, come into sight, arrive, turn up. **2** seem, look. *You appear to be sad.*

appetite NOUN hunger, taste, craving, desire.

applaud VERB clap, praise, congratulate, acclaim. An *opposite word* is criticize.

appoint VERB name, nominate, select, choose, designate.

appointment NOUN meeting, engagement, date, rendezvous.

appreciate VERB **1** enjoy, value, relish, like, respect. **2** grow in value, increase, rise.

approach VERB get near, advance, move towards.

appropriate ADJECTIVE suitable, proper, relevant, right. *Opposite words* are inappropriate, unsuitable.

approximately ADVERB nearly, roughly, almost, about, loosely.

apt ADJECTIVE **1** relevant, suitable, fitting. **2** clever, skilful/skillful (US), intelligent. **3** liable, prone, likely to. *She's apt to be a bit aloof.*

arduous ADJECTIVE difficult, hard, strenuous, tough, laborious, harsh. An *opposite word* is easy.

argue VERB discuss, debate, row, bicker, quarrel, quibble, disagree. An *opposite word* is agree.

argument NOUN dispute, debate, row, disagreement, quarrel.

army NOUN troops, soldiers, force, legions, multitude, host.

around PREPOSITION **1** encircling, surrounding, on all sides. **2** about, approximately.

arrange VERB **1** plan, organize, fix, settle. **2** order, group, classify, sort, tidy, position.

arrest VERB seize, capture, catch, take prisoner, hold, detain, stop, block, hinder.

arrive VERB reach, get to, attain, enter, come, appear, happen.

arrogant ADJECTIVE superior, patronizing, insolent, condescending, disdainful, supercilious. An *opposite word* is modest.

art NOUN Different kinds of art: painting, drawing, sketching, sculpture, pottery, woodcarving, metalwork, engraving, printing, photography.

artificial ADJECTIVE synthetic, fake, false, bogus, unnatural, fictitious. Some *opposite words* are genuine, real.

artist NOUN Some different types of artist: painter, photographer, potter, printer, sculptor.

ashamed ADJECTIVE sorry, embarrassed, guilty, sheepish, mortified, shame-faced, humbled.

ask VERB **1** enquire, find out, beg, demand, query, request. **2** invite. An *opposite word* is answer.

asleep ADJECTIVE sleeping, napping, snoozing, resting, dozing.

assassinate VERB murder, kill, slaughter, slay.

assault VERB attack, strike, hit, set upon, beat up, invade, charge. An *opposite word* is defend.

assistant NOUN helper, partner, colleague, aide.

associate VERB **1** mix, mingle, join in. *Associate with thieves.* **2** connect, link, relate, combine, couple.

association NOUN group, club, organization, society, company, partnership, confederation.

astonish VERB amaze, astound, surprise, alarm, stun, shock.

athletic ADJECTIVE fit, strong, muscular, energetic, active, good at sports, sporty.

attach VERB fasten, tie, fix, join, connect, stick, link, unite. An *opposite word* is detach.

attack VERB assault, charge, set on, storm, bomb, raid, invade. *Opposite words* are retreat, withdraw.

attempt VERB try, endeavour/ endeavor (US), struggle, have a go, undertake, tackle.

attend VERB **1** visit, be present, go to. **2** escort, accompany, look after, nurse. **3** listen to, pay attention, heed.

attentive ADJECTIVE **1** careful, mindful, alert, heedful. **2** considerate, kind, polite.

attitude NOUN position, point of view, outlook, disposition, bearing.

attract VERB **1** appeal, fascinate, enchant, interest, lure, tempt. **2** pull, drag, entice.

attractive ADJECTIVE lovely, beautiful, handsome, pretty, good-looking, gorgeous, charming, tempting, nice. *Opposite words* are plain, ugly.

Here are some **athletic** sports.

high jump

running

javelin

audience NOUN listeners, onlookers, spectators, viewers, fans.

available ADJECTIVE obtainable, accessible, on sale, handy. An *opposite word* is unavailable.

average ADJECTIVE normal, usual, ordinary, moderate, mediocre, medium, standard, everyday, fair, not bad. An *opposite word* is exceptional.

awake ADJECTIVE alert, attentive, watchful, aware, conscious. An *opposite word* is asleep.

aware ADJECTIVE conscious, informed, knowing, on the ball. An *opposite word* is unaware, ignorant.

awful ADJECTIVE dreadful, terrible, vile, fearful, horrible, ghastly.

awkward ADJECTIVE **1** clumsy, inept, sloppy, unskilful, gawky. *Awkward with her hands.* **2** fiddly, difficult. *Awkward to clean.* **3** embarrassed, uncomfortable. *An awkward silence.* **4** difficult, unhelpful. *Don't be so awkward.*

baby NOUN infant, child, tot, toddler.

back NOUN rear, end, stern, posterior.

back VERB **1** reverse, go backwards. **2** support, aid, endorse, help, champion. *We backed the project.*

bad ADJECTIVE **1** evil, wicked, wrong, dangerous, vile. *Bad dreams.* **2** harmful, damaging, unhealthy. *Smoking is bad for you.* **3** naughty, disobedient, ill-behaved. **4** rotten, sour. *Bad apples.* **5** unpleasant, nasty, offensive. *A bad smell.* **6** serious, severe, dreadful. *A bad cold. A bad accident.* **7** shoddy, inferior, poor, careless. *A bad drawing.*

badge NOUN crest, symbol, emblem, trademark.

bad-mannered ADJECTIVE impolite, discourteous, rude. *Opposite words* are polite, well-mannered.

bad-tempered ADJECTIVE angry, irritable, grumpy.

Ball can mean both a grand party, or a ball that you can play with.

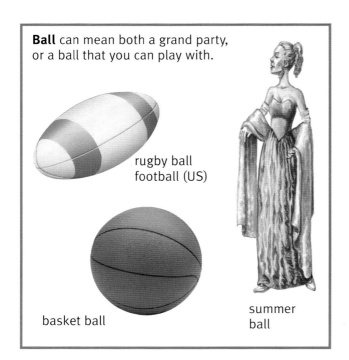

rugby ball
football (US)

basket ball

summer
ball

baggage NOUN luggage, bags, suitcases, gear.

balance VERB weigh, steady, poise, counteract.

bald VERB hairless, bare, uncovered. **2** plain, stark.

ball NOUN **1** sphere, globe. **2** dance, party.

ban VERB forbid, stop, prohibit, bar, banish, outlaw. *Opposite words* are allow, permit.

band NOUN **1** strip, belt, ribbon, zone. *A rubber band.* **2** orchestra, group. *Strike up the band.* **3** gang, group, troop. *A band of robbers.*

bang NOUN **1** blast, explosion, crash, boom. **2** bump, hit, knock. *A bang on the door.*

bang VERB hit, beat, thump, pound, hammer.

banish VERB expel, exclude, exile, deport, cast out, send away, dismiss, outlaw.

bank NOUN **1** shore, edge, embankment, coast, mound, pile. **2** treasury, fund, deposit, savings.

banner NOUN flag, standard, streamer, ensign.

bar NOUN **1** barricade, barrier, obstacle. **2** counter, pub, inn. **3** block, slab. *A bar of soap.* **4** rod, stick, rail. *Bars of a cage.*

bar VERB stop, block, prevent, seal off, bolt, lock, hinder. **2** ban, forbid, exclude.

barbaric ADJECTIVE fierce, savage, cruel, brutal, uncivilized, wild, rude. *Barbaric manner.*

bare ADJECTIVE **1** naked, unclothed, nude. **2** barren, empty.

barely ADVERB hardly, scarcely, only just, almost.

bashful ADJECTIVE shy, modest. An *opposite word* is confident.

basically 1 ADVERB fundamentally, essentially. **2** importantly, principally.

basin NOUN bowl, sink, dish.

bathe VERB swim, wet, immerse, wash, soak, cleanse.

battle NOUN fight, struggle, war, raid, conflict, contest, clash, strife, combat, brawl, scuffle.

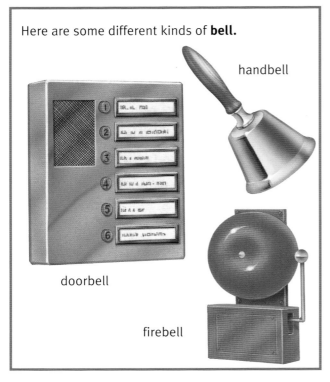

Here are some different kinds of **bell**.

handbell

doorbell

firebell

bay NOUN **1** gulf, inlet, bight. **2** alcove, niche, recess.

beach NOUN coast, shore, seaside, sands, seashore. A similar sounding word is beech.

beam NOUN **1** gleam, ray. **2** plank, girder, joist.

beam VERB **1** gleam, shine, glow, radiate. **2** smile, grin.

bear VERB **1** put up with, tolerate, stand, endure, suffer. **2** carry, lift, support, haul.

beat VERB **1** hit, strike, whip, flog, smack. **2** throb.

beast NOUN animal, brute, creature, monster.

beastly ADJECTIVE brutal, cruel, unpleasant, nasty.

beautiful ADJECTIVE lovely, pretty, handsome, gorgeous, attractive, sweet, cute, elegant.

beauty NOUN loveliness, charm, elegance.

beckon VERB call, summon, signal, wave, gesture.

become VERB change into, turn into, be transformed.

bed NOUN Some kinds of bed: **1** berth, bunk, divan, couch, four-poster. **2** floor, bottom. *The sea-bed.*

beg VERB ask, plead, entreat, request, implore.

belief NOUN **1** trust, faith. **2** creed, principle. **3** conviction, opinion.

believe VERB **1** accept, trust, depend on, count on, maintain. **2** think, feel, reckon.

belittle VERB play down, minimize, scorn, laugh at, underestimate.

bell NOUN Some different kinds of bell: bicycle bell, church bell, doorbell. How bells sound: chime, clang, peal, ring, tinkle and toll.

belongings NOUN possessions, property.

belt NOUN band, strap, sash, strip, zone.

bend VERB curve, turn, incline, bow, twist, buckle. An *opposite word* is straighten.

beneath PREPOSITION under, underneath, below, lower than.

bet VERB stake, wager, gamble.

betray VERB mislead, double-cross, deceive, delude, play false.

beware VERB take care, be careful, look out.

bewilder VERB confuse, muddle, baffle, puzzle, perplex. An *opposite word* is clarify.

bewitched VERB charmed, enchanted, spellbound, captivated.

biased VERB prejudiced, one-sided, bigoted, unfair, angled. *Opposite words* are impartial, fair.

bicker VERB quarrel, argue, disagree, wrangle.

big ADJECTIVE **1** enormous, great, heavy, huge, vast, immense, massive. **2** important, serious.

bigoted NOUN prejudiced, narrow-minded, intolerant. *See also* **biased.**

bill NOUN **1** account, receipt, charges, invoice. **2** law, legislation, proposal. **3** beak.

bind VERB fasten, attach, tie up, secure.

bird NOUN Some different kinds of bird: **birds of prey**: eagle, falcon, hawk, kestrel, kite, owl. **songbirds**: robin, thrush, lark. **flightless birds**: emu, kiwi, ostrich, penguin.

birth NOUN creation, start, origin, beginning, delivery, nativity. An *opposite word* is death.

bit NOUN piece, scrap, shred, crumb, morsel, fragment, chip, portion.

bitter VERB **1** acid, sour, sharp, harsh. *Bitter medicine.* **2** fierce, angry, savage. *Bitter enemies.* **3** sarcastic. *Bitter remarks.* An *opposite word* is sweet.

blade NOUN Some things that have blades: axe, dagger, knife, razor, scalpel, scissors, scythe, sword.

blame VERB accuse, condemn, find fault with, scold, reproach, rebuke, chide, criticize.

blameless ADJECTIVE innocent, faultless, guiltless, sinless. An *opposite word* is guilty.

blank ADJECTIVE empty, vacant, void, bare, unmarked, unused. An *opposite word* is full.

blare VERB blast, boom, clang, roar, crash, shriek, thunder, hoot.

blast VERB explode, burst, erupt, bang, boom, split.

blaze VERB burn, flare, flash.

bleak VERB **1** gloomy, dismal, cheerless, desolate, dreary. *A bleak future.* **2** bare, desolate, windswept, barren.

blend VERB mix, combine, whisk, stir together. An *opposite word* is separate.

blessed ADJECTIVE holy, sacred, revered, lucky, favoured/favored (US).

blessing NOUN advantage, godsend, boon, gain, benefit.

blind ADJECTIVE **1** unseeing, sightless, eyeless. **2** ignorant, oblivious, unaware. *Blind to her unhappiness. Opposite words* are sighted, aware.

block NOUN lump, chunk, mass. *A block of ice.*

eagle

There are many species of **bird.**

penguin

cockatoo

peacock

block VERB obstruct, bar, stop, hinder, impede, clog, seal off.

bloom NOUN flower, blossom, bud. VERB grow, develop, thrive, flourish.

blow NOUN hit, smack, clout, bang, bash. *A blow to the head.* VERB **1** puff, pant, breathe, gust, blast. **2** sound, play.

blow up VERB **1** explode, go off, burst. **2** inflate, pump up. *Blow up the balloon.*

blue VERB **1** azure, sapphire, indigo, cyan. **2** sad, glum, unhappy, depressed, miserable.

blunder NOUN mistake, error, howler, stupidity, gaffe.

blunt ADJECTIVE **1** dull, unsharpened. **2** direct, plain, abrupt, forthright, frank.

blurred ADJECTIVE dimmed, smeared, fuzzy, hazy, obscure, indistinct, foggy, out of focus.

blurt-out VERB say, let slip, reveal, blab.

board NOUN **1** plank, strip, beam, table. **2** panel, committee. *A board of directors.*

boast VERB brag, show off, swank, swagger.

boat NOUN vessel, bark, ship. Some different types of boat or ship: **rowing boats:** dinghy, kayak, gondola, raft. **sailing boats:** dhow, catamaran, clipper, galleon, junk, sampan, yacht. **steam ships:** ferry, liner, submarine, trawler, tanker. **motorboats:** cabin cruiser, lifeboat, speedboat. **warships:** aircraft carrier, battleship, cruiser, destroyer, frigate, minesweeper.

body NOUN **1** (dead) corpse, cadaver, carcass, trunk. **2** group, collection, corporation, party, band, council, committee.

bog NOUN marsh, swamp, quagmire, morass.

bogus ADJECTIVE fake, spurious, false, sham, phoney, artificial.

boisterous ADJECTIVE noisy, loud, stormy, lively, rowdy, wild.

bold ADJECTIVE **1** brave, daring, valiant, fearless, courageous, adventurous, confident. **2** strong, striking, eye-catching.

book NOUN Some different kinds of book: album, annual, atlas, autobiography, diary, dictionary, directory, encyclopedia, exercise book, guidebook.

boom NOUN **1** blast, explosion, thunder, roar, rumble. **2** growth, expansion, boost, improvement, upturn. *A boom in exports.*

boring ADJECTIVE dull, dreary, tedious, tiresome, monotonous, uneventful, uninteresting.

boss NOUN chief, employer, leader, governor, manager, supervisor.

bossy ADJECTIVE demanding, high-handed, autocratic, dictatorial, domineering, arrogant.

bother VERB annoy, distress, pester, irritate, trouble, harass, disturb, hassle, upset.

bottom NOUN **1** base, foot, foundation. **2** seabed. **3** backside, rear, behind, buttocks.

boulder NOUN stone, slab, rock.

bounce VERB rebound, spring, leap, bound.

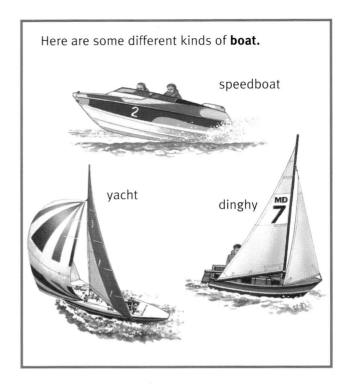

Here are some different kinds of **boat.**

speedboat

yacht

dinghy

bound VERB leap, jump, spring, vault. *The rabbits bounded away.*

boundary NOUN border, verge, edge, frontier.

bow VERB **1** bend, nod, buckle, incline. *He bowed his head.* **2** give in, surrender, submit.

bowl NOUN basin, sink, dish, vessel.

box NOUN **1** crate, carton, case, chest, trunk. **2** (slang) television.

box VERB **1** enclose, pack. *She boxed the apples in a wooden crate.* **2** fight, punch, hit, clout, spar.

brainy ADJECTIVE clever, smart (US), intelligent, intellectual, talented. An *opposite word* is stupid.

brake VERB slow down, check, curb, halt.

branch NOUN **1** bough, shoot, sprig, twig, arm. **2** department, division, section.

branch out VERB expand, develop, enlarge, extend, diversify.

brand NOUN stamp, trademark, make, mark, logo, label, tag, class, kind.

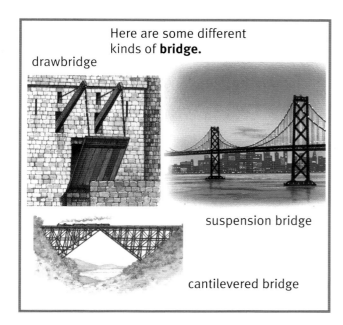

Here are some different kinds of **bridge.**

drawbridge

suspension bridge

cantilevered bridge

brash ADJECTIVE overconfident, hasty, reckless, cocky, bold, rude.

brave ADJECTIVE daring, bold, fearless, audacious, valiant. An *opposite word* is cowardly.

bread NOUN Some different kinds of bread: loaf, roll, bagel, chapati, ciabatta, crispbread, croissant, focaccia, matzo, rye, soda, wholemeal.

break NOUN rest, interval, half-time, gap, opening. VERB **1** smash, crack, fracture, snap, split, shatter, splinter, destroy, demolish, wreck, ruin.

break in VERB **1** interrupt, butt in. **2** invade, burgle.

break loose/out VERB escape, flee.

break up VERB **1** split, divide. **2** end, adjourn, stop.

breathe VERB exhale, inhale, emit, respire. Some ways we can breathe: puff, pant, gasp, wheeze.

breed NOUN kind, type, variety, pedigree, stock.

breed VERB reproduce, bear, hatch, propagate, create, generate, nurture, make.

bribe NOUN incentive, inducement.

bridge NOUN Some different kinds of bridges: arched, beam, drawbridge, footbridge, suspension, cantilever, viaduct.

brief ADJECTIVE short, little, concise, terse, pithy, crisp, curt. An *opposite word* is lengthy.

bright ADJECTIVE **1** sparkling, radiant, shining, luminous, brilliant, gleaming, clear. **2** clever, intelligent, keen, smart, ingenious. An *opposite word* is dull.

brilliant ADJECTIVE shining, radiant, dazzling, glittering, sparkling, bright. **2** gifted, talented, outstanding, witty, clever. *Opposite words* are **1** dull. **2** unimportant.

brim NOUN full to the brim, edge, brink, rim, border.

bring VERB carry, take, convey, bear, fetch, get, lead.

bring about VERB cause, make happen, achieve.

bring up VERB rear, train, educate.

brink NOUN edge, border, boundary, limit.

brisk ADJECTIVE alert, fast, quick, rapid, agile, keen, energetic, nimble, refreshing, invigorating.

brittle ADJECTIVE fragile, frail, delicate, weak.
broad ADJECTIVE wide, large, roomy, extensive.

broken-down ADJECTIVE worn-out, dilapidated, not working.

broken-hearted ADJECTIVE unhappy, grief-stricken, inconsolable, miserable, sad.

brush NOUN broom. Some different types of brush: toothbrush, clothes brush, paintbrush, hairbrush.

brush aside VERB ignore, dismiss, disregard.

brusque ADJECTIVE abrupt, gruff, blunt, rude. An *opposite word* is polite.

brutal VERB cruel, ruthless, merciless, savage, callous, hard, bestial. *Opposite words* are kind, humane.

bubbles NOUN foam, droplets, lather, suds, froth.

bubbly VERB fizzy, sparkling, foaming, lively, effervescent. An *opposite word* is flat.

budge VERB move, shift, push, roll, stir, dislodge.

Buildings are all sorts of sizes and shapes.

a building site

Arabian palace

museum

build VERB construct, erect, assemble, put up, raise, fabricate. An *opposite word* is destroy.

building NOUN construction, erection, structure, edifice. Some different kinds of building:
1 apartment block/apartment building (US), block of flats (UK), bungalow, castle, chalet, chateau, cottage, dwelling, house, mansion, villa.
2 basilica, cathedral, chapel, church, mosque, synagogue, temple. **3** college, hospital, library, museum, police station, prison, school, town hall/city hall. **4** cafe, hotel, inn, pub.

bulge NOUN swelling, bump, projection, lump.

bully VERB torment, threaten, intimidate, browbeat, oppress, frighten, bosss.

bump VERB hit, knock, bang, strike, jolt, collide.

bump into VERB meet, come across.

bunch NOUN bundle, batch, lot, cluster, collection.

bundle NOUN bunch, group, mass, parcel, package, roll. *A bundle of newspapers.*

bungle VERB botch, blunder, fumble, mess up, mismanage.

buoyant ADJECTIVE floating, afloat, light-hearted, carefree.

burden NOUN **1** load, weight, encumbrance. **2** responsibility, trouble, hardship.

burglar NOUN robber, thief, housebreaker.

burn VERB **1** blaze, flare, smoulder. **2** scorch, singe, char, toast. **3** cremate, incinerate, kindle.

bury VERB inter, hide, conceal, immerse. An *opposite word* is unearth.

burst VERB explode, erupt, break open, blow up, crack, spout, gush, pop.

business NOUN **1** trade, job, occupation, work, profession, employment. **2** commerce, trading, industry. **3** firm, company, organization, office.

busy VERB employed, active, occupied, working, tied up, industrious, on the go. *Opposite words* are idle, lazy

buy VERB purchase, procure, obtain, get. An *opposite word* is sell.

cabin NOUN **1** hut, shed, shack, shelter. **2** berth, compartment.

cable NOUN flex, rope, line, wire, lead.

cafe NOUN restaurant.

cake NOUN pastry, gateau, tart.

cake VERB cover, coat, encrust, harden, solidify.

calamity NOUN disaster, tragedy, catastrophe, accident, mishap, misfortune.

calculate VERB count, reckon, compute, work out, estimate.

call VERB **1** name, baptise, christen, term, style, dub. **2** cry, cry out, shout, yell, exclaim. **3** summon, invite, assemble muster. **4** telephone, phone, ring. **5** visit.

call for VERB request, demand, need.

call off VERB cancel, stop.

calling NOUN profession, vocation, job, work, business, trade.

callous ADJECTIVE hard, unfeeling, harsh, hard-bitten, indifferent.

calm ADJECTIVE **1** peaceful, quiet, cool, patient, unruffled, laid back. **2** smooth, peaceful, mild, windless, still, tranquil.

cancel VERB stop, abandon, call off, postpone, give up, drop, quash, repeal.

candid ADJECTIVE open, frank, blunt, truthful, straightforward.

capable ADJECTIVE able, efficient, competent, clever, skilled, gifted, qualified, suited.

capacity NOUN **1** volume, space, size. *A seating capacity of 1000.* **2** ability, capability, aptitude.

captain NOUN leader, commander, boss.

capture VERB seize, take, catch, grab, trap, arrest.

car NOUN automobile, vehicle.

carcass NOUN corpse, body, cadaver, shell, remains.

care NOUN **1** worry, anxiety, trouble. **2** attention, protection.

care VERB **1** mind, be bothered about. **2** mind, watch out, beware, heed. *Take care!* **3** look after, nurse, mind, protect. *Take care of her!*

care for VERB be fond of, like, love.

careful ADJECTIVE **1** cautious, wary, watchful. **2** thorough, precise, thoughtful.

caress VERB hug, cuddle, stroke, embrace, touch, kiss.

carry VERB convey, bring, take, move. **2** lift, support, bear.

carve VERB cut, chisel, sculpt.

castle NOUN fort, fortress, chateau.

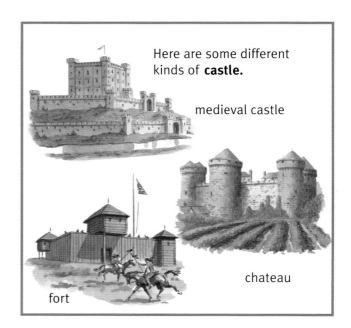

Here are some different kinds of **castle.**

medieval castle

chateau

fort

casual ADJECTIVE **1** informal. *Casual clothes.* **2** uninterested. *Casual manner.* **3** accidental, chance, random. *Casual meeting.*

catastrophe NOUN disaster, calamity, blow.

catch VERB capture, grab, seize, grasp, snatch, take hold of, arrest, stop, trap, get.

cause NOUN **1** reason, motive, source, origin. **2** purpose, object, undertaking. *A good cause.*

cause VERB bring about, produce, create, result in.

cautious ADJECTIVE careful, watchful, prudent, wary. An *opposite word* is careless.

cease VERB stop, end, finish, break off, terminate, conclude. An *opposite word* is begin.

cell NOUN prison, room, den, dungeon.

cellar NOUN vault, basement, crypt, store.

cemetery NOUN graveyard, churchyard, burial-ground, necropolis.

centre/center (US) NOUN middle, heart, nucleus, core.

cereal NOUN grain, corn. Some different kinds of cereal: barley maize, oats, rice, rye, wheat.

certain ADJECTIVE **1** sure, positive, definite, unquestionable, confident. An *opposite word* is doubtful. **2** particular, regular, fixed.

challenge VERB dare, defy, brave, threaten, question.

champion NOUN **1** guardian. An *opposite word* is loser. **2** protector, defender, supporter.

chance NOUN **1** opportunity, occasion, opening. *A chance to get on.* **2** accident, luck, fortune, fluke. *By pure chance.* **3** risk, hazard. *Take a chance.*

change VERB adjust, alter, make different, modify, amend, revise, convert, vary, replace, swap.

chaos NOUN turmoil, disorder, confusion, anarchy, bedlam.

character NOUN **1** letter, sign, symbol, emblem, hieroglyph. **2** nature, personality, quality, feature, reputation. **3** person, individual, part, role.

Here are some different aspects of **character.**

sad

happy

charge NOUN cost, price.

charge VERB attack, assault, storm.

charming ADJECTIVE appealing, attractive, pleasant, delightful, nice.

chase VERB follow, pursue, run after, hunt, tail.

chaste ADJECTIVE modest, pure.

chat VERB talk, gossip.

cheap ADJECTIVE **1** inexpensive, bargain, cut-price, low-cost. **2** paltry, inferior, shoddy, tatty.

cheat VERB swindle, defraud, con, diddle, trick, fool.

check VERB **1** examine, inspect, test, look over. **2** stop, restrain, curb, hinder. *Check your feelings.*

cheeky ADJECTIVE impertinent, saucy, rude, insolent.

cheerful ADJECTIVE happy, glad, contented, bright, merry, jolly. *Opposite words* are sad, gloomy.

cherish VERB treasure, care for, hold close, prize.

chest NOUN **1** case, coffer, trunk, casket. **2** bosom.

chief ADJECTIVE main, principal, prime, key, important. *Opposite words* are unimportant, minor.

chief NOUN boss, leader, governor, commander.

chilly ADJECTIVE **1** cool, cold, crisp, fresh. **2** unfriendly, unwelcoming.

chip NOUN piece, fragment, sliver.

choke VERB **1** strangle, throttle, suffocate,

choose VERB pick, select, vote for, prefer, settle on.

A **church** is a place of worship.

cathedral

altar

chop VERB hack, hew, fell. *See also* **cut.**

chuckle VERB laugh, titter, giggle.

chunk NOUN lump, piece, block.

church NOUN cathedral, chapel, temple.

churlish ADJECTIVE rude, uncivil, brusque, sullen.

circle NOUN **1** ring, hoop, disk, band. **2** company, group, set, fellowship. *A circle of friends.*

circulate VERB broadcast, spread, publicize, publish, diffuse.

civil ADJECTIVE **1** polite, courteous, well-mannered. **2** public, state, political. *Civil rights.*

civilize VERB educate, tame, train, cultivate.

claim VERB ask for, call for, demand, require, request.

clap VERB **1** applaud, cheer.

clarify VERB **1** make clear, explain, define, elucidate. **2** purify, refine.

clash VERB **1** disagree, conflict, quarrel.

clasp VERB grasp, hold, embrace, clutch.

class NOUN **1** group, set, category, rank. **2** form, grade (US).

classify VERB sort, set in order, group, arrange, categorize, file.

clean ADJECTIVE spotless, sparkling, unsoiled, unstained, immaculate, fresh, unused, blank.

clear ADJECTIVE **1** fine, sunny, bright, cloudless. *Clear weather.* **2** obvious, plain, evident, simple, straightforward. **3** transparent, clean. **4** empty, bare, unobstructed. **5** audible, distinct.

clever ADJECTIVE bright, intelligent, brainy, brilliant, sharp, skilled, gifted, talented.

climax NOUN peak, apex, high point, culmination.

climb VERB mount, ascent, scale, go up.

cling VERB adhere, stick, attach, embrace, grasp, clasp, hold.

clip VERB trim, prune. *See also* **cut.**

Here are some different types of **clock.**

sundial

longcase clock

sports watch

alarm clock

clock NOUN watch, timepiece, chronometer.

clog VERB block up, choke, obstruct.

close ADJECTIVE **1** nearby, adjacent, neighbouring/neighboring (US), imminent. **2** intimate, friendly. *Close friends.* **4** stuffy, muggy, heavy. *The weather is close.* **5** careful, thorough.

close VERB shut, end, cease, finish, lock, fasten.

cloth NOUN material, fabric, stuff.

clothes NOUN clothing, gear, outfit, garments, attire.

cloud NOUN haze, mist, fog, nebula. cumulonimbus, nimbostratus, stratocumulus, stratus.

cloudy ADJECTIVE hazy, overcast, dim, obscure, dull, murky, blurred. An *opposite word* is clear.

clumsy ADJECTIVE awkward, ungainly, gawky, gauche, blundering, unwieldy, lumbering. An *opposite word* is graceful.

cluster NOUN bunch, clump, group, collection.

clutch VERB *See* **clasp.**

clutter NOUN mess, muddle, jumble, disorder.

coarse ADJECTIVE **1** rough, unrefined, unpolished. **2** rude, uncivil, bawdy, vulgar. An *opposite word* is refined. A word that sounds similar is course.

coast NOUN shore, seaside, beach.

coax VERB persuade, urge, wheedle, entice.

coil VERB curl, twist, loop, wind.

cold ADJECTIVE **1** cool, chilly, unheated, fresh, frosty, nippy, raw, wintry. **2** frigid, unfriendly.

collapse VERB fall down, drop, break down, crumple, fail.

colleague NOUN workmate, partner, companion, associate.

collect VERB gather together, amass, accumulate, save, hoard.

collide VERB bang into, crash into, smash into, hit.

colossal ADJECTIVE gigantic, huge, enormous, massive, immense, vast. An *opposite word* is tiny.

colour/color (US) NOUN tint, shade, hue, tinge, dye, pigment.

colourful/colorful (US) ADJECTIVE **1** bright, rich, vivid, brilliant, flashy. **2** interesting, exciting.

column NOUN post, pillar. Types of column: Corinthian, Doric, Egyptian, Ionic.

combat VERB oppose, resist, contest, battle, fight.

combine VERB unite, join, put together, mix, blend, merge. An *opposite word* is separate.

come VERB arrive, appear, reach, get to, approach, draw near.

come across VERB find by chance, discover, meet.

come by VERB get, obtain.

come down VERB drop, decrease, fall, decline.

come round VERB **1** visit. **2** recover, awake.

comfort NOUN rest, ease, enjoyment, consolation.

comfort VERB soothe, console, calm.

comfortable ADJECTIVE restful, snug, luxurious.

comforting ADJECTIVE cheering, consoling.

comic ADJECTIVE funny.

command VERB **1** order, tell, instruct, direct. **2** to control, be in charge of, manage, rule.

commence VERB begin, start.

comment VERB remark, observe, point out, mention, criticize.

commit VERB carry out, perform, enact, be guilty of.

common ADJECTIVE **1** everyday, regular, usual, ordinary, normal. **2** vulgar, coarse, loutish.

commotion NOUN upset, turmoil, upheaval, disturbance, bustle, bother.

communicate VERB **1** contact, talk, write, telephone. **2** tell, reveal, declare, proclaim, announce.

communications NOUN Some different kinds of communication: advertising, braille, circular, fax, Internet, letter, memo, mobile phone, newspaper, radio, satellite, telephone, television.

community NOUN society, district, hamlet, village.

compact ADJECTIVE small, neat, concise.

mobile phone

radio

newspaper

Here are some different methods of **communication.**

companion NOUN *See* **friend.**

company NOUN **1** firm, business, association, syndicate. **2** society, companionship, party, crowd, group.

comparable ADJECTIVE similar, like, equal, alike. *Opposite words* are incomparable, different.

compare VERB liken, contrast.

compassion NOUN pity, kindness, sympathy. An *opposite word* is indifference.

compel VERB force, order, make, urge, browbeat.

compete VERB contest, rival, strive, emulate.

competent ADJECTIVE capable, clever, able, qualified, skilled, trained.

competition NOUN contest, match, rivalry, tournament.

compile VERB put together, amass, gather, combine, compose, arrange.

complain VERB grumble, protest, object, whine.

complete ADJECTIVE **1** whole, total, entire, full. **2** utter, absolute. *Complete nonsense.*

complete VERB finish, accomplish, achieve, carry out, conclude, end.

complex ADJECTIVE involved, difficult, hard, complicated, confused, intricate.

complex NOUN organization, structure, network.

complicated ADJECTIVE *See* **complex.**

component NOUN part, element, ingredient, piece.

comprehend VERB understand, grasp, fathom, know, appreciate, take in, perceive.

comprehensive ADJECTIVE complete, thorough, extensive, general.

comprise VERB consist of, contain, be made up of, include, form part of. *Great Britain comprises England, Scotland and Wales.*

compulsory ADJECTIVE obligatory, forced, necessary. An *opposite word* is optional.

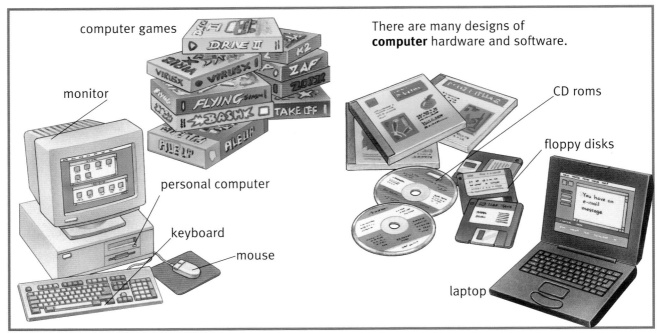

computer games

There are many designs of **computer** hardware and software.

monitor

CD roms

floppy disks

personal computer

keyboard

mouse

laptop

computer NOUN personal computer, PC, word processor, microprocessor, laptop, calculator. Some words connected with computers: bit, bug, byte, cursor, CD, data, file, floppy disk, hacker, hard disk, hardware, keyboard, memory, microchip, modem, monitor, mouse, peripheral, printer, printout, program, RAM, ROM, software, virus.

conceal VERB hide, mask, camouflage, cover. *Opposite words* are reveal, show, display.

conceited ADJECTIVE arrogant, bigheaded, smug, self-important, boastful, vain.

concentrate VERB **1** think about, pay attention to, heed, focus on. **2** condense, reduce.

concept NOUN idea, notion, theory, thought, plan.

concern NOUN **1** matter, affair, consequence. *No concern of yours.* **2** company, business, organization, firm.

concern VERB **1** trouble, disturb, upset, worry. **2** interest, affect, involve, be of importance.

concerned ADJECTIVE worried, anxious, upset.

concerning PREPOSITION regarding, about, respecting.

concise ADJECTIVE brief, condensed, short, pithy, compact. *Opposite words* are rambling, diffuse, wordy.

conclude VERB *See* **end**.

condemn VERB blame, judge, convict, punish. *Condemn to death.* **2** disapprove, criticize.

condense VERB reduce, compress, concentrate, shorten, abridge, abbreviate.

condition NOUN **1** state, plight, situation, case. **2** terms, requirement. *Conditions of the treaty.* **3** health, fitness, shape.

conduct NOUN behaviour/behavior (US), attitude, manner, bearing. *Bad conduct.* **2** management, guidance, control, leadership. *Conduct of affairs.*

conduct VERB lead, guide, direct, command, control.

conference NOUN meeting, convention, forum, get-together.

confess VERB admit, own up, acknowledge, tell, declare, admit, concede. An *opposite word* is deny.

confident ADJECTIVE sure, certain, positive, assured, fearless, bold, composed.

confiscate VERB seize, take away, commandeer, appropriate. An *opposite word* is restore.

conflict NOUN **1** struggle, fight, battle. **2** difference, disagreement. *A conflict of interests.*

confront VERB meet, face, encounter, challenge.

confuse VERB **1** puzzle, bewilder, perplex, baffle, mislead. **2** mix up, muddle, jumble.

confusing ADJECTIVE muddling, puzzling, perplexing.

confusion NOUN **1** disorder, mess, upheaval, disarray. 2 misunderstanding.

congested ADJECTIVE crowded, jammed, blocked, packed.

congregate VERB meet, assemble, come together, gather, converge.

connect VERB join, unite, link, combine. *Opposite words* are disconnect, separate.

conquer VERB overcome, beat, defeat, vanquish, overrun, crush, trounce, thrash.

conqueror NOUN winner, victor, champion.

consent NOUN permission, agreement, approval. VERB allow, permit, agree, approve.

consequence NOUN **1** outcome, result, effect, upshot. **2** importance, influence.

conserve VERB keep, safeguard, protect, save.

consider VERB think about, ponder, reflect, contemplate, examine, muse.

considerate ADJECTIVE thoughtful, kind, helpful.

consist of VERB comprise, be made up of, contain.

console VERB comfort, sympathize with, soothe.

conspire VERB plot, intrigue, scheme.

constant ADJECTIVE **1** endless, never-ending, continuous, ceaseless, incessant, unchanging. **2** stable, loyal, true, trustworthy.

construction NOUN building, structure, erection.

constructive ADJECTIVE helpful, useful, productive.

consult VERB discuss, confer, question.

consume VERB **1** use, eat, devour, waste, squander. **2** destroy, ravage. *Consumed by fire.*

contain VERB include, comprise, hold, enclose.

container NOUN Some different kinds of container: basin, bucket, cup, glass, jug, pail, vase.

contempt NOUN scorn, disdain, derision. An *opposite word* is respect.

contented ADJECTIVE happy, satisfied, pleased, cheerful. An *opposite word* is unhappy.

contest NOUN competition, match, fight.

continent NOUN Africa, Asia, Australasia, Europe, North America, South America.

continual ADJECTIVE endless, ceaseless, non-stop, constant, incessant. An *opposite word* is occasional.

continue VERB carry on, last, endure, persist, go on, remain. *Opposite words* are stop, discontinue.

continuous ADJECTIVE uninterrupted, unbroken, non-stop, constant.

This diagram shows how the position of the world's **continents** has changed over millions of years.

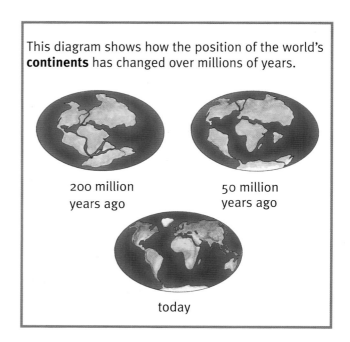

200 million years ago

50 million years ago

today

Here are some different types of **costume.**

duck costume

Santa Claus outfit

matador

angel costume

contract NOUN agreement, treaty, pact, deal, understanding.

contract VERB reduce, condense, shrink, lessen, abbreviate. An *opposite word* is expand.

control VERB manage, command, restrain, direct, guide, supervise.

convenient ADJECTIVE **1** appropriate, suitable. *A convenient time to visit.* **2** handy, helpful, useful.

conversation NOUN talk, chat, discussion.

convert VERB change, alter, adapt, modify.

convey VERB carry, take, transport, bear, escort.

convict NOUN prisoner, criminal, felon, captive.

convict VERB condemn, pass judgement, sentence, find guilty.

convince VERB persuade, satisfy, prove, win over, demonstrate.

cook VERB Some different ways of cooking: bake, barbecue, boil, broil, fry, grill, poach, roast, stir-fry, stew, toast. Some things we use for cooking: bowl, casserole, colander, food processor, frying-pan, grater, kettle, ladle, pan, peeler, ramekin.

cool ADJECTIVE *See* **cold.**

cooperate VERB collaborate, help, assist, join forces, participate, work together, combine. An *opposite word* is oppose.

cope VERB manage, deal with, grapple, handle, make do.

copy VERB **1** imitate, mimic, ape. **2** duplicate, reproduce, photocopy, trace, Xerox. **3** fake, forge.

cord NOUN rope, string, line, twine, flex. A word with a similar sound is chord.

corn NOUN maize, sweet corn. *See also* **cereal.**

corpse NOUN carcass, dead body, cadaver.

correct ADJECTIVE true, right, actual, accurate, faultless. *Opposite words* are wrong, incorrect.

corridor NOUN passageway, aisle, gallery.

corrode VERB rust, decay, erode, waste away, crumble, waste.

corrupt ADJECTIVE crooked, dishonest, fraudulent, depraved, immoral, bad, wicked.

cost NOUN **1** expense, amount, charge, price. **2** loss, damage, penalty, sacrifice. *At the cost of his good reputation.*

costly ADJECTIVE expensive, dear, precious, valuable, rich. An *opposite word* is cheap.

costumes NOUN outfit, dress, fancy dress, attire, uniform, robes.

count VERB add up, total, reckon, number, list, estimate.

counterfeit ADJECTIVE forged, sham, mock, fake, bogus, feigned, spurious.

couple NOUN pair, two, brace, duo.

courage NOUN bravery, valour/valor (US), daring.

course NOUN **1** way, road, track, trail. **2** syllabus, studies. A word with a similar sound is coarse.

courteous ADJECTIVE polite, civil, well-mannered, considerate.

cover VERB **1** hide, camouflage, secrete, bury, screen, cloak, veil. **2** include, incorporate, embrace. *Covers the cost of insurance.*

coward NOUN funk, weakling, wimp, chicken.

coy ADJECTIVE shy, bashful, timid, demure.

crack NOUN gap, split, crevice, break, flaw, fissure.

crack VERB break, burst, snap, split, splinter.

crack up VERB collapse, go to pieces.

craft NOUN **1** skill, talent, ability, expertise, handicraft. **2** boat, vessel, aircraft, spacecraft.

crafty ADJECTIVE clever, cunning, deceitful, sly.

cram VERB fill, stuff, ram, squeeze.

crash VERB **1** shatter, break, splinter, dash. **2** collide, bump into. 3 fall down, topple.

crawl VERB **1** creep, glide, slither. **2** grovel.

crazy ADJECTIVE **1** mad, insane, lunatic, idiotic, demented, deranged, foolish. **2** ridiculous, absurd, weird, impractical. *A crazy idea.* **3** keen, fanatical, enthusiastic. *Crazy about football.*

creak VERB grate, grind, scrape, squeak.

crease VERB or NOUN pleat, fold, wrinkle, groove, crumple.

create VERB make, form, originate, devise, think up, invent, bring into being, compose, concoct.

creative ADJECTIVE inventive, artistic, imaginative, original.

credible ADJECTIVE believable, reliable.

creep VERB **1** crawl, slither. **2** grovel, cringe.

crew NOUN team, gang, party, company, band.

crime NOUN felony, offence, wrong, misdemeanour/misdemeanor (US), law-breaking.

Here are some jobs which are **creative** in different ways.
painter
sculptor
actor
writer

criminal NOUN offender, felon, law-breaker, wrongdoer, convict, culprit, crook.

crisis NOUN emergency, danger, problem, calamity.

crisp ADJECTIVE **1** brittle, crunchy, firm.

criticize VERB **1** judge, examine, review, estimate, assess. **2** knock, condemn, find fault.

crockery NOUN pots, dishes, earthenware.

crooked ADJECTIVE **1** bent, curved, bowed, askew, twisted.

cross ADJECTIVE (old-fashioned, US) grumpy, bad-tempered, snappy, short. *See also* **angry**.

cross VERB go across, traverse, bridge, pass over.

cross out VERB delete, draw a line through.

crowd NOUN mass, group, throng, gang, mob, assembly, company, flock, swarm, herd.

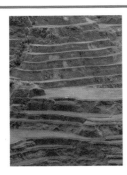

terraces cut into the hillside

hothouse flowers

rows of crops

grassland

Here are some different ways we can **cultivate** the land.

crucial ADJECTIVE critical, urgent, vital, decisive.

crude ADJECTIVE **1** raw, rough, unrefined, unpolished. **2** coarse, rude, vulgar.

cruel ADJECTIVE harsh, fierce, heartless, merciless, vicious, brutal, cold-hearted, barbarous.

crumble VERB decay, disintegrate, break up, powder.

crumple VERB crease, wrinkle, crush.

crush VERB **1** squash, squeeze, compress, mash, grind, crumple. **2** conquer, overcome, overrun, subdue, quash.

cry VERB **1** sob, weep, shed tears. **2** shout, call out, yell, exclaim, scream, shriek.

cuddle VERB hug, embrace, hold, fondle, nestle.

cue NOUN hint, sign, signal, suggestion.

cultivate VERB **1** grow, farm, till. **2** educate, train, encourage, help.

cultivated ADJECTIVE refined, educated, cultured.

cunning ADJECTIVE sly, shrewd, wily, artful, astute, canny, clever.

curb VERB restrain, hold back, control, bridle.

cure NOUN remedy, drug, medicine, antidote, treatment.

cure VERB **1** heal, remedy, restore, relieve, fix.

curious ADJECTIVE **1** inquisitive, interested, nosy, prying. **2** strange, odd, peculiar, queer, funny.

curl VERB twist, coil, wind, bend, curve, loop.

currency NOUN money, coins.

current NOUN **1** stream, water course, flow, drift, trend. **2** present, up to date, modern, common, widespread.

curtail VERB shorten, cut, abridge, clip, trim, lop.

curve VERB bend, twist, coil, wind, arch.

custom NOUN habit, tradition, usage, practice, rite.

cut VERB slice, crop, reduce.

cute ADJECTIVE **1** charming, pretty, attractive. **2** clever, cunning.

cutlery NOUN Some items of cutlery: dessertspoon, fork, knife, soupspoon, spoon, tablespoon, teaspoon.

cutting ADJECTIVE bitter, sharp, sardonic, sarcastic.

cynical ADJECTIVE scornful, sneering, pessimistic, scoffing, sour, morose, contemptuous.

Here are some different types of **dance.**

ballet dance

belly dance

daft ADJECTIVE silly, soppy, stupid, foolish.

dainty ADJECTIVE delicate, neat, small, pretty, fine.

damage VERB harm, hurt, injure, vandalize, deface, wreck, destroy, demolish.

damp ADJECTIVE moist, humid, dank, soggy.

dance NOUN ball, caper, hop. Some different kinds of dance: ballet, ballroom, country, line dancing, jive, morris dancing, tap. Some different dances: bolero, bossa nova, flamenco, limbo, cha cha, foxtrot, rumba, tango, waltz.

danger NOUN risk, threat, peril, hazard.

dangerous ADJECTIVE unsafe, hazardous, perilous, risky, harmful. *Opposite words* are safe, secure.

dare VERB venture, risk, brave, challenge, defy.

daring ADJECTIVE fearless, brave, adventurous.

dark ADJECTIVE **1** murky, dingy, overcast, shadowy, sunless, cloudy. *A dark room.* **2** gloomy, dismal, grim, mournful, sorrowful. *Dark looks.* *Opposite words* are bright, cheerful.

dart VERB dash, hurtle, charge, rush, spring.

dash VERB **1** dart, rush, race. **2** hurl, throw, cast.

date NOUN **1** time, age, epoch, period. **2** appointment, engagement.

dated ADJECTIVE out of date, old-fashioned, obsolete, archaic.

dawdle VERB loiter, linger, lag, hang about/hang around (US), dally. An *opposite word* is hurry.

day NOUN daytime, daylight. The *opposite word* is night. The days of the week are Monday, Tuesday, Wednesday, Thursday, Friday, Saturday, Sunday. *What day is it today?*

dazed ADJECTIVE confused, bewildered, dazzled, stunned. *He was dazed after the crash.*

dazzle VERB **1** amaze, overwhelm, astonish, surprise. *The young actress was dazzled by her success.* **2** blind, confuse, blur. *The rabbit was dazzled by the headlights.*

dazzling ADJECTIVE sparkling, bright.

dead NOUN **1** lifeless, deceased. **2** dull, cold, frigid, cheerless. *Opposite words* are **1** alive. **2** lively.

deal VERB **1** trade, transact, traffic. **2** share out, divide, distribute. *Deal out the cards.* **3** handle, attend to, cope with. *She doesn't like dealing with*

dealer NOUN merchant, trader, retailer, shopkeeper. *A secondhand car dealer.*

dear ADJECTIVE **1** expensive, costly, pricey. An *opposite word* is cheap. **2** darling, beloved, pet, precious. *She's a dear child.*

debate NOUN discussion, dialogue, talk, argument, dispute, controversy.

debris NOUN rubbish, remains, ruins, junk.

decay VERB rot, decompose, go bad, waste away, perish, disintegrate, wither, putrefy.

deceive VERB mislead, cheat, trick, betray, fool, con, swindle.

decent ADJECTIVE proper, respectable, fit, seemly.

deceptive ADJECTIVE misleading, deceiving, false.

decide VERB resolve, determine, elect, choose to.

decipher VERB solve, explain, unravel, figure out.

declare VERB assert, state, announce, maintain, claim.

decorate VERB **1** adorn, embellish, trim, ornament, paint, paper. **2** honour/honor (US), reward. *Decorated with medals.*

decrease VERB diminish, dwindle, decline, go down, lessen, reduce. An *opposite word* is increase.

decree NOUN law, order, edict, act, edict, command.

decrepit ADJECTIVE weak, aged, tottering, worn-out, dilapidated.

deduct VERB take away, subtract, withdraw, remove.

deed NOUN act, achievement, action, feat.

deep ADJECTIVE **1** profound. **2** mysterious, difficult, wise, learned, sagacious. *Deep thoughts.* An *opposite word* is shallow.

A person can be **decorated** with a medal. We can also **decorate** objects, like Christmas trees and brighten up walls.

medal

Christmas tree

deface VERB disfigure, deform, damage, spoil, vandalize.

defeat VERB conquer, overcome, beat, vanquish, get the better of, thwart.

defect NOUN flaw, blemish, imperfection, fault, failing, weakness.

defect VERB desert, abandon, rat on.

defective ADJECTIVE faulty, imperfect, deficient, not working. An *opposite word* is perfect.

defence/defense (US) NOUN **1** guard, protection, fortification, barricade, bulwark. An *opposite word* is attack. **2** justification, explanation.

defend VERB guard, protect, shield, resist, stand up for. An *opposite word* is attack.

defer VERB delay, put off, postpone.

deficient ADJECTIVE lacking, wanting, incomplete, inadequate. An *opposite word* is superfluous.

define VERB explain, describe, clarify, specify.

definite ADJECTIVE **1** certain, positive, decided, fixed. **2** clear, obvious, precise, exact.

definition NOUN **1** explanation description, meaning. **2** clarity, distinctness, sharp focus.

deformed ADJECTIVE misshaped, disfigured, mutilated, distorted, contorted, warped.

defraud VERB swindle, cheat, trick, dupe, cheat, con.

defy VERB disregard, flout, spurn, ignore, scorn, challenge. An *opposite word* is obey.

dejected ADJECTIVE depressed, downcast, despondent, dispirited, gloomy, glum, blue.

delay VERB **1** dawdle, hang about/ hang around (US), linger, loiter. **2** put off, postpone, defer. **3** hinder, obstruct, hold up. *Fog delayed the train.*

delete VERB rub out, erase, cancel.

deliberate ADJECTIVE **1** careful, cautious. **2** planned, intentional.

delicate ADJECTIVE **1** frail, dainty, fragile. An *opposite word* is rough. **2** weak, unhealthy, ailing. *Delicate health.* An *opposite word* is strong.

delicious ADJECTIVE tasty, palatable, scrumptious, appetizing, delightful, enjoyable.

delighted ADJECTIVE pleased, happy, charmed.

delightful ADJECTIVE enjoyable, charming, enchanting, pleasant, agreeable. An *opposite word* is horrid.

deliver VERB **1** convey, carry, hand over, transfer, yield, grant, surrender. **2** free, release.

deluge NOUN flood, inundation, downpour, overflow. An *opposite word* is drought.

demand VERB **1** request, ask, require, beg, want. **2** require, involve. *Demanding a lot of hard work.*

demented ADJECTIVE *See* **crazy**

demolish VERB destroy, raze, wreak, smash, pull down, knock down, dismantle.

demon NOUN devil, fiend, evil-spirit, monster, rogue.

demonstrate VERB **1** show, prove, establish, exhibit. **2** protest, march.

den NOUN Places where wild animals live: a rabbit's burrow, a lion's den, a squirrel's drey, a fox's earth, a hare's form, a wolf's lair, an otter's lodge, a bird's nest, a badger's sett.

denounce VERB condemn, blame, accuse, defame, brand, attack. An *opposite word* is commend.

dense ADJECTIVE **1** thick, compact, compressed. **2** stupid, dull. *He appeared to be very dense.*

deny VERB refute, contradict, reject, not agree, gainsay. *Deny the truth.*

depart VERB leave, go away, set out, quit, vanish. An *opposite word* is arrive.

department NOUN section, part, branch, division.

depend on VERB **1** rely on, count on, trust. **2** revolves round, turns on, hinges on. *It depends on the weather.*

Here are some different methods of **descent**.

abseiler

deep sea diver

depict VERB portray, sketch, paint, draw, outline, describe. *The poem depicts a tree.*

deplorable ADJECTIVE **1** sad, regrettable, distressing. **2** scandalous, disgraceful, shocking.

deplore VERB condemn, denounce, regret.

deposit VERB **1** put, place, lay down. **2** save, bank, entrust.

depressed ADJECTIVE miserable, unhappy, dejected, gloomy, upset. *See also* **sad**.

depression NOUN **1** slump, stagnation, decline. **2** dip, hollow, dent. **3** gloominess, dumps, unhappiness. *Opposite words* are **1** boom. **2** concavity. **3** cheerfulness.

deprive VERB deny, refuse, take away, rob, strip, divest. An *opposite word* is provide.

deride VERB laugh at, jeer, mock, scoff, knock. An *opposite word* is praise.

derive VERB **1** get, obtain, gain. **2** spring from, arise, originate, stem from.

descent NOUN **1** fall, drop, plunge. **2** slope, decline. *Opposite words* are ascent, rise.

descendant NOUN offspring, family, issue, progeny. *Opposite words* are forebears, ancestors.

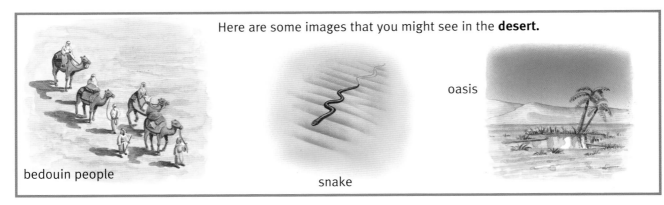

Here are some images that you might see in the **desert.**

bedouin people

snake

oasis

describe VERB define, explain, tell, narrate, relate, portray, characterize, detail, depict, specify.

descriptive ADJECTIVE graphic, colourful/colorful (US), illustrative

desert NOUN wasteland, wilderness, solitude.

desert VERB abandon, leave, quit, forsake, renounce, defect.

deserted ADJECTIVE barren, desolate, wild, forsaken, empty. *A deserted village.*

deserve VERB merit, be worthy of, justify, earn, be entitled to, warrant.

design NOUN **1** plan, drawing, draught, sketch, pattern, outline, scheme. **2** aim, goal, purpose.

desire VERB want, fancy, wish for, long for, crave, yearn after, ask for.

despair NOUN despondency, misery, hopelessness, desperation, distress. An *opposite word* is hope.

desperate ADJECTIVE **1** hopeless, despondent, despairing, serious. *A desperate situation.*
2 reckless, rash, daring, foolhardy.

despise VERB look down on, dislike, disdain, spurn, scorn, detest, abhor.

despite PREPOSITION notwithstanding, in spite of, regardless of.

dessert NOUN sweet, pudding (UK). Some different kinds of dessert and pudding: apple dumpling, cake, cassata, crème brûlée, crepe suzette, gateau.

destitute ADJECTIVE needy, penniless, poverty-stricken, down and out, bankrupt.

destroy VERB **1** demolish, break, knock down, wreck, raze, pull down, smash, ruin, devour.
2 kill off, wipe out, exterminate, eliminate.

detach VERB separate, undo, unfasten, disconnect, divide, remove. An *opposite word* is attach.

detail NOUN component, portion, part, item, feature.

detailed ADJECTIVE thorough, exhaustive, comprehensive, exact.

detain VERB keep, delay, stop, retain, hold back.

detect VERB **1** discover, expose, reveal. **2** notice, observe, spy.

deteriorate VERB decline, worsen, go downhill, weaken, degenerate. An *opposite word* is improve.

devastate VERB wreck, ravage, lay waste, ransack.

develop VERB improve, progress, grow, expand, get better, evolve, flourish.

device NOUN tool, implement, gadget, instrument, apparatus, contrivance, contraption.

devise VERB scheme, contrive, invent, plot.

devoted ADJECTIVE loyal, trusted, loving, dedicated, faithful, true.

devour VERB destroy, ravage. *See also* **eat.**

diagram NOUN plan, drawing, sketch, graph, chart.

dictate VERB speak, utter, say, read out, command, instruct, order, decree.

die VERB expire, pass away, perish, decease.

different ADJECTIVE dissimilar, unlike, opposite, contrasting, clashing. **2** varied, various, mixed, assorted. *Different kinds of nut.* **3** distinct, separate, original, unusual.

difficult ADJECTIVE hard, complex, complicated, intricate, tricky, tough, laborious, demanding.

difficulty NOUN problem, snag, trouble, predicament, plight, dilemma.

dig VERB **1** tunnel, burrow, excavate, delve. **2** investigate.

dilapidated ADJECTIVE broken-down, ruined, ramshackle, battered, crumbling, uncared for.

dilemma NOUN quandary, predicament, problem, plight, difficulty.

dilute VERB water down, make weaker, thin, lessen.

dim VERB dark, shadowy, obscure, blurred, misty, cloudy, murky, unfocused, faint, vague.

diminish VERB reduce, lessen, decrease, become smaller, shrink. An *opposite word* is increase.

din NOUN noise, uproar, racket, clatter.

dingy ADJECTIVE drab, dull, dreary, dirty, grimy, shabby. An *opposite word* is bright.

dinosaur NOUN Some different kinds of dinosaur: Apatsaurus, Ankylosaurus, Brachiosaurus, Camptosaurus, Diplodocus.

direct ADJECTIVE straightforward, frank, candid, outspoken.

direct VERB **1** show, point, guide, conduct. **2** manage, control. **3** tell, command, order.

direction NOUN **1** course, road, way, bearing. **2** control, management, guidance.

directly ADVERB straightaway, immediately, soon, presently.

dirt NOUN filth, muck, grime, mud, mire.

dirty ADJECTIVE filthy, grubby, grimy, mucky, foul.

disabled ADJECTIVE handicapped, incapacitated, disadvantaged, maimed, crippled, lame, impaired, immobilized. The *opposite word* is able-bodied.

disagree VERB quarrel, differ, oppose, argue, dispute, squabble.

disagreeable ADJECTIVE **1** crabby, surly, bad-tempered. *A disagreeable woman.* **2** nasty, offensive, repulsive. *A disagreeable smell.*

disappear VERB vanish, fade away, depart, leave, recede. An *opposite word* is appear.

disappoint VERB let down, displease, fail, frustrate, deceive, betray.

disaster NOUN catastrophe, calamity, misfortune, accident, blow, fiasco.

discard VERB throw away, get rid of, scrap, reject, dump, shed. *Discard the outer wrapping.*

Here are some different kinds of **dinosaur.**

ouranosaurus

yangchuanosaurus

troodon

disclose VERB uncover, reveal, expose, show, divulge, tell, betray.

discontinue VERB stop, cease, interrupt, abandon.

discord NOUN disagreement, strife, wrangling, contention.

discount NOUN reduction, cut, deduction, rebate.

discover VERB **1** find, come across, come upon, uncover. **2** learn, detect, track down.

discrimination NOUN **1** judgement, assessment, discernment, insight, perception. **2** prejudice, bias, bigotry. *Racial discrimination.*

discuss VERB talk about, consider, argue about.

disease NOUN illness, disorder, ailment, infection, malady, sickness, complaint.

disguise VERB camouflage, hide, mask, pretend to be, dress up.

disgusting ADJECTIVE offensive, revolting, repellent, loathsome, distasteful.

dislike VERB loathe, hate, detest, abhor, disapprove of. An *opposite word* is like.

dismal ADJECTIVE gloomy, dreary, drab, depressing, cheerless. An *opposite word* is cheerful.

dismay NOUN fright, fear, alarm, concern, distress.

dismiss VERB sack (UK), fire, send away, discharge, release. An *opposite word* is retain.

disobey VERB rebel, defy, ignore, disregard.

disorder NOUN upheaval, mess, muddle, confusion, untidiness. *See also* **disease**.

dispense VERB distribute, hand out, share out, supply, administer.

display VERB show, exhibit, flaunt, parade.

dispute NOUN disagreement, argument, discussion, debate, quarrel, squabble.

disrupt VERB disturb, upset, put into disorder.

dissolve VERB melt, thaw, evaporate, disintegrate, break up, fade away.

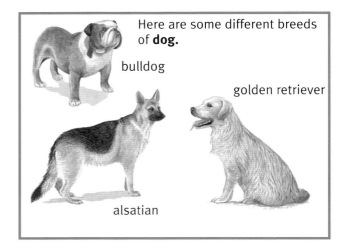

Here are some different breeds of **dog.**

bulldog

golden retriever

alsatian

distant ADJECTIVE far away, remote.

distinct ADJECTIVE **1** clear, lucid, obvious, plain. **2** separate, contrasting, different, detached, independent.

distress VERB upset, trouble, bother, worry, harass, frighten. *The news distressed them.*

distribute VERB allot, share out, hand out, dispense, circulate. An *opposite word* is collect.

disturb VERB upset, worry, trouble, bother, annoy, interrupt, pester, disorder, frighten, move.

dither VERB hesitate, waver, oscillate.

dive VERB plunge, leap, nose-dive, jump, drop.

divert VERB **1** amuse, entertain, please. **2** distract, deflect, switch, reroute.

divide VERB **1** distribute, allot, share, dispense, deal out. **2** split, separate, cleave, fork, branch.

divulge VERB disclose, reveal, expose, show, release, uncover, betray.

do VERB **1** perform, accomplish, carry out, complete, end, finish. **2** make, deal with, prepare, producing, creating. **3** be enough, suffice.

dodge VERB avoid, evade, elude, duck, side-step.

dog NOUN hound, cur, pup, whelp, mongrel, bitch. Some different breeds of dog: beagle, boxer, bull-terrier, bulldog, chow, cocker-spaniel, collie, corgie, dachshund, foxhound, German shepherd.

donate VERB give, present, contribute, subscribe to.

doubtful ADJECTIVE uncertain, undecided, dubious, unsure. An *opposite word* is certain.

dowdy ADJECTIVE drab, dreary, dull, frumpish, unfashionable.

downfall NOUN defeat, collapse, destruction.

down-hearted ADJECTIVE downcast, gloomy, miserable, unhappy, sad, depressed, dejected.

drag VERB tow, pull, draw, tug, heave.

dramatic ADJECTIVE stirring, thrilling, exciting, flamboyant, important.

drastic ADJECTIVE violent, extreme, powerful, harsh, severe, far-reaching.

draw VERB **1** sketch, trace, depict. **2** haul, tug, tow, pull. **3** attract, entice, persuade. **4** equal, be even.

dreadful ADJECTIVE terrible, awful, frightening, shocking, bad, tragic.

drench VERB soak, wet, immerse, steep, douse (or dowse).

drift VERB float, move off, wander, stray.

drill VERB **1** teach, train, coach, discipline. **2** pierce, bore, perforate, penetrate.

drink NOUN imbibe, sip, swig, lap, swallow, gulp, quaff.

drip VERB dribble, trickle, drop, ooze, flow, slobber, drool.

drive VERB **1** direct, control, steer, operate, propel. **2** force, send, push, hurl, impel.

droop VERB sag, flop, dangle, hang, wilt, wither. An *opposite word* is flourish.

drop VERB **1** lower, let fall, dump, shed, discard. **2** fall, descend, sink, plunge, cascade. **3** decrease, diminish, go down. *Dropping sales.* **4** abandon, desert, leave.

drowsy ADJECTIVE sleepy, tired, heavy.

drum VERB beat, tap, rap, bang. Some different kinds of drum:bass, bongo, snare.

dry ADJECTIVE **1** arid, parched, waterless, thirsty. **2** boring, tedious.

duck NOUN drake (male), duckling (baby).

dull ADJECTIVE **1** boring, tedious, uninteresting, drab. **2** muffled. **3** gloomy, dingy, grey. **4** slow, stupid.

dumb ADJECTIVE **1** silent, soundless, speechless, mute. **2** foolish.

duplicate NOUN copy, double, replica, reproduction, facsimile, photocopy.

durable ADJECTIVE lasting, endurable, reliable, strong, sturdy.

dusk NOUN twilight, sunset, nightfall, evening, gloaming, eventide.

duty NOUN **1** obligation, responsibility, task, job, work. **2** tax. *Duty free.*

dwindle VERB diminish, decrease, get smaller.

dye VERB colour/color (US), stain, tint, hue, pigment. A word with a similar sound is die.

dynamic ADJECTIVE energetic, active.

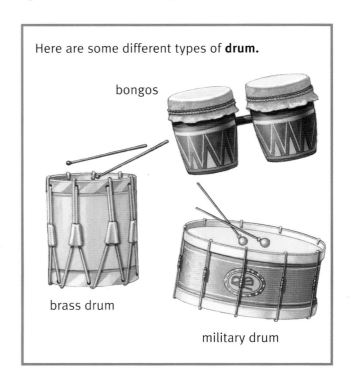

Here are some different types of **drum.**

bongos

brass drum

military drum

eager ADJECTIVE keen, enthusiastic, zealous, impatient, ardent.

early ADJECTIVE and ADVERB **1** soon, recent, forward, advanced, premature. **2** primeval.

earn VERB receive, get, gain, deserve, merit, acquire.

earnest ADJECTIVE **1** serious, solemn. *Earnest looks.* **2** determined, conscientious, sincere.

easy ADJECTIVE **1** simple, uncomplicated, smooth, trouble-free, obvious, effortless, straightforward. **2** carefree, restful, relaxed, comfortable.

eat VERB **1** consume, swallow, feed. **2** erode, wear away, corrode. Some of the different ways we can eat: chew, chomp, devour, gobble, gulp, guzzle.

ebb VERB recede, fall back, wane, decline, subside.

eccentric ADJECTIVE strange, odd, peculiar, weird, erratic, abnormal, quirkish, wayward.

edge NOUN border, margin, boundary, rim, side, periphery.

edible ADJECTIVE eatable, wholesome, good, palatable.

educate VERB teach, train, instruct, tutor, coach, bring up.

effective ADJECTIVE **1** useful, efficient, productive. **2** functioning, operative.

efficient ADJECTIVE able, effective, capable, competent, working well, skilful/skillful (US).

effort NOUN **1** toil, trouble, work, exertion. **2** endeavour/endeavor (US), attempt.

elaborate NOUN complex, intricate, complicated, ornate, detailed.

elect VERB choose, pick, opt for, vote for.

elegant ADJECTIVE smart, chic, elegant, stylish, graceful, refined.

eliminate VERB abolish, do away with, remove, delete, get rid of, exclude.

eloquent ADJECTIVE articulate, expressive, flowing.

embarrassed ADJE7CTIVE ashamed, upset, shy, awkward, distressed.

embrace VERB **1** hug, hold, caress, fondle, clasp. **2** include, contain.

emerge VERB come out, appear, surface.

emergency NOUN crisis, difficulty, extremity, plight, dilemma, predicament.

eminent ADJECTIVE famous, distinguished, celebrated, prominent, outstanding, well-known.

emotion NOUN feeling, passion, sentiment, excitement, agitation.

emphasize VERB stress, accentuate, accent, underline, highlight.

Here are some **edible** objects.

bread and cheese

banana

fruit

chocolate cake

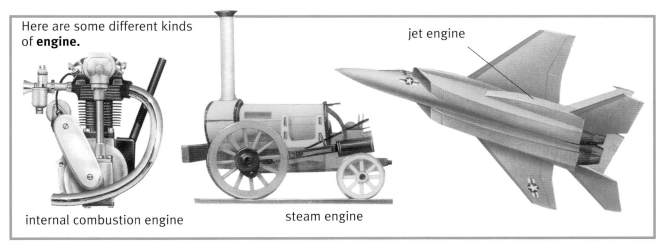

Here are some different kinds of **engine.**

jet engine

internal combustion engine

steam engine

employ VERB **1** engage, hire, recruit. **2** use, adopt.

employee NOUN worker, member of staff, servant.

employment NOUN work, occupation, job, trade, profession, vocation, calling.

empty ADJECTIVE unoccupied, unfilled, deserted, vacant, void, clear, blank, hollow.

enchant VERB entrance, bewitch, enthral.

encourage VERB exhort, urge on, support, inspire.

end NOUN **1** conclusion, ending, finish, termination. **2** purpose, aim, goal. **3** tip, point.

end VERB **1** finish, conclude, terminate, close, cease, stop, achieve. **2** abolish, destroy.

endeavour/endeavor (US) VERB attempt, try, strive, aim, struggle, essay.

endless ADJECTIVE unending, ceaseless, continuous, perpetual, unlimited.

energetic ADJECTIVE active, lively, vigorous, enthusiastic, forceful. An *opposite word* is sluggish.

energy NOUN strength, power, force, might, drive, vitality, muscle.

engaging ADJECTIVE charming, attractive, delightful, agreeable. An *opposite word* is repulsive.

engine NOUN **1** machine, motor. **2** locomotive. Some different engines: diesel, fuel injection, internal combustion, ramjet, steam, turbine.

enjoy VERB like, love, delight in, appreciate.

enlarge VERB expand, extend, make bigger, grow, add to, increase.

enormous ADJECTIVE huge, vast, gigantic, massive, colossal, tremendous. *The blue whale was enormous.*

enough ADJECTIVE sufficient, adequate, plenty, abundant. *Is there enough food?*

enter VERB **1** go into, come into, board, invade, penetrate. **2** record, register, inscribe.

entertain VERB **1** amuse, divert, cheer. **2** receive guests. **3** consider. *Entertaining an idea.*

entertainers NOUN Some different types of entertainers: acrobat, clown, comedian, dancer.

entertaining ADJECTIVE interesting, amusing, fun.

entertainment NOUN amusement, diversion, enjoyment, fun, distraction.

enthusiasm NOUN eagerness, fervour/fervor (US), zeal, passion.

entire ADJECTIVE complete, whole, intact.

entrance NOUN opening, way in, entry.

entry NOUN **1** admittance. access. **2** record, note.

environment NOUN surroundings, neighbourhood/neighborhood (US), setting, habitat.

envy VERB covet, desire, crave, be jealous of.

episode NOUN **1** part, instalment/ installment (US), chapter. **2** incident, occurrence, happening.

epoch NOUN period, age, era.

equal ADJECTIVE **1** alike, matching, the same, equivalent. **2** even, level, regular. **3** fit, up to, suitable, able.

equipment NOUN gear, apparatus, tackle, tools.

erase VERB rub out, delete, remove, eradicate.

erect ADJECTIVE upright. rigid, firm, vertical. VERB build, construct, put up, set up, raise.

errand NOUN job, task, chore, mission, assignment.

error NOUN mistake, fault, slip, blunder, fallacy.

escape VERB **1** flee, get away, break free, abscond. **2** avoid, dodge, elude.

essential ADJECTIVE necessary, vital, important.

establish VERB set up, organize, found, place, institute, fix, secure.

estate NOUN property, land, possessions, inheritance.

esteem VERB admire, value, prize.

estimate VERB assess, work out, value, reckon.

eternal ADJECTIVE endless, everlasting, incessant, ceaseless, continuous, unending, infinite.

evacuate VERB leave, abandon, depart, empty.

evade VERB avoid, escape, elude, dodge.

evaporate VERB vanish, disappear, melt away, dissolve, vaporize. An *opposite word* is appear.

even ADJECTIVE **1** calm, placid, steady, equal. *Even tempered.* **2** flat, smooth, level. ADVERB still, yet.

event NOUN happening, incident, occurrence.

evidence NOUN facts, proof, testimony, information, sign.

evil ADJECTIVE wicked, wrong, harmful, bad, sinful.

exact ADJECTIVE **1** accurate, correct, faultless.

exaggerate VERB overemphasize, magnify, amplify.

examination NOUN test, inspection, inquiry, investigation, search, survey, check-up.

examine VERB inspect, test, scrutinize, question.

excavate VERB dig, delve, unearth, burrow.

exceed VERB beat, surpass, outstrip.

excel VERB outdo, surpass, shine at, exceed.

excellent ADJECTIVE outstanding, first-class, superb, superlative, marvellous/marvelous (US).

exchange VERB trade, swap, replace, substitute.

excitement NOUN commotion, agitation, action, activity, unrest, suspense, ferment.

exciting ADJECTIVE thrilling, inspiring, stimulating, rousing, exhilarating.

exclaim VERB cry out, shout, proclaim, declare.

exclude VERB shut out, expel, evict, keep out.

excursion NOUN outing, trip, journey, tour, expedition.

excuse VERB **1** pardon, forgive, overlook. **2** let off, exempt, relieve, free.

exercise VERB **1** use, employ, utilize. **2** train, practise/practice (US), work out.

exhausted ADJECTIVE **1** tired, dog-tired, worn-out, weary. **2** empty, used up, consumed.

Here are some different ways to **exercise.**

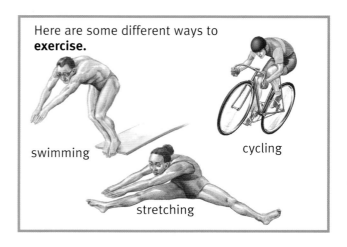

swimming

cycling

stretching

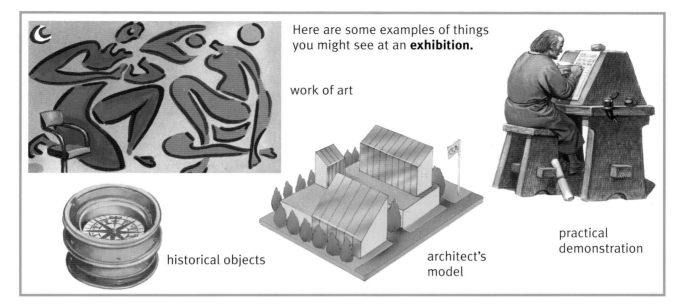

Here are some examples of things you might see at an **exhibition.**

work of art

historical objects

architect's model

practical demonstration

exhibition NOUN show, display, exposition.

exist VERB live, be, continue, survive, be present.

expect VERB **1** forecast, foresee, await, hope, look out for, anticipate. **2** require, insist on, demand.

expel VERB banish, exile, eject, exclude, throw out, deport, evict, bar.

expensive ADJECTIVE dear, costly, precious, high-priced. An *opposite word* is cheap.

experience NOUN undergo, encounter, endure, feel, suffer.

experienced ADJECTIVE skilled, practised/practiced (US), expert, trained, accomplished.

explain VERB make clear, show, describe, spell out, elucidate.

explore VERB search, investigate, look around, hunt, probe, pry.

explosion NOUN blast, bang, eruption, detonation.

expose VERB reveal, disclose, uncover, show, lay bare. **2** betray.

express VERB say, speak, utter, state, assert. **2** show, signify, stand for.

express ADJECTIVE fast, rapid, quick.

extend VERB stretch, expand, lengthen, reach, continue, prolong.

exterior ADJECTIVE external, outside, outer.

exterminate VERB destroy, get rid of, wipe out, kill, eliminate.

extinct ADJECTIVE dead, defunct, vanished, exterminated, ended.

extra ADJECTIVE **1** additional, more. **2** spare, surplus, excess.

extract VERB remove, pull out, draw out, select.

extraordinary ADJECTIVE outstanding, remarkable, amazing, unusual, strange, incredible.

extravagant ADJECTIVE wasteful, reckless, expensive, flamboyant, lavish.

eye NOUN Parts of the eye: cornea, eyebrow, eyelid, eyelash, iris, lens, optic nerve, pupil, retina, sclera.

fame NOUN renown, distinction, stardom, celebrity, glory, repute.

familiar ADJECTIVE **1** common, well-known, normal, usual. **2** intimate, friendly, easy.

family NOUN ancestors, tribe, race, relations.

famine NOUN shortage, scarcity, hunger, want, starvation. An *opposite word* is plenty.

famous ADJECTIVE renowned, well-known, celebrated. An *opposite word* is unknown.

fan NOUN admirer, follower, enthusiast, supporter.

fanatical ADJECTIVE enthusiastic, extreme, wild, frenzied.

fancy VERB **1** like, wish for, long for, yearn for, be attracted to. **2** imagine, dream, suppose, think.

fantastic ADJECTIVE amazing, wonderful, incredible, tremendous, strange, good.

far ADJECTIVE distant, remote, out of the way.

far ADVERB much, greatly, decidedly.

farm VERB cultivate, grow, till, husband.

fascinating ADJECTIVE interesting, engrossing, absorbing, attractive.

fashion NOUN **1** style, vogue, craze, mode, trend. **2** way, method, manner. VERB make, mould/mold (US), create.

fast ADJECTIVE quick, speedy, swift, hurried, rapid, brisk. An *opposite word* is slow.

fast ADVERB **1** rapidly, speedily, like lightning. **2** tightly, firm, securely. *Hold fast to the rope.*

fasten VERB do up, attach, tie up, secure, bind.

fat ADJECTIVE plump, stocky, well-built, stout, chubby, overweight, corpulent, obese.

fatigue ADJECTIVE tiredness, exhaustion, weariness.

fault NOUN **1** mistake, error, blunder, flaw, weakness, defect, imperfection, failing. **2** blame, responsibility. *Whose fault is it?*

fault VERB criticize. *Find fault with.*

favourite/favorite (US) ADJECTIVE preferred, best-liked, chosen.

fear NOUN terror, dread, fright, alarm, panic, distress. *A fear of heights.*

fearless ADJECTIVE brave, courageous, gallant. An *opposite word* is fearful.

feat NOUN brave action, deed, exploit, achievement, accomplishment. A word with a similar sound is feet.

There are many different types of **farm**.

arable farm

dairy farm

feeble ADJECTIVE weak, frail, delicate, puny, powerless. An *opposite word* is strong.

feed VERB nourish, foster, supply, provide, nurture, eat.

feel VERB **1** touch, handle, stroke, caress, grope. **2** experience, suffer from, notice, perceive, think, consider. *She feels the heat.*

feeling NOUN **1** sense, sensation, instinct. **2** emotion, sympathy, passion, pity, concern, warmth. **3** belief, opinion.

female ADJECTIVE feminine, womanly.

fence NOUN barrier, hedge, wall, railing, paling.

ferocious ADJECTIVE fierce, savage, vicious, cruel, barbaric, wild. An *opposite word* is harmless.

fertile ADJECTIVE productive, fruitful, plentiful, abundant, rich. An *opposite word* is barren.

festival NOUN feast, holiday, celebration, jubilee, anniversary.

fetch VERB carry, bring, get, collect, convey.

feud NOUN row, quarrel, dispute, disagreement, squabble, vendetta.

few ADJECTIVE not many, scarce, scanty, rare.

fib NOUN lie, falsehood, untruth.

fiddle VERB **1** tinker, play about with, fidget. **2** swindle, cheat.

fidget VERB fret, fuss, be nervous, wriggle, fiddle.

field NOUN paddock, meadow, playing field.

fiery ADJECTIVE passionate, hot, excitable, fervent, ardent, violent, heated. An *opposite word* is cool.

fight VERB **1** combat, battle, strive, struggle, row, quarrel, brawl. **2** wrestle, box. **3** oppose, resist.

fighter NOUN **1** combatant, warrior. **2** boxer, wrestler.

figure NOUN **1** number, numeral, digit, symbol.

fill VERB cram, load, stuff, pack, replenish.

A **festival** is a time for celebration.

Shinto festival

carnival

Easter basket

Chinese dragon

filter VERB sieve, sift, refine, strain, purify.

final ADJECTIVE closing, last, latest, concluding.

find VERB discover, come upon, recover, locate.

fine ADJECTIVE **1** excellent, good, splendid, attractive, great. **2** thin, slender, delicate, powdery, fragile. **3** bright, sunny, dry. **4** all right, OK.

finish VERB **1** complete, end, stop, accomplish. **2** use up, eat, consume.

fire VERB **1** ignite, kindle, light. **2** let off, shoot, discharge, detonate. **3** dismiss.

firm ADJECTIVE steady, solid, secure, fixed, rigid. NOUN company, business, concern.

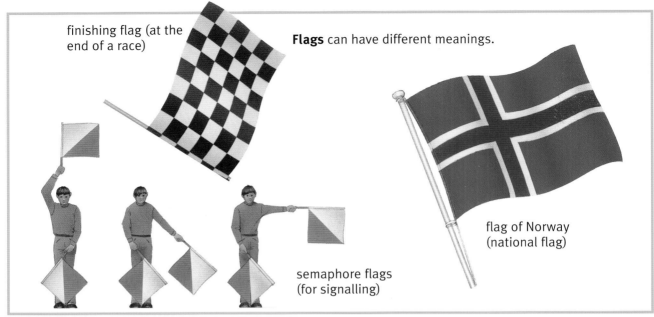

finishing flag (at the end of a race)

Flags can have different meanings.

flag of Norway (national flag)

semaphore flags (for signalling)

first-rate ADJECTIVE supreme, excellent, matchless, superb, first class. An *opposite word* is inferior.

fish NOUN Some different types of fish: cod, Dover sole, eel, goldfish, haddock, hake, halibut.

fishy ADJECTIVE suspicious, dubious, doubtful.

fit ADJECTIVE **1** well, healthy, strong, robust. **2** apt, suitable, able, competent, qualified. VERB assemble, put together, adjust, adapt, alter.

fix NOUN dilemma, predicament, jam, hole, plight.

fix VERB **1** fasten, connect, attach, secure, stick, establish, settle. **2** repair, mend, adjust.

fizzy ADJECTIVE sparkling, bubbly, carbonated, gassy.

flabby ADJECTIVE soft, sagging, floppy, drooping.

flag NOUN ensign. Some different kinds of flag: banner, bunting, ensign, jack, pennant, standard, streamer.

flag VERB droop, tire, weaken.

flair NOUN talent, gift, knack, ability, aptitude.

flake NOUN slice, sliver, chip, shaving, scale.

flap VERB flutter, wave, shake, beat.

flash VERB **1** flare, flicker, gleam, sparkle. **2** speed, dash, fly. *Flashed past.*

flat ADJECTIVE **1** level, plain, even, smooth, horizontal. **2** dull, lifeless, insipid, tame, boring.

flatter VERB praise, compliment, humour/humor (US), butter up.

flavour/flavor (US) NOUN taste, savour/savor (US), tang, relish, seasoning.

flee VERB run away, escape, bolt, vanish, scarper.

fleeting ADJECTIVE passing, brief, transient, momentary. An *opposite word* is lasting.

flexible ADJECTIVE bendy, pliable, bendable, stretchy, supple, elastic, adjustable.

flicker VERB twinkle, flash, flutter, waver, sparkle.

flimsy ADJECTIVE fragile, frail, meagre/meager (US), insubstantial, thin, weak.

flip VERB toss, flick, spin, pitch.

flippant ADJECTIVE frivolous, light-hearted, facetious, impertinent, pert.

float VERB waft, drift, hover, glide.

Here are some different kinds of **flower.**

orchids

primroses

tiger lilies

tulips

flock NOUN gathering, collection, set.

flourish VERB thrive, do well, succeed, prosper.

flow VERB run, pour, stream, glide, lap, trickle.

flower NOUN bloom, blossom.

fluent ADJECTIVE articulate, eloquent, glib, flowing.

fluid ADJECTIVE watery, liquid, runny, molten, flowing.

flutter VERB wave, beat, flap, flit, shake.

fly VERB glide, soar, rise up, ascend, hover, sail.

foam NOUN froth, lather, surf, suds.

fog NOUN mist, cloud, smog, haze.

fold VERB crease, bend, double.

follow VERB **1** pursue, come after, trail, track, go along. **2** come next, succeed, supersede. **3** understand, comprehend.

food NOUN nourishment, nutriment, provisions, refreshments.

foolhardy ADJECTIVE reckless, rash, bold, irresponsible. *What a foolhardy thing to do!*

foolish ADJECTIVE idiotic, stupid, daft, silly, unwise, senseless, inept, crazy.

forbid VERB ban, prohibit, stop, disallow, veto.

forbidding ADJECTIVE threatening, menacing, hostile, grim, stern, awesome.

force VERB make, compel, order, coerce, push.

forecast VERB predict, foresee, foretell, prophesy, expect.

foreign ADJECTIVE strange, alien, outlandish, imported, overseas.

forgery NOUN fake, counterfeit, dud, copy, imitation.

forget VERB overlook, omit, neglect, leave behind.

forgetful ADJECTIVE absent-minded, neglectful, inattentive, thoughtless.

forgive VERB pardon, excuse, let off, absolve.

form NOUN **1** shape, appearance, outline, pattern. **2** method, system, practice, variety, kind of.

forsake VERB abandon, desert, reject, jilt.

forthright ADJECTIVE frank, candid, straightforward, direct.

fortify VERB strengthen, reinforce, confirm, protect.

fortunate ADJECTIVE lucky, happy, successful, favourable/favorable (US).

found VERB set up, start, originate, establish, create. *Founded in 1888.*

fountain NOUN well head, spring, source, spray, spout, jet.

fraction NOUN part, division, piece, fragment.

fragile ADJECTIVE frail, weak, flimsy, delicate.

fragment NOUN piece, bit, chip, morsel, scrap, sliver, segment.

fragrance NOUN scent, smell, aroma, odour/odor (US).

frank ADJECTIVE candid, open, honest, direct.

fraud NOUN deception, deceit, dishonesty, forgery, swindle.

freak ADJECTIVE strange, abnormal, unusual.

free ADJECTIVE **1** unoccupied, vacant, available. *Is this chair free?* **2** liberated, at large, independent. *A free country.* **3** no charge, gratis.

free VERB release, liberate, let loose, dismiss, acquit.

freeze VERB ice up, refrigerate, chill, congeal.

frequent ADJECTIVE **1** many, numerous, repeated, regular. **2** common, usual, everyday.

fresh ADJECTIVE **1** new, unused, different. **2** lively, energetic, refreshed

friction NOUN **1** chaffing, abrasion, grating, rubbing. **2** hostility, discord, ill-feeling.

friend NOUN mate, pal, chum, partner, companion, acquaintance, ally, colleague.

frighten VERB alarm, startle, daunt, terrify, scare.

frill NOUN edging, border, ruffle.

fringe NOUN edging, trimming, edge, border.

frivolous ADJECTIVE trivial.

frontier NOUN border, boundary, margin, limit.

froth NOUN foam, lather, bubbles, suds.

frugal ADJECTIVE economical, sparing, thrifty, stingy, meagre/meager (US).

fruit NOUN crop, harvest, produce.

fruitful ADJECTIVE productive, fertile, abundant, plentiful, successful. *An opposite word* is barren.

frustrate VERB thwart, hinder, foil, defeat, baffle.

fuel NOUN Some different kinds of fuel: wood, coal, diesel, electricity, gas, hydroelectric power, nuclear power, oil, petrol/gasoline.

fugitive NOUN refugee, deserter, runaway.

fulfil/fulfill (US) VERB achieve, accomplish, complete, conclude.

full ADJECTIVE packed, filled, loaded, bulging, complete.

fun NOUN enjoyment, amusement, pleasure, sport, recreation, jollity.

function NOUN **1** purpose, use, part, role. **2** meeting, gathering, party. *A business function.* VERB operate, go, run, drive.

fundamental ADJECTIVE basic, essential, rudimentary, important, crucial.

funeral NOUN burial, cremation, interment.

funny ADJECTIVE **1** amusing, comic, humorous, ridiculous, witty, laughable, droll. **2** strange, weird, peculiar, odd, curious.

furtive ADJECTIVE stealthy, sly, secretive, clandestine, sneaky.

fury NOUN rage, ferocity, anger, frenzy, passion.

fuse NOUN blend, join, weld.

futile ADJECTIVE useless, pointless, fruitless.

fuzzy ADJECTIVE misty, blurred, hazy, unclear.

Here are some different kinds of **fruit.**

strawberries

cherries

lemon and lime

grapes

bananas

gabble VERB chatter, prattle, babble.

gadget NOUN device, instrument, tool, contraption.

gag NOUN joke, jest.

gag VERB choke, silence, throttle, stifle.

gain VERB earn, get, acquire receive, obtain, win.

galleon NOUN *See* **boat, ship.**

gallery NOUN museum, arcade, corridor, passage.

gallop VERB run, speed, race.

gamble VERB bet, risk, wager, chance, hazard.

game ADJECTIVE courageous, brave, gallant, valiant.

game NOUN **1** pastime, sport, amusement, play, entertainment, recreation, contest. Some different kinds of game: badminton, baseball, basketball, cricket, football, hockey, pool, table tennis, golf, chess, ice hockey, cards. **2** prey, quarry.

gang NOUN band, group, mob, clique.

gaol (UK) NOUN jail, prison, lock-up, penitentiary.

gap NOUN hole, space, opening, break, crevice.

garden NOUN plot, allotment, orchard. Some things used in gardening: fork, hoe, rake, secateurs, shears. shovel. spade, trowel, watering-can, wheelbarrow.

garish ADJECTIVE gaudy, loud, vulgar, flashy, showy. An *opposite word* is tasteful.

garment NOUN dress, attire. *See also* **clothes.**

garnish VERB decorate, embellish adorn.

gas NOUN vapour/vapor (US), fumes, smoke. Some different kinds of gas: ammonia, carbon dioxide, carbon monoxide, helium, hydrogen, nitrous oxide (laughing gas), methane, neon, oxygen, ozone.

gash NOUN slash, cut, slit, wound.

gasp VERB pant, puff, choke.

gate NOUN portal, doorway, barrier, entrance, way in, way out.

gather VERB **1** collect, accumulate, put together. *Gather facts.* **2** pick, pluck. *Gather apples.* **3** come together, congregate, assemble. *Gather round the fire.* **4** understand, deduce, infer. *We gather you'll be away.*

gathering NOUN meeting, assembly, collection.

gaudy ADJECTIVE cheap, tawdry. *See also* **garish.**

gaunt ADJECTIVE thin, haggard, skinny, emaciated.

gaze VERB stare, contemplate, look steadily at.

gem NOUN jewel, precious stone, treasure.

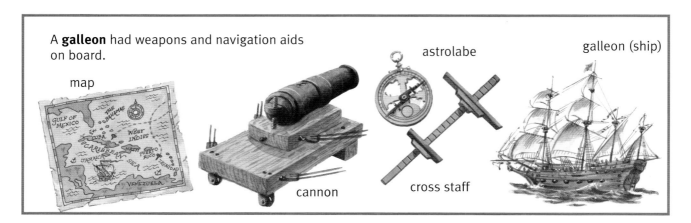

A **galleon** had weapons and navigation aids on board.

map

astrolabe

galleon (ship)

cannon

cross staff

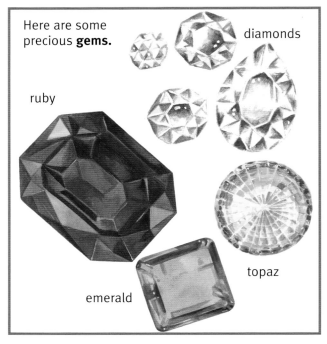

Here are some precious **gems.**

diamonds

ruby

topaz

emerald

general ADJECTIVE **1** usual, widespread, common. *What's the general feeling about it?* **2** vague, inaccurate, broad.

generous ADJECTIVE **1** kind, giving, unselfish, open-handed, charitable. **2** big, large, abundant, copious.

genius NOUN brilliance, cleverness, talent, flair, ability.

gentle ADJECTIVE **1** kind, tender, mild, good-hearted. **2** smooth, moderate, slight. *Some gentle exercise.* **3** pleasant, soft, peaceful, restful.

genuine ADJECTIVE real, authentic, natural.

gesture NOUN signal, motion, nod, movement, indication.

get VERB **1** obtain, gain, win, earn, secure. **2** become, turn, grow. **3** fetch, bring, collect. **4** arrive, come, reach. *When did you get here?* **5** understand. *Did you get the joke?* **6** receive. *We got a big welcome.*

ghastly ADJECTIVE horrible, awful, hideous.

ghostly ADJECTIVE spooky, eerie, shadowy, haunted, weird.

giant ADJECTIVE huge, enormous, gigantic, colossal, immense, big. An *opposite word* is tiny.

gibberish NOUN nonsense, drivel, gabble.

giddy ADJECTIVE **1** dizzy, unsteady, light-headed. **2** flighty, wild, reckless.

gift NOUN **1** present, donation, offering. **2** talent, ability, flair, aptitude, bent.

gingerly ADJECTIVE cautiously, carefully, delicately, tentatively.

give VERB **1** offer, hand over, present. **2** contribute, donate. **3** deliver, convey, pass on. **4** supply, issue, grant, distribute, hand out. **5** make, do. *He gave a deep chuckle.* **6** present, perform. *She gave a talk.* **7** bend, yield.

glad ADJECTIVE pleased, happy, delighted.

glamour/glamor (US) NOUN appeal, attraction, charm, fascination.

glare VERB **1** frown, glower, scowl. *See also* **look.** **2** dazzle, shine, glitter.

glaring ADJECTIVE obvious, blatant, barefaced, terrible. *A glaring mistake.*

glaze VERB gloss, varnish, polish, enamel.

gleam VERB sparkle, flash, glow, glitter, glint

glib ADJECTIVE easy, smooth, slick, talkative, facile.

glide VERB slide, soar, sail, skim, float, drift.

glimmer VERB gleam, shine, glow, flicker, glitter.

glimpse VERB see, spot, spy, catch sight of.

glisten VERB glimmer, gleam, shine.

glitter VERB shine, sparkle, flash, glisten, glimmer, gleam, scintillate.

gloat VERB exult, revel, crow, triumph, relish.

global ADJECTIVE worldwide, international.

globe NOUN ball, sphere, orb, planet.

gloomy ADJECTIVE **1** depressing, dismal, dark, dreary. **2** unhappy, sad, miserable, glum.

glorious ADJECTIVE **1** brilliant, splendid, bright, beautiful, superb. **2** famous, noted, noble, exalted.

glory NOUN **1** fame, honour/honor (US), praise, greatness. **2** beauty, splendour/splendor (US), brilliance. **3** praise, worship.

glossy ADJECTIVE shiny, polished, burnished, sheeny.

glow VERB **1** gleam, shine, burn, smoulder. **2** flush.

glue NOUN and VERB gum, adhesive, paste, cement.

glum ADJECTIVE sad, depressed, sullen, morose, miserable.

glut NOUN surplus, excess, abundance, plenty.

gnaw VERB nibble, bite, chew. *See also* **eat**.

go VERB **1** leave, depart, set out. **2** escape, flee, run away. **3** become, grow, turn, get. *He went pale with fear.* **4** continue, extend, lead, reach. *Most rivers go to the sea.* **5** belong, fit. *The nut goes with the bolt.* **6** travel, journey. **7** work, operate, function. *The car won't go. An opposite word* is stop.

goal NOUN aim, ambition, target, purpose.

good ADJECTIVE **1** correct, faultless, perfect, excellent, admirable. **2** caring, generous, honest, loyal, reliable. **3** kind, considerate, virtuous. **4** obedient, well-behaved, polite. **5** skilled, clever, capable, talented. **6** interesting, exciting, thrilling.

goods NOUN belongings, property, merchandise, cargo.

gorgeous ADJECTIVE superb, magnificent, brilliant, splendid, beautiful.

gossip VERB talk, tittle-tattle, chatter, tell tales.

govern VERB rule, manage, control, run, supervise, direct.

government NOUN rule, management, administration, authority, state, parliament.

gown NOUN robe. *See also* **clothes**.

grab VERB seize, clutch, take hold of, snatch, grasp.

graceful ADJECTIVE elegant, flowing, natural, attractive.

gracious ADJECTIVE polite, kindly, friendly, gentle, generous, urbane. *Opposite words are* ungracious, churlish.

grade NOUN rank, position, degree, status, category, class.

grade VERB sort, group, classify, rank, assess.

gradient NOUN slope, incline, ascent, descent.

gradual ADJECTIVE slow, continuous, steady, little by little. *Opposite words are* abrupt, sudden.

grand ADJECTIVE impressive, important, splendid, superb, magnificent, majestic, imposing.

grant VERB **1** give, donate, bestow, award. **2** allow.

grasp VERB **1** hold, clasp. *See also* **grab**. **2** understand.

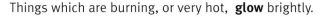
Things which are burning, or very hot, **glow** brightly.

candle flame

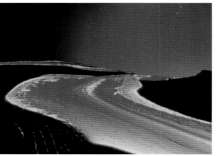
volcanic lava

glow worm

grateful ADJECTIVE thankful, indebted, appreciative.

grave ADJECTIVE **1** serious, solemn, thoughtful. *A grave moment.* **2** important, essential. *Grave news.*

greasy ADJECTIVE fatty, oily, slimy, slippery.

great ADJECTIVE **1** large, huge, tremendous, immense. **2** important, spectacular, splendid, grand. **3** classic, famous, well-known, leading. **4** excellent, wonderful, marvellous/ marvelous (US).

greedy ADJECTIVE **1** gluttonous, ravenous, piggish. **2** grasping, selfish, avaricious.

greet VERB salute, hail, welcome, meet.

grief NOUN sadness, sorrow, distress, heartache, woe, misery, suffering, unhappiness.

grieve VERB mourn, sorrow, lament.

grim ADJECTIVE **1** serious, harsh, solemn. **2** frightening, horrid, gruesome, unpleasant.

grime NOUN smut, dust. *See also* **dirt**.

grin VERB smile, beam, smirk, simper, laugh.

grind VERB **1** crush, pulverize, crunch. **2** sharpen.

grip VERB seize, clasp, grasp, clutch, hold.

groan NOUN and VERB moan, sigh, whine, wail, lament, grumble.

groom VERB tidy, smarten, clean, brush, preen.

grope VERB hold, feel, handle, touch, fumble.

ground NOUN **1** earth, soil, clay. **2** base, foundation.

grounds NOUN **1** justification, cause, excuse, reason. **2** dregs, sediment. **3** land, estate, territory, parkland.

group NOUN division, section, collection.

grow VERB **1** develop, expand, enlarge, get bigger, get taller, increase. **2** become. *It grew late.* **3** plant, raise, cultivate, germinate, sprout.

growl VERB snarl, grumble, threaten.

gruesome ADJECTIVE horrible, hideous, nasty.

gruff ADJECTIVE **1** rough, harsh, hoarse. *A gruff voice.* **2** rude, grumpy, curt, churlish.

grumble VERB complain, moan, protest, carp.

grumpy ADJECTIVE bad-tempered, snappish, surly, sullen. An *opposite word* is affable.

guarantee VERB promise, vouch for, warrant, assure, make sure.

guard VERB protect, shield, defend, watch over, look after, shelter.

guess VERB **1** estimate, surmise, conjecture, reckon. **2** think, suppose, assume.

guest NOUN visitor, caller.

guide VERB lead, direct, conduct, manage, control, escort. An *opposite word* is mislead.

guilty ADJECTIVE blameworthy, responsible, wrong, wicked. An *opposite word* is innocent.

gulf NOUN bay, gap, rift, breach, chasm.

gun NOUN some different types of gun: bazooka, blunderbuss, cannon, carbine, firearm, musket.

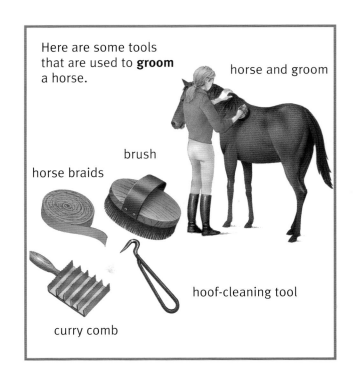

Here are some tools that are used to **groom** a horse.

horse and groom

brush

horse braids

hoof-cleaning tool

curry comb

habit NOUN **1** custom, usage, tradition, practice, way, addiction. **2** mannerism.

haggle VERB bargain, barter, argue.

hairy ADJECTIVE furry, shaggy, bushy, woolly.

hall NOUN vestibule, foyer, lobby, corridor, entrance, auditorium, concert-hall.

halt VERB stop, pull up, wait, cease, end.

halve VERB divide, bisect, dissect, split in two.

hammer VERB beat, hit, pound, bang, knock.

hamper VERB hinder, prevent, obstruct, get in the way, impede, restrict, curb.

hand NOUN mitt. Parts of a hand: finger, fingernail, fist, knuckle, palm, thumb, wrist.

hand VERB give, pass, transmit, deliver.

handicap NOUN disability, disadvantage, hindrance, drawback, restriction.

handle VERB **1** feel, hold, fondle, touch. **2** manage, control, manipulate, look after, wield.

handsome ADJECTIVE **1** good-looking, attractive, elegant. **2** generous, liberal, ample.

handy ADJECTIVE **1** useful, helpful, convenient, accessible, to hand, compact. **2** skilful, practical.

hang VERB **1** dangle, sag, droop, suspend, drape.

hanker VERB crave, long for, want, desire, yearn, thirst for.

haphazard ADJECTIVE accidental, chance, random.

happen VERB occur, take place, come about, transpire.

happy ADJECTIVE merry, cheerful, joyful, delighted, glad, pleased, contented.

harass VERB pester, annoy, tease, badger, disturb, bother, hassle.

harbour/harbor (US) NOUN port, docks, quay, haven, mooring, anchorage.

hard ADJECTIVE **1** solid, rigid, dense, stiff, tough. **2** difficult, complicated, baffling, complex, intricate. **3** severe, harsh, cruel. *A hard punishment.* **4** exhausting, tiring, tough, arduous.

hardly ADVERB just, barely, not quite, only just.

hardy ADJECTIVE strong, rugged, robust, sturdy, tough. An *opposite word* is weak.

harm VERB injure, hurt, damage, spoil, ill-treat.

harmful ADJECTIVE damaging, dangerous, injurious.

harsh ADJECTIVE **1** rough, grating, rasping, jarring. *A harsh noise.* **2** hard, cruel, pitiless, strict. **3** glaring, dazzling, bright.

hasten VERB hurry, speed up, rush, dash, fly.

hasty ADJECTIVE hurried, speedy, brisk, impulsive, careless, sloppy. *Opposite words* are slow, careful.

hat NOUN headgear, millinery. Some different kinds of hats and headgear: balaclava, bearskin, beret, biretta, boater, bonnet, bowler, cap, cloche, crown, fez, helmet, kepi, mitre, shako, skullcap, sombrero, tricorn, trilby, tiara, turban.

Here are some different kinds of **hat.**

hard hat

decorative hat

military hat

hate VERB dislike, loathe, detest, despise.

haul VERB drag, pull, tow, heave, tug.

have VERB **1** own, possess. **2** contain, consist of, be made up of, include. *The castle has a hundred rooms.* **3** get, obtain, receive. *How many Christmas cards did you have?* **4** allow, put up with, tolerate. *She wouldn't have the dog in the house.* **5** produce, give birth to. *The cat had eight beautiful kittens.* **6** experience, go through, enjoy. *We had a lovely time at the coast.*

havoc NOUN chaos, disturbance, upset, disorder, mayhem.

hazy ADJECTIVE misty, cloudy, foggy, blurred, dim.

head ADJECTIVE leading, main, principal.

head NOUN **1** skull, mind, brains. **2** top, summit, peak, apex. **3** leader, boss, chief, commander, ruler.

heady ADJECTIVE thrilling, exciting.

heal VERB cure, make better, restore, remedy.

health NOUN fitness, strength, wellbeing.

healthy ADJECTIVE fit, well, sound, robust.

heap NOUN pile, mound, mass, collection.

There are many varieties of **herb.**

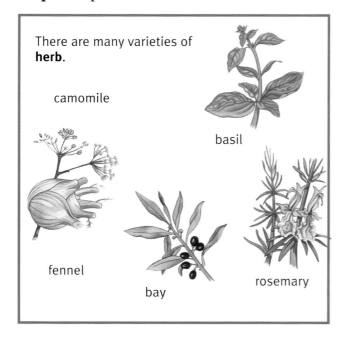

camomile

basil

fennel

bay

rosemary

hear VERB listen, eavesdrop, pay attention.

heart NOUN centre/center (US), middle, core, kernel, nucleus. **2** kindness, sympathy, feeling.

heartless ADJECTIVE cruel, pitiless, callous, harsh, brutal, unkind. *Opposite words* are kind, merciful.

hearty ADJECTIVE **1** enthusiastic, warm, friendly, sincere. **2** large, nourishing, ample. *A hearty meal.*

heat NOUN warmth, fervour, fever, excitement.

heat VERB warm, boil, cook. *See also* **cook.**

heavy ADJECTIVE **1** weighty, ponderous, bulky. **2** hard, difficult. An *opposite word* is light.

hectic ADJECTIVE busy, frenetic, frenzied, heated.

hedge NOUN fence, barrier, boundary.

heed VERB pay attention to, observe, follow, obey.

heir NOUN inheritor, offspring, child.

help VERB **1** aid, assist, give a hand, serve. **2** improve, make better.

helpful ADJECTIVE **1** useful, beneficial, worthwhile. **2** kind, friendly, considerate, caring.

helpless ADJECTIVE weak, powerless, incapable.

hem NOUN edge, margin, border.

hence ADVERB therefore, thus, accordingly.

herb NOUN plant, seasoning, flavouring/flavoring (US). Some different kinds of herb: basil, bay leaf, camomile, chives, fennel, mint, oregano, rosemary, sage, tarragon, thyme.

heritage NOUN **1** inheritance, legacy, bequest. **2** tradition, culture.

heroic ADJECTIVE brave, valiant, courageous, gallant, fearless.

hesitate VERB delay, pause, waver, falter, hold back.

hide VERB conceal, cover, put away, veil, mask. *Opposite words* are show and find.

hideous ADJECTIVE ugly, ghastly, frightful, horrible, repulsive. An *opposite word* is beautiful.

Hh

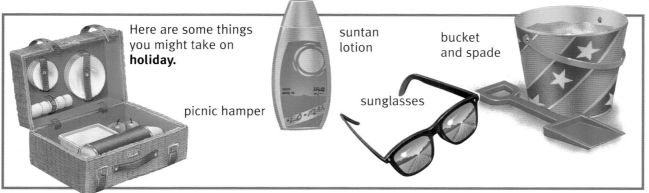

Here are some things you might take on **holiday.**

picnic hamper

suntan lotion

sunglasses

bucket and spade

high ADJECTIVE **1** tall, lofty, elevated, towering. **2** eminent, important, distinguished. **3** shrill, sharp, piercing.

highbrow ADJECTIVE intellectual, clever, cultivated, brainy. An *opposite word* is lowbrow.

highly ADVERB very, extremely, decidedly.

highly-strung ADJECTIVE sensitive, nervous, tense.

high-powered ADJECTIVE dynamic, go-ahead, forceful.

hike VERB ramble. *See also* **walk**.

hilarious ADJECTIVE funny, amusing, entertaining, hysterical. An *opposite word* is serious.

hill NOUN mound, rise, elevation, peak, slope.

hinder VERB check, impede. *See also* **hamper**.

hint VERB suggest, mention, insinuate, allude to.

hire VERB rent, lease, charter, let, book. A word that sounds similar is higher.

hit VERB **1** beat, thrash. **2** punch, clout, sock, clobber, batter, wallop. **3** tap, touch, tip, knock. **4** collide with, crash into, smash into, bump into.

hoard VERB collect, amass, save, accumulate.

hoarse ADJECTIVE husky, raucous, croaking, gruff, rough. A word that sounds similar is horse.

hoax NOUN prank, trick, joke, deception, con.

hobble VERB limp, totter, stagger, stumble, shuffle.

hobby NOUN pastime, interest, recreation, pursuit, sideline.

hoist VERB raise, lift, elevate.

hold VERB **1** clutch, grip, grasp, seize. **2** possess, admit. **3** contain. *The box holds a lot.* **4** think, believe, judge, reckon. **5** imprison, arrest, detain.

hole NOUN opening, cavity, crater, gap, puncture, tear, split, burrow.

holiday NOUN vacation, festival, anniversary, leave, time off.

hollow ADJECTIVE **1** sunken, concave, empty. **2** insincere, sham, artificial. *It was nothing but a hollow promise.* An *opposite word* is sincere.

hollow NOUN dip, depression, cavity, hole.

home NOUN **1** house, dwelling, residence, abode. **2** institution, asylum.

homonym NOUN homonyms are words with the same spelling but different meanings, as in bank (a place money is kept) and bank (the side of a river).

homophone NOUN homophones are words that have the same sound but a different spelling and a different meaning: allowed/aloud, altar/alter, bail/bale, band/banned, bare/bear, be/bee.

honest ADJECTIVE truthful, sincere, genuine.

hooligan NOUN lout, ruffian, thug, yob (UK), hoodlum.

hop VERB leap, jump, spring, dance, hobble, limp.

hope VERB wish, long for, look forward to, await, desire, yearn, believe. An *opposite word* is despair.

hopeful ADJECTIVE expectant, optimistic.

hopeless ADJECTIVE **1** despairing, pessimistic, despondent. **2** useless, no good. **3** unattainable.

horde NOUN crowd, mob, gang, swarm, throng.

horizontal ADJECTIVE flat, level, straight, plane.

horrible ADJECTIVE nasty, unpleasant, disgusting, horrid, frightful, frightening, terrible.

horrify VERB terrify, alarm, shock, appal, outrage.

horror NOUN fear, dread, fright, terror, loathing.

horse NOUN hack, mount, charger, cob, stallion, mare, filly, colt.

hospital NOUN clinic, nursing home, sanitorium, infirmary.

hostile ADJECTIVE unfriendly, aggressive.

hot ADJECTIVE **1** warm, scalding, boiling, sweltering, scorching, sizzling, blazing. **2** peppery, pungent. *A hot sauce.*

hotel NOUN inn, boarding house, guest house, bed and breakfast, motel, hostel.

hound VERB chase, pursue, harry, persecute.

house NOUN building, dwelling, home, residence.

hovel NOUN shack, cabin, hut, dump, shanty.

hover VERB fly, float, flutter, rift, linger.

however CONJUNCTION still, yet, nonetheless, nevertheless, notwithstanding.

howl VERB hoot, shriek, cry, scream, wail.

huddle VERB cluster, crowd, flock, gather, snuggle.

hug VERB cuddle, embrace, hold, cling to.

huge ADJECTIVE colossal, gigantic. *See also* **big**.

hum VERB drone, purr, buzz, murmur.

humane ADJECTIVE kind, merciful, forgiving, compassionate, sympathetic.

humble ADJECTIVE meek, modest, submissive, simple, unassuming. An *opposite word* is proud.

humiliate VERB mortify, degrade, embarrass, crush, deflate. An *opposite word* is dignify.

hump NOUN lump, bulge, bump, mound.

hunch NOUN suspicion, notion, feeling, intuition, premonition.

hunger NOUN **1** famine, starvation, appetite. **2** greed, desire, yearning, thirst.

hunt VERB **1** chase, stalk, pursue, track down, hound. **2** look for, search, probe, seek.

hurdle NOUN fence, barrier, obstacle.

hurl VERB throw, fling, propel, chuck, toss, cast.

hurry VERB hasten, speed, dash, race, run, scurry.

hurt VERB **1** harm, damage, wound, injure. **2** ache, pain, throb. **3** upset, distress, offend.

hush VERB silence, quieten, soothe.

hush-hush ADJECTIVE secret.

hut NOUN shed, cabin, shanty, shack.

hymn NOUN religious song, psalm.

These animals are **huge.**

elephant

sperm whale

icon NOUN picture, image, symbol.

icy ADJECTIVE chilly, cold, freezing, frosty.

idea NOUN thought, notion, suggestion, plan, opinion, belief.

ideal ADJECTIVE perfect, complete, model, excellent, best.

identical ADJECTIVE same, indistinguishable, duplicate, matching.

identify VERB know, recognize, distinguish, discern, pick out.

idiom NOUN turn of phrase, expression.

idiot NOUN fool, moron, dunce, halfwit, imbecile, simpleton.

idle ADJECTIVE lazy, unoccupied, inactive.

idol NOUN **1** image, god, statue. **2** favourite/favorite (US), hero, heroine, darling.

ignite VERB light, set fire to, kindle, spark off.

ignorant ADJECTIVE **1** stupid, unintelligent, illiterate, uneducated, clueless. **2** unaware.

ignore VERB disregard, disobey, overlook, neglect, pay no attention to.

ill ADJECTIVE **1** unwell, sick, poorly, under the weather, infirm. **2** harmful, damaging.

ill-treat VERB injure, abuse, harm.

illegal ADJECTIVE unlawful, forbidden, banned, prohibited, illicit. *Opposite words* are legal, lawful.

illegible ADJECTIVE unreadable, indecipherable, indistinct.

illness NOUN sickness, ailment, disease, complaint, disorder, disability, malady.

illuminate VERB shed light on, enlighten, explain, elucidate, clarify. An *opposite word* is darken.

illustration NOUN picture, drawing, sketch, decoration, representation, example.

image NOUN picture, likeness, representation, statue, concept, idea.

imaginary ADJECTIVE unreal, made-up, fictitious, imagined, make-believe, illusory, fanciful.

imagination NOUN fancy, idea, vision, creativity, inspiration.

imagine VERB **1** picture, dream, fancy, invent, make up, envisage. **2** think, believe, suppose.

imitate VERB copy, ape, parody, simulate, reproduce, follow, caricature, impersonate, forge.

Here are some **imaginary** creatures.

pixie

elf

fairy

goblin

troll

immature ADJECTIVE raw, crude, unripe, unformed, young, childish, puerile.

immediately ADVERB straightaway, at once, without delay, forthwith.

immense ADJECTIVE huge, enormous, vast, massive.

immerse VERB plunge, submerge, dip, dunk, douse.

imminent ADJECTIVE impending, looming, approaching, threatening.

immortal ADJECTIVE eternal, everlasting, undying.

immune ADJECTIVE resistant, invulnerable, free.

impact NOUN **1** effect, influence, repercussions. **2** collision, crash, bang, shock, blow.

impartial ADJECTIVE objective, unbiased, disinterested, neutral, fair.

impassive ADJECTIVE calm, unruffled, composed, indifferent, unmoved.

impatient ADJECTIVE eager, anxious, fidgety, restless, hasty intolerant, bad-tempered.

impede VERB hinder, obstruct, get in the way of, interrupt, block, stop.

impending ADJECTIVE imminent, threatening, approaching, coming.

impenetrable ADJECTIVE **1** dense, thick, solid, impassable. **2** mysterious, incomprensible.

imperfect ADJECTIVE faulty, defective, flawed, unsound, damaged.

impersonal ADJECTIVE formal, official, remote, aloof. An *opposite word* is friendly.

impertinent ADJECTIVE rude, impudent, insolent.

impetuous ADJECTIVE hasty, impulsive, rash, reckless.

imply VERB hint, insinuate, suggest, intimate.

import VERB bring in, introduce.

important ADJECTIVE **1** chief, essential, main. **2** famous, well-known, notable, great. **3** big, major, significant, special.

imposing ADJECTIVE impressive, magnificent.

impossible ADJECTIVE unworkable, inconceivable, hopeless, impracticable, absurd.

impractical ADJECTIVE unworkable, unrealistic, unusable, idealistic.

impression NOUN **1** mark, stamp, brand. **2** feeling, idea, a vague idea. opinion. *I have the impression she's unhappy.* **3** impersonation, imitation, take-off.

impressive ADJECTIVE splendid, magnificent, wonderful, overpowering.

imprison VERB jail, lock up, incarcerate, confine.

improve VERB correct, get better, make better, develop, amend, perfect.

improvize VERB make up, extemporize, invent, ad-lib.

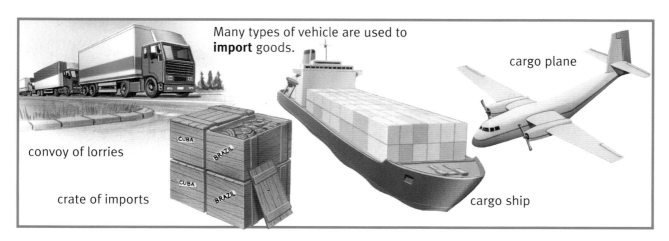

Many types of vehicle are used to **import** goods.

cargo plane

convoy of lorries

crate of imports

CUBA BRAZIL CUBA BRAZIL

cargo ship

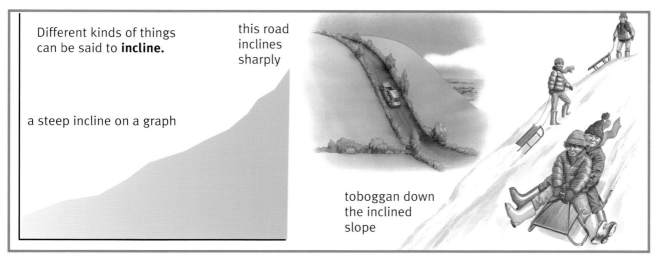

Different kinds of things can be said to **incline.**

a steep incline on a graph

this road inclines sharply

toboggan down the inclined slope

impudent ADJECTIVE saucy, impertinent, cocky, insolent. An *opposite word* is polite.

impure ADJECTIVE contaminated, unclean, polluted, dirty, indecent.

inaccessible ADJECTIVE remote, isolated, unreachable, unobtainable.

inaccurate ADJECTIVE wrong, incorrect, faulty, imprecise, inexact.

inarticulate ADJECTIVE unintelligible, incoherent, tongue-tied.

inaudible ADJECTIVE silent, noiseless, faint, muffled, indistinct.

incapable ADJECTIVE unable, helpless, unfit, weak, incompetent.

incentive NOUN spur, motive, encouragement, bait, inducement.

incessant ADJECTIVE unending, interminable, continual, ceaseless, non-stop.

incident NOUN event, happening, occurrence, experience.

incline VERB tend, lean, slope, veer, favour/favor (US), be disposed.

include VERB contain, consist of, comprise, hold, enclose. *Opposite words* are exclude, omit.

incomparable ADJECTIVE superb, unequalled/unequaled (US), matchless, superlative.

incompetent ADJECTIVE incapable, helpless, inept.

incorrect ADJECTIVE faulty, mistaken, wrong, erroneous, untrue, inaccurate.

increase VERB expand, extend, enlarge, boost, add to, swell, enhance, develop.

incredible ADJECTIVE unbelievable, amazing, extraordinary, far-fetched.

independent ADJECTIVE free, self-governing, self-reliant, separate, self-sufficient.

indicate VERB show, point to, denote, suggest.

indifference NOUN disregard, negligence, unconcern, apathy, lack of interest.

indispensable ADJECTIVE essential, vital, necessary.

indulge VERB pander to, give in to, yield, gratify, pamper, satisfy, humour/humor (US), spoil.

inefficient ADJECTIVE incompetent, unworkable, wasteful, time-consuming.

inevitable ADJECTIVE unavoidable, doomed, inescapable, destined, certain, sure.

infallible ADJECTIVE unfailing, unerring, sure, dependable, trustworthy.

infamous ADJECTIVE notorious, disreputable.

infatuated ADJECTIVE besotted, fascinated.

infectious ADJECTIVE contagious, catching.

inferior ADJECTIVE mediocre, second-rate, shoddy, minor, subordinate, secondary, lesser.

infinite ADJECTIVE unending, endless, eternal, boundless, limitless, immeasurable, vast.

inflexible ADJECTIVE unbending, rigid, stiff, fixed, stubborn, adamant.

inflict VERB burden, impose, deliver, give, put.

influence VERB affect, impress, inspire, sway, persuade, manipulate.

inform VERB tell, notify, let know, instruct, communicate, relate. An *opposite word* is conceal.

informal ADJECTIVE casual, relaxed, easy-going, unceremonious, simple, friendly.

information NOUN news, knowledge, intelligence, advice, facts, data.

infuriate VERB anger, enrage, vex, madden, annoy.

ingenious ADJECTIVE clever, cunning, shrewd.

inhabit VERB live in, occupy, dwell, reside.

initial ADJECTIVE first, beginning, introductory.

initiative NOUN resourcefulness, drive, energy, ambition, go, innovativeness.

inject VERB insert, inoculate, vaccinate.

injure VERB harm, damage, hurt, wound, maltreat.

injustice NOUN unfairness, discrimination, oppression, prejudice.

innocent ADJECTIVE **1** blameless, guiltless, sinless, faultless, pure. **2** naive, simple, unworldly, gullible, harmless.

innovation NOUN change, novelty, variation.

inquisitive ADJECTIVE curious, prying, nosy, enquiring, snooping.

insanity NOUN madness, mental illness, craziness, lunacy, mania.

inscribe VERB engrave, etch, carve, cut, incise, stamp, write, dedicate.

insect NOUN Some different kinds of insect: ant, bee, beetle, butterfly, cricket, earwig, fly, gnat, grasshopper, ladybird/ladybug (US), mosquito, moth, wasp.

insert VERB put in, implant, introduce, inject.

insincere ADJECTIVE false, two-faced, deceptive, hypocritical, devious, faithless.

insinuate VERB hint at, suggest, imply, intimate.

insipid ADJECTIVE tasteless, flavourless/flavorless (US), flat, bland, weak, dull, lifeless.

inspect VERB look over, check, examine.

inspire VERB excite, provoke, hearten, cheer, stimulate, stir, arouse, spur.

instal/install (US) VERB fix, set, establish, set up.

instantly ADVERB immediately, without delay, at once, now.

institute VERB found, start, establish, originate.

There are many species of **insect.**

cricket

ladybird/ladybug (US)

bee

instruct VERB **1** order, command, direct, tell, inform. **2** teach, train, educate, coach, tutor.

instrument NOUN tool, utensil, device, contraption, appliance, implement.

insulate VERB protect, pad, cocoon, shield, isolate,

insult NOUN abuse, offence/offense (US), rudeness, slander, snub.

intact ADJECTIVE whole, complete, unharmed.

integrity NOUN honour/honor (US), honesty, goodness, uprightness.

intelligent ADJECTIVE clever, astute, bright, quick, brainy, smart, alert.

intense ADJECTIVE **1** strong, great, very, extreme. *Intense heat.* **2** eager, ardent, passionate.

intercept VERB interrupt, stop, seize, catch, arrest.

interesting ADJECTIVE fascinating, amazing, intriguing, entertaining, amusing, exciting.

interfere VERB pry, intrude, meddle, disturb.

interior ADJECTIVE internal, inside, secret, hidden.

internal ADJECTIVE inner, inside, inward, interior.

interrupt VERB interfere, intrude, disturb.

interval NOUN interlude, break, gap, pause, intermission, recess, delay.

intervene VERB **1** interrupt, intrude, break in, interfere. **2** mediate, arbitrate.

interview NOUN meeting, consultation, talk, conference, press conference.

intolerant ADJECTIVE bigoted, narrow-minded, unfair, impatient, prejudiced, arrogant.

intrepid ADJECTIVE brave, bold, fearless, valiant.

intrigue VERB **1** fascinate, attract. **2** scheme, plot.

introduce VERB **1** start, inaugurate, launch, institute. **2** acquaint, make known, present.

intrude VERB interrupt, meddle, interfere, trespass.

inundate VERB flood, drown, submerge, swamp.

invade VERB overrun, conquer, occupy, march into.

invalid NOUN patient, victim, sufferer.

invaluable ADJECTIVE precious, priceless, valuable.

invent VERB conceive, think up, create, devise.

invention NOUN creation, discovery, development, design, gadget, device.

investigate VERB inquire into, examine, study, inspect, explore, research, probe.

invisible ADJECTIVE out of sight, unseen, hidden, concealed, undetectable.

invite VERB ask, request, summon, call, encourage.

involve VERB **1** mean, result in, require, include, take in. **2** take part in, connect with, concern with. **3** confuse, confound.

irrigate VERB water, inundate, flood.

irritate VERB **1** annoy, upset, bother, enrage, vex. **2** chafe.

isolate VERB insulate, detach, set apart, keep apart, segregate.

item NOUN **1** object, article, thing, detail. **2** entry, report. *An item in the newspaper.*

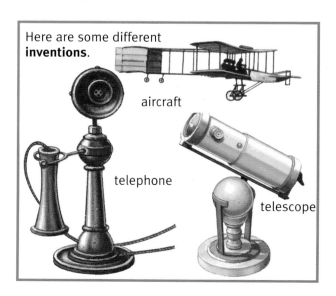

Here are some different **inventions**.

aircraft

telephone

telescope

jab VERB poke, prod, stab, thrust, elbow.

jacket NOUN coat, cover, case, wrapping.

jaded ADJECTIVE exhausted, tired, weary.

jagged ADJECTIVE uneven, ragged, notched, serrated, toothed.

jam NOUN preserve, conserve, jelly, marmalade.

jam VERB **1** stick, clog, block. **2** cram, crush, squeeze, press, block, fill, squeeze.

jangle VERB clatter, clank, clash, ring, rattle.

jar NOUN pot, beaker (UK). *See also* **container**.

javelin NOUN spear. *See also* **weapon**.

jealous ADJECTIVE envious, bitter, resentful, covetous, suspicious, possessive.

jeer VERB mock, sneer, laugh at, scoff, ridicule.

jeopardy NOUN danger, risk, peril, hazard.

jest VERB joke, fool, banter, quip.

jet NOUN spray, fountain, spout, gush.

jewel NOUN gem, precious stone, ornament.

jingle VERB tinkle, chime, jangle.

job NOUN **1** work, occupation, profession, trade, employment, business, position, post. **2** chore, task, pursuit, function.

jocular ADJECTIVE jolly, funny, jovial, witty, humorous. An *opposite word* is serious.

jog VERB **1** run, trot, sprint. **2** prod, jolt, nudge.

join VERB **1** connect, link, unite, fasten, attach. **2** come together, meet, merge. **3** enter, enrol, become a member of, enlist. *Join a club.*

joke NOUN jest, wisecrack, quip, gag, prank, trick.

jostle VERB shove, push, crowd, elbow, jolt.

journal NOUN **1** newspaper, magazine, review, periodical, monthly, weekly. **2** diary, log.

journey NOUN trip, excursion, outing, tour, voyage.

jovial ADJECTIVE cheery, cordial, jolly.

joy NOUN happiness, pleasure, delight, rapture, bliss, glee. *Opposite words* are gloom, sadness, grief.

judge VERB assess, decide, appraise, evaluate, consider, examine, convict, sentence, adjudicate.

juggle VERB conjure, manipulate, rig, rearrange.

jump VERB **1** bounce, leap, bound, hurdle, pounce, vault, hop. **2** start, flinch, wince. *You made me jump.*

jumpy ADJECTIVE nervous, fidgety, tense.

junk NOUN rubbish, trash, scrap, garbage, waste.

just ADJECTIVE fair, unbiased, objective, impartial,

just ADVERB exactly, precisely.

jut VERB protrude, stick out, project, extend.

These pictures show some different kinds of **job.**

surgeon

office worker

photographer

electrician

Kk

keen ADJECTIVE **1** eager, enthusiasic, ardent. **2** clever, perceptive, sharp, penetrating. *A keen sense of smell.*

keep VERB **1** hold, guard, detain. **2** look after, save, mind, support. **3** save, put away, store. **4** obey, follow, observe. **5** continue. *She keeps asking questions.* **6** remain, stay. *Keep quiet.*

keep off VERB stay away. *Keep off the grass.*

keep on VERB continue, persist.

keep out VERB not to enter. *Keep out!*

key ADJECTIVE important, principal, essential, crucial. A word that sounds similar is quay.

key NOUN guide, clue, lead.

kick NOUN excitement, stimulation, thrill.

kick VERB boot, strike with foot, punt.

kidnap VERB abduct, capture, seize, hijack.

kill VERB slay, put to death, murder, massacre, assassinate, slaughter, destroy, put to sleep.

kind ADJECTIVE good-natured, friendly, considerate, thoughtful, generous, helpful, gentle, amiable. NOUN type, sort, species, breed, make, category.

kindle VERB set light to, start burning, ignite, inflame, stir, thrill.

kindness NOUN tenderness, good nature, generosity, friendliness.

kiss VERB embrace, caress, greet, smooch.

kit NOUN equipment, gear.

knack NOUN skill, ability, facility, flair, gift.

knave NOUN rascal, scoundrel, rogue, scamp.

knock VERB hit, strike, beat, rap, tap, smite.

knot VERB tie, loop, entwine, secure.

know VERB **1** recognize, identify, be acquainted with. **2** remember, recall, recollect. **3** understand, perceive, comprehend, see, realize.

know-how NOUN knowledge, talent, ability.

knowing ADJECTIVE astute, perceptive, shrewd, knowledgeable. An *opposite word* is ignorant.

knowledge NOUN experience, understanding, learning, education, wisdom, facts, information.

kudos NOUN honour/honor (US), praise, fame.

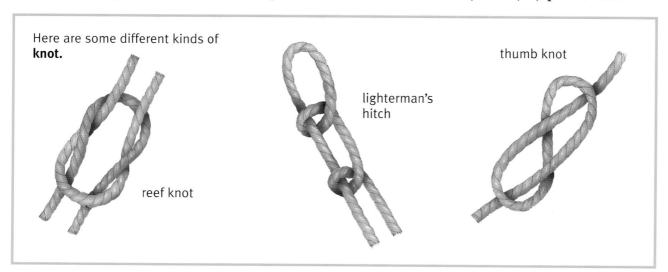

Here are some different kinds of **knot.**

reef knot

lighterman's hitch

thumb knot

label NOUN badge, tag, ticket.

labour/labor (US) NOUN work, job, chore, task, slog, toil, effort, exertion, drudgery.

lack NOUN shortage, need, scarcity, dearth, want.

lag VERB linger, dawdle, loiter.

lair NOUN nest, den, burrow, earth, hole.

lake NOUN loch, lagoon, mere, reservoir.

lame ADJECTIVE **1** limping, disabled, crippled, hobbling. **2** weak, poor. *A lame excuse.*

lament VERB mourn, feel sorry for, grieve, sorrow.

lamp NOUN lantern, torch, flare, light.

lance NOUN spear, javelin, shaft, scalpel, lancet.

lance VERB cut, penetrate, pierce.

land NOUN **1** earth, ground, soil. **2** country, nation, district, region, province. VERB come down to earth, alight, arrive, touch down, go ashore, disembark.

landscape NOUN scenery, view, panorama, countryside. *A beautiful landscape.*

language NOUN speech, dialect, tongue, talk, jargon.

lanky ADJECTIVE tall, gangly.

lap NOUN orbit, circuit, loop, circle.

lapse NOUN error, fault, failing, slip.

lapse VERB slip, slide, sink, decline. deteriorate, die.

large ADJECTIVE big, sizeable, bulky, great, ample, broad, fat, huge, vast, massive.

last ADJECTIVE final, concluding, ultimate.

last VERB endure, stay, go on, remain, continue, survive. *Opposite words* are fade, vanish, cease.

late ADJECTIVE overdue, delayed, slow, behind-time, tardy. *Opposite words* are early, prompt, punctual.

lately ADVERB recently, latterly.

lather NOUN foam, bubbles, froth, suds.

laugh VERB chuckle, giggle, snigger, chortle, titter smile, guffaw. An *opposite word* is cry.

launch VERB **1** send off, propel, set in motion. **2** begin, start, inaugurate, embark on. *They launched a new magazine.*

lavish ADJECTIVE plentiful, luxuriant, abundant, profuse, liberal, generous, extravagant. An *opposite word* is frugal.

law NOUN rule, regulation, edict, decree, statute, legislation.

lawyer NOUN solicitor (UK), barrister (UK), advocate, counsel, attorney.

lax ADJECTIVE careless, negligent, slack, relaxed. *Opposite words* are strict, rigid.

lay VERB put, set down, place, leave. *Lay the basket on the ground.* **2** arrange, present. **3** produce an egg.

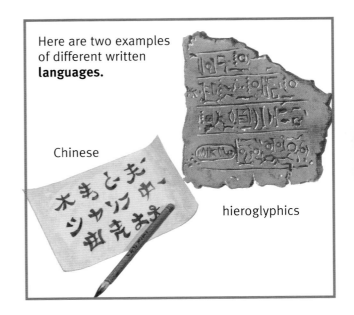

Here are two examples of different written **languages.**

Chinese

hieroglyphics

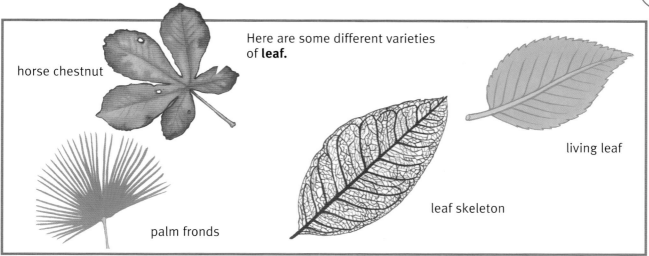

horse chestnut

Here are some different varieties of **leaf.**

living leaf

leaf skeleton

palm fronds

lay on VERB supply.

lay out VERB display, exhibit, arrange.

layer NOUN seam, stratum, thickness, coating.

lazy ADJECTIVE idle, indolent, work-shy, slothful.

lead VERB **1** conduct, guide, steer, take. An *opposite word* is follow. **2** be in charge of, rule, command, manage, direct. **3** outstrip, surpass.

leader NOUN chief, ruler, commander, guide.

leaf NOUN **1** page, sheet. **2** part of a plant or tree.

league NOUN union, alliance, association, federation, group, category.

leak VERB drip, ooze, percolate, dribble, trickle, seep. *The shower leaks.*

lean ADJECTIVE thin, slim, scrawny.

lean VERB **1** bend, slant, tilt, slope, list, tend. *The Leaning Tower of Pisa.* **2** prop, rest, recline.

leap VERB **1** jump, spring, skip, vault, bound. **2** rise, increase.

learn VERB discover, find out, hear, memorize, understand, comprehend, grasp.

learned ADJECTIVE erudite, educated, scholarly. An *opposite word* is ignorant.

leave VERB **1** depart, quit, go. **2** abandon, forsake, desert. **3** put down, place. **4** bequeath, entrust.

lecture NOUN talk, discourse, address, sermon.

legal ADJECTIVE lawful, legitimate, permitted, allowed, above board. An *opposite word* is illegal.

legible ADJECTIVE readable, clear, decipherable.

leisure NOUN time off, spare time, freedom, liberty, holiday.

lend VERB loan, grant, give, lease.

lengthen VERB extend, elongate, stretch, prolong.

lenient ADJECTIVE mild, gentle, tolerant, forgiving, merciful, clement. An *opposite word* is harsh.

lessen VERB cut, reduce, decrease, shrink, dwindle. *Opposite words* are increase, grow. A word that sounds similar is lesson.

let VERB **1** allow, permit, consent. An *opposite word* is forbid. **2** hire, lease, rent.

level ADJECTIVE **1** flat, smooth, even, horizontal. *A level teaspoon of sugar.* **2** equal. *The buildings are level with each other.*

liberate VERB free, set free, release. An *opposite word* is imprison.

liberty NOUN freedom, release, emancipation.

lie VERB **1** tell a lie, fib. **2** be located, be situated. **3** recline, sprawl. *He lay on the sofa.*

lift VERB hoist, raise, pick up.

light ADJECTIVE **1** lightweight, buoyant. **2** bright. **3** faint, pale.

light NOUN Some different kinds of light: candle light, daylight, electric light, firelight, gas light, lamp light, moonlight, street light, torch light, sunlight. VERB **1** kindle, set fire to, burn, ignite. **2** illuminate, lighten, brighten.

like ADJECTIVE similar, alike, identical. VERB **1** love, adore, have a soft spot for, be fond of, admire, respect, cherish. **2** prefer, choose, wish for, want.

likely ADJECTIVE probable, expected, liable.

likeness NOUN similarity, resemblance, image, portrait.

limit VERB restrict, curb, confine, hinder.

limp ADJECTIVE hobble, stumble, shuffle.

linger VERB dawdle, loiter, delay, hang about/hang around (US), tarry, lag. An *opposite word* is hurry.

link VERB connect, join, unite, bind, fasten, attach.

liquid ADJECTIVE fluid, flowing, runny.

lithe ADJECTIVE flexible, supple, pliable.

litter NOUN rubbish, debris, junk, waste, garbage.

little ADJECTIVE **1** small, compact, tiny, minute, wee. **2** brief, fleeting.

live VERB **1** exist, survive. **2** dwell, reside, inhabit, occupy.

livelihood NOUN living, occupation. *See also* **job**.

lively 1 ADJECTIVE energetic, active, sprightly, animated, agile, frisky, busy, bustling. An *opposite word* is lazy. **2** bright, vivid. *Lively patterns.*

livid ADJECTIVE enraged. *See also* **angry**.

load VERB fill, pack, burden, pile up, encumber.

loathe VERB despise, abhor. *See also* **hate**.

local ADJECTIVE district, regional, provincial, parish, community.

locate VERB **1** discover, detect, unearth, find. **2** situate, establish, place.

lock NOUN and VERB bolt, latch, padlock. An *opposite word* is unlock.

lodge VERB **1** stay, reside, dwell, inhabit, settle, shelter. **2** fix, get stuck in. *A fishbone lodged in his throat.*

lonely ADJECTIVE **1** lonesome, unhappy. **2** remote, isolated, solitary, out of the way.

long ADJECTIVE lengthy, extensive, extended, prolonged, protracted, endless.

long for VERB want, wish, yearn for, fancy, crave.

look VERB **1** gaze, see, regard, watch, stare, peer, observe, notice. **2** seem, appear.

look after VERB protect.

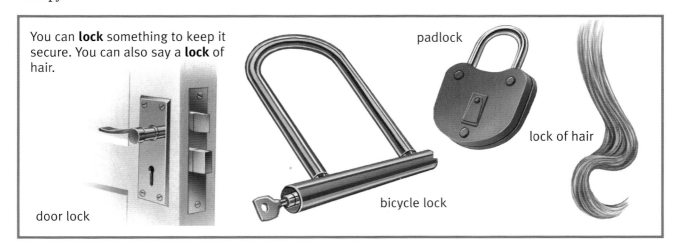

You can **lock** something to keep it secure. You can also say a **lock** of hair.

door lock

padlock

bicycle lock

lock of hair

look for VERB search, try to find.

look up to VERB admire, respect. *He's always looked up to his older brother.*

loom VERB appear, threaten, menace.

loop NOUN circle, noose, ring, hoop.

loose ADJECTIVE **1** flabby, baggy, slack, hanging, not tight, wobbly. *My little sister has another loose tooth.* **2** free, unattached. *The horse got loose and nearly ran out into the road.* **3** vague, indefinite, inaccurate.

lose VERB **1** misplace, mislay. **2** fail, to be beaten, be defeated.

lot NOUN **1** plenty, abundance. **2** fate, fortune.

loud ADJECTIVE **1** noisy, deafening, earpiercing, shrill, raucous. **2** strong, clear, powerful. *She has got such a loud voice.* **3** showy, brash, garish. *Opposite words* are **1**, **2** quiet, soft. **3** subdued, tasteful. Some different sounds: bang, boom, crash, howl, roar, shriek, uproar.

lovable ADJECTIVE dear, likeable, attractive, endearing, charming, sweet, amiable, winning.

love VERB adore, like, worship. *See also* **like**.

lovely ADJECTIVE *See* **beautiful**.

low ADJECTIVE squat, shallow, short, stunted.

lower ADJECTIVE inferior, lesser.

lower VERB **1** let down, fall, descend, sink. **2** reduce, lessen, decrease.

loyal ADJECTIVE faithful, staunch, true, trustworthy. *Opposite words* are disloyal, treacherous.

lubricate VERB grease, oil, smoothe, ease.

lucid ADJECTIVE clear, plain, easy to understand, intelligible.

luck NOUN fortune, chance, fate, accident, coincidence, success.

lucky ADJECTIVE fortunate, favoured/favored (US), happy, timely.

lug VERB drag, heave, tow, tug, haul, pull.

There are many symbols and tokens of **love.**

engagement ring
(a token of love)

heart
(a symbol of love)

Romeo and Juliet fell in love

luggage NOUN baggage, belongings, suitcase.

lump NOUN **1** swelling, bump, tumour. **2** chunk, clump, block, mass, piece.

lunge VERB thrust, attack, charge at, pounce.

lure VERB attract, tempt, ensnare, seduce.

lurid ADJECTIVE shocking, startling, grisly, graphic, sensational, dismal.

lurk VERB prowl, slink, snoop, skulk.

lush ADJECTIVE rich, abundant, luxuriant, prolific, green.

lusty ADJECTIVE robust, tough, sturdy, vigorous, strong, rugged.

luxury NOUN comfort, ease, pleasure, opulence, splendour/splendor (US).

macabre ADJECTIVE hideous, gruesome, grim, horrible, sinister.

macaroni NOUN pasta. Some different kinds of pasta: cannelloni, conchiglie, fettucini.

machine NOUN apparatus, instrument, tool, contrivance, engine, machinery.

mad ADJECTIVE **1** insane, deranged, lunatic, mentally ill, unbalanced. **2** angry. **3** stupid, irrational, foolish, absurd.

magazine NOUN periodical, journal, review.

magic NOUN sorcery, wizardry, witchcraft, enchantment, spells.

magnificent NOUN grand, majestic, impressive, splendid, imposing.

magnify VERB enlarge, increase, amplify, boost, increase. An *opposite word* is reduce.

mail NOUN **1** post, correspondence, letters.

main ADJECTIVE principal, key, chief, basic, first, leading, most important.

maintain VERB **1** look after, care for, support, provide for. **2** state, insist, assert, declare, affirm.

majestic ADJECTIVE splendid, imposing, grand, noble, dignified.

major ADJECTIVE leading, important, bigger, larger, chief. An *opposite word* is minor.

majority NOUN most, bulk, mass, greater number.

make VERB **1** create, invent. **2** build, construct, put up. **3** manufacture, put together, form, mould/mold (US), shape. **4** add up, total, equal. **5** force, oblige, compel. **6** cause, produce, bring about. **7** prepare. **8** compose, comprise. **9** get, earn. *He makes a lot of money.*

make for VERB go towards.

make believe NOUN fantasy.

makeshift ADJECTIVE rough and ready, temporary.

male NOUN masculine, manly.

malicious ADJECTIVE spiteful, bitter, hateful, bad, evil. *They've been spreading malicious stories.*

maltreat VERB abuse, injure, ill-treat, harm, hurt, bully. An *opposite word* is help.

mammoth ADJECTIVE huge, enormous, massive, giant.

Here are three very different kinds of **machine.**

bicycle

computer

gears

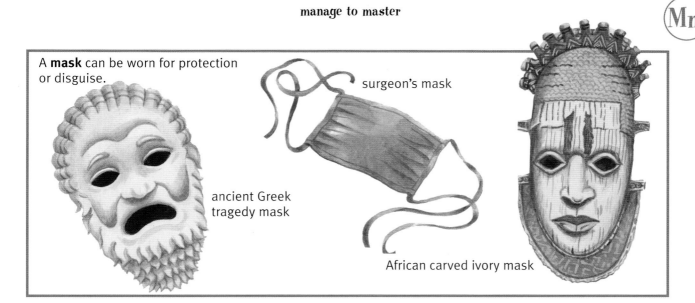

A **mask** can be worn for protection or disguise.

ancient Greek tragedy mask

surgeon's mask

African carved ivory mask

manage VERB **1** control, run, direct, be in charge of, look after, administer. **2** succeed, accomplish. **3** cope with, get along.

manager NOUN boss, director, controller, overseer, chief.

mangle VERB maim, disfigure, twist, maul.

mania NOUN craze, obsession, fad, enthusiasm.

manifest VERB show, reveal, declare, signify.

manner NOUN style, way, fashion. *He has a rude manner.* A word that sounds similar is manor.

manners plural NOUN conduct, behaviour/behavior (US).

manual ADJECTIVE automatic, by hand, hand-operated.

manual NOUN handbook, guide.

manufacture VERB make, produce, fabricate, build, turn out.

many ADJECTIVE numerous, various, a large number, sundry. An *opposite word* is few.

map NOUN chart, plan, diagram.

mar VERB damage, spoil, blemish, disfigure, scar.

march VERB **1** stride, walk, step out, trek. **2** parade, demonstration.

margin NOUN edge, limit, verge, border, rim.

marine ADJECTIVE maritime, naval, oceanic, nautical.

mariner NOUN sailor, seafarer, deckhand, seadog.

mark VERB **1** notice, observe, note, see. **2** scratch, stain, blot. **3** grade, assess.

maroon VERB abandon, desert, leave.

marriage NOUN wedding, wedlock, matrimony, nuptials. An *opposite word* is divorce.

marry VERB get married, wed, join in matrimony.

marsh NOUN swamp, bog, morass, quagmire.

martial ADJECTIVE military, warlike, militant, belligerent. An *opposite word* is peaceful.

marvel NOUN wonder, spectacle, miracle.

marvellous/marvelous (US) ADJECTIVE wonderful, spectacular, splendid, fabulous, extraordinary.

mask NOUN conceal, disguise, camouflage, cloak, veil, cover.

mass NOUN **1** load, lump, pile, quantity, mound. *A mass of paperwork.* **2** majority.

massive ADJECTIVE huge, bulky, heavy, enormous.

master VERB **1** control, tame, overcome, defeat. **2** learn, understand, grasp, get the hang of.

match VERB **1** equal, copy, resemble, measure up to. **2** go with, suit, tone with.

match NOUN contest, competition, game.

mate NOUN companion, friend, pal, colleague, spouse, husband, wife. VERB breed, pair, couple.

material NOUN **1** cloth, fabric, textile, stuff. **2** substance, matter, stuff. **3** information.

mathematics NOUN Words used in mathematics: **1** add up, divide, multiply, subtract, take away, times. **2** calculate, count, measure, work out.

matrimony NOUN marriage, wedlock, nuptials.

matted ADJECTIVE tangled, twisted.

matter NOUN **1** substance, material. **2** problem, difficulty, worry, trouble. **3** topic, subject.

mature ADJECTIVE adult, grown-up, fully grown, developed, ripe. An *opposite word* is immature.

maul VERB injure, hurt, beat, deform, abuse.

meadow NOUN field, paddock, pasture, grassland.

meagre/meager (US) ADJECTIVE poor, scanty, sparse, insubstantial.

meal NOUN **1** snack, banquet, feast **2** breakfast, brunch lunch, tea (UK), dinner, supper, picnic.

mean ADJECTIVE **1** stingy, selfish. **2** cruel, unkind.

mean VERB **1** stand for, convey, indicate. *What does this Italian word mean?* **2** intend, plan. *I meant to give you this.*

measurement NOUN size, dimension, height, depth, width, volume.

mechanism NOUN **1** motor, machinery, workings, contrivance. **2** method, means, procedure, functioning.

meddle VERB interfere, tamper, butt in.

media NOUN press, newspapers, radio, television.

medicine NOUN drug, medication, remedy, potion, tablet, pill, suppository, injection.

mediocre ADJECTIVE average, ordinary, middling, medium, inferior, commonplace.

medium ADJECTIVE average, normal, mediocre.

medley NOUN mixture, assortment, variety, collection, miscellany, jumble.

meek ADJECTIVE humble, modest, lowly, unassuming, docile. An *opposite word* is arrogant.

meet VERB **1** join, come together, converge. **2** encounter, run into, bump into. **3** gather.

meeting NOUN assembly, gathering, congregation.

melancholy NOUN sad, unhappy, dejected, gloomy.

mellow ADJECTIVE mature, mild, melodious, smooth.

melt VERB thaw, dissolve, liquefy.

memorable ADJECTIVE unforgettable, famous, celebrated, outstanding.

memory NOUN remembrance, recall, recollection.

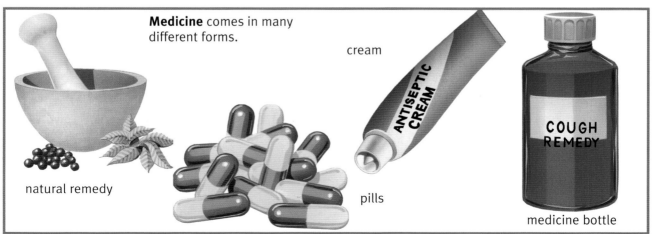

Medicine comes in many different forms.

cream

natural remedy

pills

medicine bottle

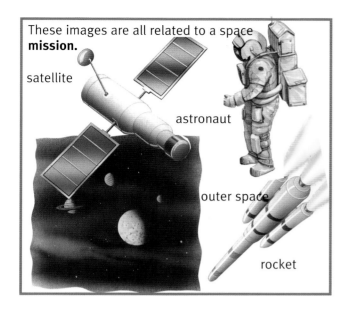

These images are all related to a space **mission.**

satellite

astronaut

outer space

rocket

menace VERB threaten, frighten, intimidate.

mend VERB repair, fix, restore, rectify, heal.

mental ADJECTIVE **1** intellectual, theoretical, abstract. *Mental powers.* **2** insane.

merchandise NOUN goods, produce, wares.

merchant NOUN trader, dealer, retailer, shopkeeper, wholesaler, vendor.

merciless ADJECTIVE pitiless, callous, cruel, ruthless, unforgiving.

mercy NOUN pity, forgiveness, compassion, clemency, kindness. An *opposite word* is cruelty.

merge VERB combine, blend, amalgamate.

merry ADJECTIVE jolly, cheerful, happy, jovial.

mess NOUN **1** clutter, disorder, confusion, jumble, muddle, chaos.

message NOUN letter, note, missive.

metal NOUN Some different metals: brass, bronze, copper, chromium, gold, iron, lead, mercury.

method NOUN system, way, manner, technique.

middle NOUN centre/center (US), heart, midpoint, core.

mighty ADJECTIVE strong, powerful, dynamic.

mild ADJECTIVE gentle, pleasant, warm, slight.

militant ADJECTIVE aggressive, fighting, belligerent, contending.

mimic VERB ape, copy, imitate, impersonate.

mince VERB dice, grind, chop, cut up, hash.

mind NOUN **1** brain, understanding, wits, intelligence. **2** opinion. *She changed her mind.* VERB **1** worry, care. *Do you mind if I open the window?* **2** care for, look after. *She is minding the children.* **3** Pay attention, obey, listen to, heed. *Mind your mother!*

mindless ADJECTIVE thoughtless, stupid.

mineral NOUN Some common minerals: alabaster, asbestos, blacklead, borax, calamine, calcite.

mingle VERB mix, combine, blend, merge, join in.

minimize VERB **1** diminish, reduce. **2** belittle, discount, play down.

minimum NOUN least, smallest, slightest.

minor ADJECTIVE smaller, inferior, lesser, unimportant, trivial.

minute ADJECTIVE little, small, tiny, miniscule.

mirth NOUN laughter, fun, jollity, merriment.

misbehave VERB disobey, be naughty.

mischief NOUN naughtiness, pranks, harm, injury.

miserable ADJECTIVE **1** sad, unhappy, wretched. **2** awful, bad, poor.

misery NOUN grief, distress, sorrow, sadness.

misfortune NOUN bad luck, adversity, hardship, disaster,trouble.

mislay VERB lose, misplace.

mislead VERB trick, delude, deceive, lead astray.

miss VERB **1** avoid, dodge, steer clear of. **2** pine for. **3** omit, skip, leave out.

mission NOUN undertaking, assignment, errand, duty, job, business.

mist NOUN fog, vapour/vapor (US), cloud, haze. A word that sounds similar is missed.

mistake NOUN error, blunder, fault, gaffe, slip.

mistaken ADJECTIVE incorrect, inexact, wrong, erroneous. An *opposite word* is correct.

mistreat VERB abuse, harm, hurt, batter, maltreat.

misty ADJECTIVE hazy, dim, fuzzy, unclear.

mix VERB blend, combine, mingle, shuffle, stir.

mixture NOUN blend, combination, variety, assortment, miscellany.

moan VERB groan, lament, wail, whimper, grumble, whine.

mob NOUN crowd, throng, rabble, flock, group.

mock VERB tease, ridicule, taunt, make fun of.

model NOUN **1** pattern, prototype, copy, replica. **2** style, version, design, type.

moderate ADJECTIVE normal, ordinary, medium.

modern ADJECTIVE up-to-date, fashionable, new, recent.

modest ADJECTIVE humble, shy, bashful.

modify VERB amend, change, alter, revise, adjust.

moist ADJECTIVE damp, humid, dank, wet, clammy.

Here are two forms of **money.**

banknotes/ bills (US)

coins

molest VERB torment, tease, pester, annoy, harry, vex, upset, badger, harm, hurt.

moment NOUN second, tick, instant, jiffy.

momentous ADJECTIVE important, notable, outstanding, serious.

monarch NOUN king, queen, emperor, empress.

money NOUN **1** cash, coin, banknote (UK)/bill (US), currency, change. **2** wealth, fortune.

monotonous ADJECTIVE boring, tedious, dull, uninteresting, repetitive.

monster NOUN ogre, beast, vampire, werewolf.

month NOUN January, February, March, April, May, June, July, August, September, October, November, December.

mood NOUN temper, humour/ humor (US), feeling, state of mind, *He is in a really bad mood.*

moody ADJECTIVE temperamental, morose, peevish, perverse, sullen.

moor VERB fasten, fix, berth, tie up. *Moor the boat.*

moral ADJECTIVE honest, good, virtuous.

more ADJECTIVE additional, extra, greater, further. ADVERB **1** again. **2** longer, better.

moreover ADVERB also, in addition, besides, also.

morose ADJECTIVE sullen, sulky, brooding, moody.

morsel NOUN scrap, bit, piece, fragment, fraction.

mortal ADJECTIVE **1** human, perishable, temporal, feeble. *We are mere mortals.* **2** deadly, fatal, lethal.

mortuary NOUN morgue, necropolis, cemetery.

mostly ADVERB mainly, principally, usually.

motherly ADJECTIVE maternal, loving, caring, gentle, tender.

motion NOUN **1** movement, action, change. **2** proposal, suggestion.

motive NOUN reason, cause, purpose, inspiration.

motto NOUN axiom, saying, adage, maxim, slogan.

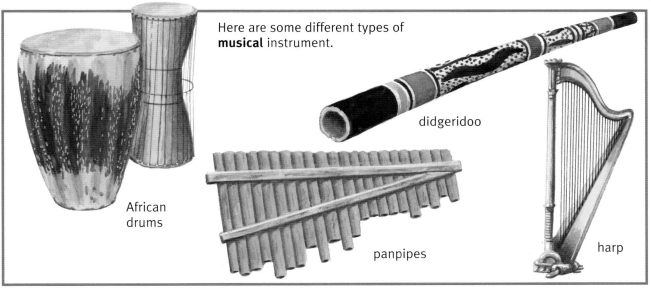

Here are some different types of **musical** instrument.

African drums

didgeridoo

panpipes

harp

mould/mold (US) VERB form, model, shape.

mouldy/moldy (US) ADJECTIVE bad, putrid, musty, off, stale, decaying.

mound NOUN pile, hillock, rise, embankment.

mount VERB 1 get on, clamber on, ascend, go up, rise. 2 exhibit, display.

mountain NOUN peak, summit, volcano, elevation.

mourn VERB grieve, sorrow, lament, regret.

mournful NOUN sad, unhappy, sombre.

mouth NOUN opening, aperture, orifice, estuary.

move VERB 1 leave, go away, depart, quit. 2 go forward, proceed, advance, travel, walk. 3 run, race, gallop, rush. 4 stir, budge, shift. 5 take away, remove, disturb, carry, transport.

movement NOUN 1 action, motion, move, change. 2 party, group, cause, crusade. 3 section of music.

moving ADJECTIVE stirring, emotional, touching.

mow VERB cut, crop, scythe.

muddle VERB 1 mix up, tangle, jumble. 2 bewilder, confuse.

multiply VERB increase, grow, spread, extend, reproduce, breed.

murky ADJECTIVE dark, gloomy, cloudy, overcast.

murmur VERB whisper, mutter, mumble.

muse VERB ponder, think about, meditate, reflect.

music NOUN tune, melody.

musical ADJECTIVE melodic, harmonious, dulcet.

musician NOUN player, performer, singer, vocalist.

mute ADJECTIVE dumb, speechless, voiceless, silent, quiet. An *opposite word* is loud.

mutiny NOUN rebellion, uprising, riot, revolt, insurrection.

mutter VERB mumble, murmur, grouse, complain.

mutual ADJECTIVE common, reciprocal, joint, shared.

mysterious ADJECTIVE 1 strange, puzzling.

musical notes

nag VERB pester, annoy, badger, go on about.

nail VERB fix, peg, fasten, hammer in.

naive ADJECTIVE innocent, simple, unsophisticated, gullible.

naked ADJECTIVE nude, bare, unclothed.

name NOUN **1** title, label, designation. **2** reputation, character, fame. *He's making a name for himself.* VERB call, christen, term, entitle, dub. **2** indicate, specify.

nap VERB sleep, doze, snooze, rest.

narrate VERB tell, describe, recount, relate.

narrow ADJECTIVE fine, thin, slender, limited, tight.

narrow-minded ADJECTIVE biased, bigoted, intolerant. An *opposite word* is broad-minded.

nasty ADJECTIVE **1** bad, dreadful, horrible, offensive, unpleasant, offensive. **2** dirty, filthy, foul. **3** unfriendly, unkind rude, mean, vicious.

natter VERB chatter, gossip.

natural ADJECTIVE **1** normal, usual, common. **2** inborn, instinctive, hereditary. **3** frank, open ,genuine, unsophisticated, artless.

naughty ADJECTIVE, unruly, disobedient, mischievous.

nausea NOUN sickness, queasiness, squeamishness.

naval ADJECTIVE maritime, nautical, marine, seafaring.

navigate VERB sail, pilot, steer, guide, direct.

nearly ADVERB almost, not quite, practically.

neat ADJECTIVE smart, tidy, orderly, spruce.

need NOUN necessity, shortage.

need VERB **1** want, require, call for. **2** rely on, depend on, count on.

needy ADJECTIVE poor, needful, penniless, destitute. An *opposite word* is rich.

neglect VERB ignore, overlook, forget.

negotiate VERB bargain, haggle, mediate, deal, talk about, discuss.

neighbourhood/neighborhood (US) NOUN district, area, locality, surroundings.

nervous ADJECTIVE anxious, fidgety, edgy.

nest NOUN burrow, den, lair.

net NOUN mesh, net, trap, snare.

neutral ADJECTIVE **1** impartial, unbiased, fair, even-minded. **2** dull, mediocre.

never ADVERB not ever, at no time, under no circumstances. An *opposite word* is always.

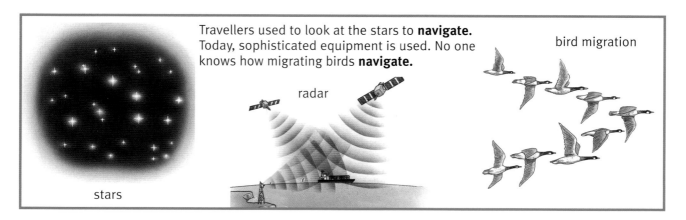

Travellers used to look at the stars to **navigate.** Today, sophisticated equipment is used. No one knows how migrating birds **navigate.**

bird migration

radar

stars

Here are some different kinds of **nut.**

coconut

walnut

horse chestnut

new ADJECTIVE **1** unused, fresh. **2** novel, original, unfamiliar. **3** modern, recent, up-to-date, latest.

news NOUN information, report, bulletin, account.

nibble VERB bite, peck, gnaw. *See also* **eat.**

nice ADJECTIVE **1** beautiful, fine, lovely, attractive, pretty, pleasant, good. **2** delicious, tasty, scrumptious **3** friendly, warm, kind, likeable, considerate, good-natured. **4** comfortable, cosy.

nimble ADJECTIVE spry, agile, nippy, lively, swift.

nip VERB cut, bite, pinch.

nobility NOUN **1** aristocracy, gentry, nobles. **2** dignity, majesty, eminence, worthiness.

nod VERB **1** beckon, signal, indicate, gesture, agree. **2** doze, sleep.

noisy ADJECTIVE loud, rowdy, deafening, boisterous. *Opposite words* are quiet, silent.

nomadic ADJECTIVE wandering, roving, migratory.

none PRONOUN not one, not any, nobody.

nonsense NOUN rubbish, drivel, gobbledegook.

nook NOUN corner, alcove, niche, recess.

normal ADJECTIVE common, ordinary, usual.

nostalgic ADJECTIVE longing, yearning, homesick, wistful, sentimental.

notable ADJECTIVE remarkable, outstanding, famous, notable, momentous.

note NOUN **1** letter, message. **2** signal, symbol.

note VERB **1** remark, notice, observe. **2** record, write down.

notice VERB see, note, perceive, detect, observe.

notify VERB inform, tell, announce, declare, advise.

nought NOUN zero, nil, nothing, naught.

nourish VERB feed, support, sustain.

novel ADJECTIVE new, fresh, original, innovative, uncommon, unusual.

novice NOUN beginner, learner, pupil, apprentice.

now ADVERB **1** instantly, at this moment, immediately. **2** at this time, at present.

nude ADJECTIVE naked, bare, undressed, unclothed.

nudge VERB elbow, prod, poke, push.

nuisance NOUN bother, pest, trouble, worry, plague.

numb ADJECTIVE insensible, dead, frozen, unfeeling.

number NOUN figure, amount, quantity, total.

numerous ADJECTIVE many, several, abundant.

nurse VERB care for, mind, tend, look after.

nut NOUN Some different kinds of nut: almond, brazil, cashew, chestnut, cobnut, coconut.

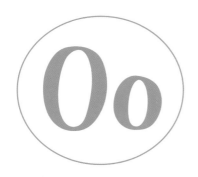

oath NOUN **1** promise, pledge, vow.

obedient ADJECTIVE well-behaved, law-abiding, deferential.

object NOUN **1** article, thing, item. **2** target, purpose, mission, reason.

object VERB complain about, disapprove, oppose.

objectionable ADJECTIVE offensive, disagreeable, unpleasant.

obliterate VERB wipe out, erase, destroy, annihilate.

obnoxious ADJECTIVE disagreeable, disgusting, repulsive, unpleasant, horrid.

obscene ADJECTIVE foul, dirty, unclean, indecent, smutty, coarse. An *opposite word* is decent.

obscure ADJECTIVE **1** dim, vague, hazy, indistinct. **2** puzzling, confusing. **3** little known.

observe VERB **1** watch, notice, perceive. **2** remark, mention. **3** keep, adhere to, comply.

observer NOUN viewer, watcher, spectator, onlooker, bystander.

obsolete ADJECTIVE antiquated, old, out-of-date, disused.

obstacle NOUN hindrance, barrier, obstruction.

obstinate ADJECTIVE stubborn, pig-headed, dogged, mulish, headstrong.

obtain VERB get, acquire, gain, achieve, earn.

obvious ADJECTIVE plain, clear, apparent, evident, unmistakable.

occasion NOUN **1** occurrence, event, incident. **2** opportunity, suitable time, chance.

occasional ADJECTIVE infrequent, rare, periodic.

occupation NOUN **1** job, work, business, employment. *See also* **job. 2** activity, hobby. **3** possession, tenancy, occupancy.

occupied ADJECTIVE **1** settled, populated. **2** busy.

occupy VERB **1** inhabit, live in, dwell, own, possess, keep. **2** engage, busy. **3** invade, capture. **4** use, fill. *Is this seat occupied?*

occur VERB happen, take place.

occurrence NOUN happening, event, incident.

ocean NOUN sea. Some famous seas and oceans: Bering Sea, Black Sea, Caspian Sea, Irish Sea, Antarctic Ocean, Atlantic Ocean, Arctic Ocean.

odd ADJECTIVE **1** curious, funny, peculiar, quaint, unusual, strange, weird. **2** extra, spare, unmatched.

odious ADJECTIVE unpleasant, objectionable, loathsome, disgusting, hateful.

odour/odor (US) NOUN smell, aroma, fragrance, stench.

The **ocean** is full of wildlife.

Atlantic Ocean

Pacific Ocean

Indian Ocean

Arctic Ocean

Antarctic Ocean

offend VERB **1** displease, insult, annoy, hurt.

offensive ADJECTIVE unpleasant, rude, hurtful, insulting.

offence/offense (US) NOUN **1** crime, sin, misdeed. **2** insult, attack, injury.

offer VERB propose, put forward, present, submit. **2** volunteer.

office NOUN **1** bureau, work place. **2** responsibility, duty, job, position.

official ADJECTIVE authorized, formal, authoritative, proper, approved.

officious ADJECTIVE meddlesome, self-important, pushy.

offspring NOUN child, children, heir, successor, descendant.

often ADVERB frequently, again and again, repeatedly. *Opposite words* are rarely, seldom.

oil NOUN grease, fat, lubricant.

old ADJECTIVE **1** aged, elderly **2** out-of-date, old-fashioned. **3** stale. **4** worn out, shabby. **5** last, previous, former.

omen NOUN sign, warning, premonition, augury.

ominous ADJECTIVE menacing, foreboding.

omit VERB leave out, exclude, drop, overlook.

once ADVERB **1** one time. **2** in the past, previously, formerly.

ooze VERB leak, exude, seep.

opaque ADJECTIVE clouded, murky, filmy, unclear, obscure. *An opposite word* is transparent.

open ADJECTIVE **1** frank, candid, sincere. **2** unfastened, unlocked, uncovered. **3** exposed, unsheltered. VERB **1** unlock, unfasten, undo. **2** begin, start.

opening NOUN **1** gap, crack, hole, space, aperture. **2** beginning, start, launch. **3** opportunity.

operate VERB use, work, handle, drive, manipulate. *Do you know how to operate a VCR?*

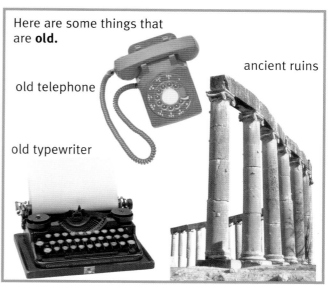

Here are some things that are **old**.

old telephone

ancient ruins

old typewriter

opinion NOUN view, thought, idea, belief, feeling.

opponent NOUN rival, competitor, adversary, challenger, enemy, foe. *An opposite word* is ally.

opportunity NOUN chance, occasion, break, scope.

oppose VERB resist, combat, stand against, confront, withstand, defy, fight.

opposite ADJECTIVE **1** facing, fronting. **2** opposed, adverse, conflicting, different contrary.

opposition NOUN **1** hostility, resistance, antagonism, obstacle. **2** rival, opponent.

oppress VERB overpower, overwhelm, crush, harass.

oppressive ADJECTIVE **1** stifling, airless, muggy, close. **2** tyrannical, overwhelming, cruel, savage.

opt VERB choose, select, prefer.

optimistic ADJECTIVE hopeful, cheerful, confident, bright. *An opposite word* is pessimistic.

option NOUN choice, selection, possibility, alternative.

opulent ADJECTIVE rich, wealthy, prosperous, affluent. *An opposite word* is poor.

oral ADJECTIVE spoken, said, verbal, unwritten.

oration NOUN speech, address, lecture, declamation.

orbit VERB circle, revolve. *Earth orbits the Sun.*

ordeal NOUN trial, torment, test, trouble, hardship.

order NOUN **1** command, regulation, law, rule. **2** plan, pattern, arrangement. **3** society, association, community. *An order of monks.* VERB **1** tell, command, instruct, direct. **2** arrange, control, classify. **3** ask for, send for.

ordinary ADJECTIVE usual, common, normal, customary, everyday, average, plain, simple.

organize VERB arrange, order, establish, set up.

organization NOUN **1** group, establishment, institute, society. **2** order, plan, pattern, system.

origin NOUN start, beginning, source, root, cause.

original ADJECTIVE **1** first. **2** new, fresh, novel imaginative.

ornament NOUN decoration, adornment, trinket.

ornate ADJECTIVE decorated, elaborate, adorned.

orthodox ADJECTIVE conventional, accepted, traditional, recognized.

oscillate VERB swing, sway, vary.

Here are some different kinds of **ornament.**

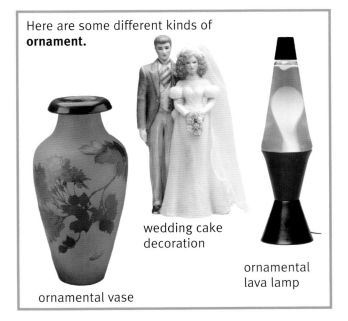

wedding cake decoration

ornamental lava lamp

ornamental vase

oust VERB expel, eject, throw out, overthrow.

outbreak NOUN **1** outburst, eruption, explosion. **2** rebellion, uprising, upsurge.

outcome NOUN result, consequence, conclusion, effect.

outing NOUN trip, day out, excursion, jaunt.

outlaw NOUN criminal, fugitive, bandit, desperado, highwayman.

outlet NOUN way out, exit, opening, vent.

outlook NOUN **1** view, scene, viewpoint, attitude. **2** chance, prospect, forecast. *The employment outlook is good.*

outrage NOUN fury, shock, anger, offence/offense (US). *The decision caused outrage.*

outskirts NOUN suburbs, borders, boundaries.

outspoken ADJECTIVE frank, open, blunt, direct.

outstanding ADJECTIVE **1** notable, exceptional, noticeable, striking. **2** owing, unpaid.

overcome VERB conquer, overwhelm, defeat, overpower, subdue.

overflow VERB spill, run over, flood, inundate.

overhead ADVERB above.

overlook VERB **1** neglect, pass over, miss, ignore. **2** pardon, excuse, turn a blind eye. **3** look over.

overseas ADJECTIVE abroad, foreign.

oversight NOUN mistake, error, omission, blunder.

overtake VERB pass, catch up with, outdo.

overthrow VERB destroy, demolish, overwhelm, defeat, topple, beat, crush.

overturn VERB capsize, overbalance, keel over, abolish, set aside.

overwhelm VERB **1** *See* **overcome**. **2** confuse, overpower, inundate.

own VERB possess, have, keep.

own up VERB confess, admit, acknowledge.

pace NOUN step, rate, speed, tempo.

pacify VERB calm, placate, soothe, appease, soften.

pack VERB put, load, fill, cram.

package NOUN parcel, packet, bundle.

packed ADJECTIVE filled, full, crowded.

packet NOUN package, pack, parcel, carton, container.

pact NOUN agreement, treaty, contract, alliance.

pad NOUN cushion, pillow, bolster.

pad VERB fill, stuff, protect.

pad out VERB lengthen fill out.

pageant NOUN parade, display, show, fair, spectacle, procession.

pain NOUN ache, sting, hurt, twinge, torment, torture, agony.

painful ADJECTIVE aching, hurting, sore, throbbing, stinging, distressing, unpleasant.

painstaking ADJECTIVE careful, diligent, thorough, scrupulous. *Opposite words* are negligent, slipshod.

paint NOUN colour/color (US), pigment, dye. VERB dye, tint, colour/color (US), embellish, decorate.

painting NOUN picture, mural, illustration, portrait, still-life, landscape.

pair NOUN two, couple, brace, twins, twain, duo.

palace NOUN mansion, castle, chateau.

pale ADJECTIVE **1** white, pasty, ashen, pallid. **2** light, colourless/colorless (US), insipid.

pamper VERB spoil, pander to, indulge, cosset.

pamphlet NOUN leaflet, booklet, brochure.

pan NOUN pot, saucepan, frying pan, container.

panel NOUN board, group, committee, forum.

panic NOUN fear, terror, alarm, consternation.

panorama NOUN view, landscape, scenery, prospect.

pant VERB puff, gasp, blow, wheeze.

paper NOUN **1** newspaper, journal, periodical, tabloid, broadsheet. **2** document, report.

parade NOUN march, display, procession, pageant.

parched ADJECTIVE dry, arid, thirsty, dehydrated.

pardon VERB forgive, let off, excuse, spare, reprieve.

pare VERB peel, skin, strip, trim, prune.

parent NOUN father, mother.

park NOUN enclosure, garden, grounds, green.

parliament NOUN assembly, congress, council.

parody NOUN caricature, imitation, satire, spoof.

part NOUN **1** piece, bit, component, fraction, portion, section, element, constituent. **2** area, district, region. **3** role, character. *A part in a play.*

part VERB **1** divide, separate, break. **2** leave, depart.

partial ADJECTIVE **1** incomplete, restricted, limited. **2** biased, favouring/favoring (US), unjust.

Here are some different things used to make packages

string

brown paper

labels

tape

participate VERB take part, co-operate, contribute, share, help, partake.

particle NOUN speck, bit, morsel, fragment.

particular ADJECTIVE **1** individual, personal, private. **2** special, distinct, specific. *A particular time of day.* **3** fussy, choosy.

parting NOUN **1** leave-taking, departure, farewell. **2** separating, split. *A parting of the ways.*

partner NOUN companion, friend, colleague.

party NOUN **1** festivity, celebration, get-together, dance, disco, ball, wedding, birthday, anniversary. **2** group, faction, company. *The Green party.*

pass VERB **1** exceed, overtake. **2** experience, suffer. **3** cease, pass away, elapse. *Time passes quickly.* **4** enact, approve, authorize. **5** hand, transmit, give. *Please pass the salt.* **6** succeed. *Pass a test.*

pass away VERB die, expire.

pass out VERB faint, collapse.

pass over VERB ignore, disregard.

passage NOUN **1** corridor, hallway. **2** extract, section, quotation

passenger NOUN traveller/traveler (US), voyager, tripper, commuter.

passion NOUN enthusiasm, emotion, feeling, mania, craze.

past ADJECTIVE **1** done, finished, over. **2** previous, former. *Past president.*

pasta NOUN spaghetti, tagliatelli, tortellini, macaroni, lasagne/lasagna (US) cannelloni.

pat VERB tap, pet, touch, stroke.

path NOUN track, trail, footpath, lane, pavement, way, walkway, bridleway.

pathetic ADJECTIVE **1** sad, pitiable, moving, lamentable. **2** worthless, useless, laughable.

patient ADJECTIVE calm, long-suffering, restrained uncomplaining.

pattern NOUN **1** decoration, design, ornament, shape. **2** model, prototype, specimen.

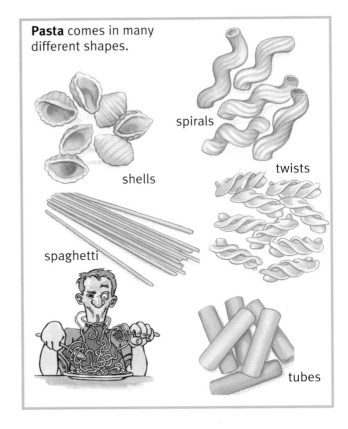

Pasta comes in many different shapes.

spirals

twists

shells

spaghetti

tubes

pause VERB rest, stop, wait, hesitate, cease.

pay VERB give, spend, settle, reward.

peaceful ADJECTIVE calm, quiet, restful, serene.

peculiar ADJECTIVE **1** odd, strange, unusual, funny, curious, bizarre. **2** special, characteristic.

peep VERB **1** look, glimpse, peer. **2** appear.

peer VERB look, examine, gaze, inspect. A word that sounds similar is pier.

penetrate VERB pierce, perforate, bore, pass through, cut, enter.

penetrating ADJECTIVE piercing, cutting, incisive, probing, perceptive, shrewd.

penniless ADJECTIVE poor, destitute, needy, broke.

people NOUN human beings, populace, population, inhabitants, folk, tribe, nation.

perceive VERB **1** observe, see, notice. **2** understand, grasp discern, appreciate.

Here are some different kinds of animals that make good **pets.**

dog

rabbit

hamster

cat

perception NOUN understanding, feeling, awareness.

perch VERB roost, rest, settle.

percussion ADJECTIVE crash, clash, collision. Some percussion instruments: bongo drums, cymbals, chimes, kettledrum, snare drum.

perfect ADJECTIVE **1** ideal, excellent, faultless, flawless. **2** exact, precise.

perform VERB act, **1** take part, play, appear in, sing. **2** do, achieve, carry out, accomplish, function.

performance NOUN **1** presentation, show, production. **2** behaviour/behavior (US), operation, work, action. *His performance at work has been disappointing.*

perfume NOUN scent. *See also* **smell.**

perhaps ADVERB possibly, maybe.

peril NOUN danger, risk, hazard, risk, jeopardy.

period NOUN time, term, span, era, age, phase.

perish VERB rot, decay, wither, shrivel, die.

permanent ADJECTIVE lasting, stable, durable, perpetual, enduring.

permission NOUN approval, consent, leave, authorization. An *opposite word* is prohibition.

permit VERB let, allow, approve of, agree to.

perpetrate VERB do, carry out, commit, execute, perform, inflict.

perplex VERB bewilder, baffle, puzzle, confound.

persecute VERB harass, hunt, chase, torment.

persist VERB continue, carry on, persevere, remain.

person NOUN individual, human, being, character, man, woman, child.

perspective NOUN outlook, view, angle, standpoint, point of view.

perspire VERB sweat, drip.

persuade VERB tempt, urge, coax, entice, cajole, talk into. An *opposite word* is dissuade.

perturb VERB bother, trouble, disturb, upset, worry, alarm, distress.

peruse VERB study, pore over, examine, inspect, scrutinize.

pervade VERB fill, permeate, spread, saturate.

perverse ADJECTIVE stubborn, obstinate, wilful, contrary. An *opposite word* is reasonable.

pessimistic ADJECTIVE gloomy, cynical, despondent, defeatist, downhearted.

pester VERB annoy, worry, harass, nag, trouble.

pet NOUN favourite/favorite (US), darling, idol. Some animals that people keep as pets: canary, cat, dog, gerbil, goldfish, hamster, parrot, rabbit.

petty ADJECTIVE **1** small, unimportant, insignificant, trifling, paltry. **2** mean (UK), miserly. *She's petty about money.*

phase NOUN angle, view, aspect, period, stage.

philanthropic ADJECTIVE kind, charitable, benevolent, generous, unselfish.

philistine ADJECTIVE vulgar, uncouth.

phobia NOUN dread, obsession, dislike, aversion. Some common phobias: acrophobia (heights), agoraphobia (open spaces), claustrophobia (confined spaces).

phone VERB telephone, call, ring.

photograph NOUN picture, snap, slide, transparency.

physician NOUN doctor, medic, healer.

pick VERB **1** choose, select, elect. **2** pluck, collect, gather, harvest.

picture NOUN drawing, illustration, painting, photograph, snapshot, portrait, sketch, diagram, mural, collage.

picturesque ADJECTIVE pretty, attractive, scenic, pictorial, quaint.

piece NOUN bit, fragment, part, portion, sliver, chip, chunk.

pierce VERB penetrate, puncture, go through, prick, perforate.

pig NOUN **1** swine, hog, boar, sow. **2** glutton.

pile NOUN heap, mound, mass, stack, collection.

pilgrim NOUN traveller, wanderer.

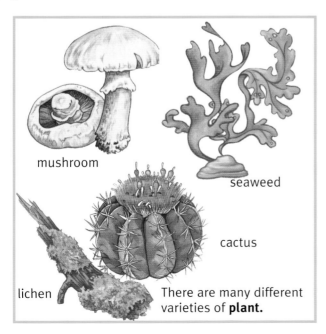

mushroom

seaweed

cactus

lichen

There are many different varieties of **plant.**

pillar NOUN column, post, support, mast.

pinch VERB **1** nip, squeeze, hurt. **2** See **steal.**

pioneer NOUN innovator, frontiers-man/woman, explorer, trail-blazer.

pious ADJECTIVE holy, religious, saintly, godly.

pipe NOUN hose, tube, conduit.

pit NOUN mine, well, hollow, hole, cavity.

pitch VERB **1** toss, hurl, throw, fling. **2** fall, plunge, drop. **3** erect, set up. *Let's pitch the tent here.*

pitiless ADJECTIVE ruthless, merciless, cruel.

pity NOUN mercy, sympathy, compassion.

place NOUN **1** site, position, location, spot. **2** area, region, district, city, town. **3** home, dwelling, residence.

placid ADJECTIVE calm, composed, serene, mild.

plague NOUN **1** disease, pestilence, epidemic. **2** nuisance, bother, affliction, thorn in the side.

plain ADJECTIVE **1** simple, ordinary, everyday. **2** clear, obvious, definite.

plan NOUN **1** project, idea, scheme, proposal. **2** map, diagram, drawing, chart.

planet NOUN The Sun's planets are: Earth, Mars, Jupiter, Saturn, Uranus, Venus, Mercury, Pluto, Neptune.

plant NOUN Some different kinds of plant: algae, aquatic plants, cacti, ferns, flowering plants.

play VERB **1** perform. *She's playing the violin.* **2** amuse yourself, have fun, sport, frolic.

plead VERB beg, implore, ask for, request.

pleasant ADJECTIVE **1** agreeable, cheerful, enjoyable, pleasing, nice. **2** friendly, kind, likeable. *They're pleasant people.* **3** fine, mild, warm. *Pleasant weather.* **4** attractive, peaceful, pretty.

pleasure NOUN enjoyment, happiness, joy, delight, amusement, entertainment.

pledge NOUN promise, guarantee, vow, undertaking.

plenty ADJECTIVE abundance, lots of, loads of, enough. *Opposite words* are scarcity, need.

pliable ADJECTIVE flexible, pliant, bendable, supple.

plight NOUN difficulty, trouble, predicament, dilemma.

plod VERB trudge, lumber, labour/labor (US), slog.

plot NOUN story, theme, outline.

plot VERB conspire, plan, scheme, devise, scheme.

pluck VERB pick, gather, collect, snatch.

plump ADJECTIVE fleshy, portly, fat, round, chubby.

plunge VERB dive, jump, leap, drop, submerge, dip.

ply VERB use, employ, practise/practice (US).

poach VERB steal, pilfer, trespass, filch.

poetry VERB verse, rhyme. Some different kinds of poetry: ballad, limerick, lyric, haiku, sonnet, ode.

poignant ADJECTIVE bitter, sharp, distressing, piercing, moving.

point NOUN **1** spike, tip, end. **2** purpose, object, intent. *The point of studying hard.* VERB aim, direct, level, indicate, show.

pointless ADJECTIVE aimless, futile, meaningless.

poison NOUN pollute, contaminate, infect, taint.

poke VERB prod, jab, dig, thrust, shove, nudge.

poky ADJECTIVE cramped, uncomfortable, small.

policy NOUN plan, tactics, stratagem, programme/program (US), strategy, procedure.

polished ADJECTIVE shiny, sparkling, bright, glossy, burnished. An *opposite word* is dull.

polite ADJECTIVE well-mannered, well-behaved, considerate, civil. *Opposite words* are rude, impolite.

polluted ADJECTIVE poisoned, contaminated, infected, defiled, adulterated.

pompous ADJECTIVE proud, pretentious, bombastic, self-important, flaunting.

ponder VERB consider, study, contemplate, reflect.

pool NOUN pond, lake, swimming pool, puddle, loch, lough, lagoon.

poor ADJECTIVE **1** hard-up, broke, poverty-stricken, impoverished, penniless, needy, destitute. **2** bad, inferior, faulty, third-rate. **3** barren, unproductive, infertile. *Poor soil.*

poorly ADJECTIVE ill, unwell, sick, under the weather. An *opposite word* is healthy.

popular ADJECTIVE liked, well-known, admired, accepted, sought after, famous.

port NOUN harbour/harbor (US), haven, dock, anchorage.

portion NOUN helping, part, piece, share, slice.

portly ADJECTIVE large, stout, plump, burly. *Opposite words* are slim, slender.

portrait NOUN picture, likeness, drawing, sketch.

pose VERB stand, affect, feign, pretend, model.

position NOUN **1** place, situation, spot, site. **2** posture, pose. **3** job, post, occupation. **4** rank, status, standing.

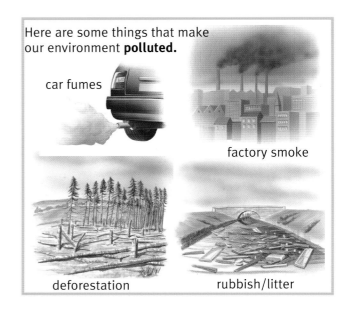

Here are some things that make our environment **polluted.**

car fumes

factory smoke

deforestation

rubbish/litter

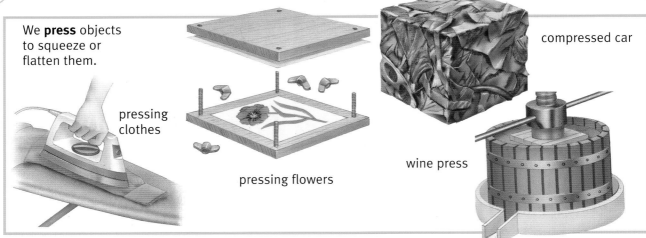

We **press** objects to squeeze or flatten them.

pressing clothes

pressing flowers

compressed car

wine press

possess VERB have, own, hold, enjoy, occupy.

possession NOUN belongings, property.

post NOUN **1** column, pillar, pole, support. **2** mail.

postpone VERB put off, defer, hold over, shelve, adjourn, delay, put on ice.

poultry NOUN Some different kinds of poultry: chicken, duck, goose, turkey.

pounce VERB strike, swoop, fall on, jump on.

pour VERB **1** empty, tip, spill. **2** flow, gush, stream.

poverty NOUN penury, hardship, impoverishment, need, distress, lack. An *opposite word* is wealth.

powerful ADJECTIVE mighty, strong, robust, potent, high-powered, leading.

practical ADJECTIVE useful, handy, efficient.

practise/practice (US) VERB **1** train, rehearse, exercise. **2** carry out, perform, do, pursue.

pragmatic ADJECTIVE realistic, sensible, business-like. *Opposite words* are romantic, unrealistic.

praise VERB congratulate, praise, admire, compliment, applaud, flatter.

prattle VERB chatter, gossip, gabble, witter.

pray VERB beg, call on, ask, entreat, worship, beseech.

precaution NOUN care, wariness, safeguard, prudence.

precede VERB lead, come before, herald, head, go first. An *opposite word* is succeed.

precious ADJECTIVE costly, expensive, valuable, priceless. An *opposite word* is worthless.

precise ADJECTIVE exact, scrupulous, accurate, formal, strict.

predict VERB foretell, forecast, prophesy, project.

prefer VERB fancy, favour/favor (US), like better, select, support.

prejudice NOUN bias, partiality, unfairness, bigotry, discrimination.

premises NOUN grounds, buildings, property, site.

preoccupied ADJECTIVE distracted, involved in, engrossed, wrapped up, day-dreaming.

prepare VERB get ready, organize, plan, arrange.

preposterous ADJECTIVE absurd, ridiculous, unbelievable, unreasonable.

prescribe VERB recommend, order, decree, rule, command, specify.

present NOUN gift, offering. VERB **1** award, hand over, give, bestow. **2** introduce. **3** exhibit, show.

presently ADVERB **1** soon, shortly, directly. **2** at present, now.

press VERB **1** push. **2** flatten, iron, smooth. **3** squeeze, compress, crush.

presume VERB suppose, take for granted, believe.

pretend VERB **1** act, impersonate, trick, imitate, bluff. **2** claim, aspire.

pretty ADJECTIVE beautiful, lovely, pleasing, dainty, attractive. *Opposite words* are plain, ugly.

prevent VERB stop, hinder, impede, slow down, ward off. *Opposite words* are cause, help.

previous ADJECTIVE former, preceding, earlier.

previously ADVERB before, formerly, earlier.

price NOUN fee, cost, charge, payment, value, expense.

priceless ADJECTIVE invaluable, precious, prized.

prick VERB pierce, puncture, bore, perforate.

pride NOUN **1** self-respect, dignity. An *opposite word* is humility. **2** conceit, vanity, arrogance.

prim ADJECTIVE formal, stiff, prudish, priggish.

primary ADJECTIVE **1** earliest, first, original, beginning, basic, fundamental. **2** main, principal, leading, chief. An *opposite word* is secondary.

prime ADJECTIVE **1** best, excellent, first-class, choice. **2** principal, chief.

primitive ADJECTIVE early, rudimentary, simple, old, crude, prehistoric.

principal ADJECTIVE chief, important, main, key, foremost. An *opposite word* is minor.

principle NOUN **1** law, rule, doctrine, code. **2** honour/honor (US), virtue, integrity.

print VERB imprint, mark, stamp, reproduce, copy.

prisoner NOUN captive, inmate, convict.

private ADJECTIVE personal, secret, confidential, hidden. An *opposite word* is public.

prize NOUN award, bounty, reward, recompense, trophy. VERB cherish, esteem, value.

probe VERB **1** investigate, explore, examine, look into. **2** poke, prod.

problem NOUN **1** difficulty, dilemma, question, worry. **2** puzzle, question, enigma.

proceed VERB **1** go forward, advance, progress. **2** arise, derive.

process NOUN method, procedure, way, technique.

procession NOUN march, parade, cavalcade, motorcade.

proclaim VERB announce, declare, make known.

procure VERB obtain, buy, get, purchase, secure, gain.

prod VERB poke, jab, dig, nudge, shove, stimulate.

prodigal ADJECTIVE wasteful, spendthrift, reckless, extravagant. An *opposite word* is thrifty.

produce VERB **1** make, create, manufacture, originate, invent. **2** publish, bring out, present.

production NOUN **1** manufacture, creation, construction, assembly. **2** presentation, staging.

productive ADJECTIVE fruitful, creative, worthwhile, constructive.

profession NOUN occupation, career, calling, employment.

profound ADJECTIVE deep, penetrating, weighty, serious, shrewd. *It was a profound concept.*

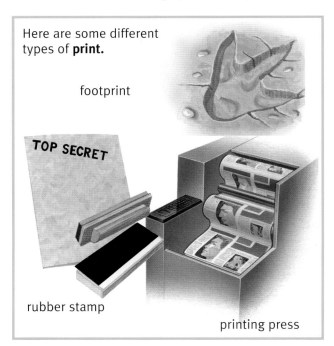

Here are some different types of **print**.

footprint

TOP SECRET

rubber stamp

printing press

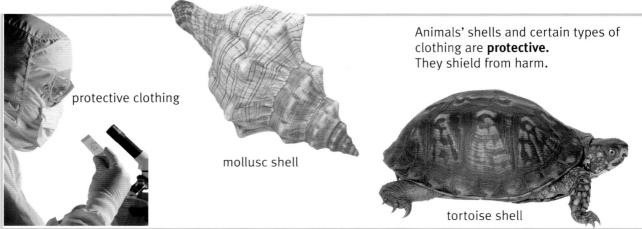

protective clothing

mollusc shell

Animals' shells and certain types of clothing are **protective.** They shield from harm**.**

tortoise shell

progress VERB move forward, proceed, advance, make headway, improve.

progressive ADJECTIVE advanced, forward-looking, increasing, growing.

prohibit VERB forbid, bar, deny, ban, hinder, veto, prevent. An *opposite word* is allow.

project NOUN plan, scheme, task, job, idea, proposal.

project VERB **1** forecast, predict, estimate. **2** protrude, jut out. **3** fling, throw.

prolong VERB lengthen, protract, draw out, extend.

prominent ADJECTIVE **1** noticeable, outstanding. *Prominent features.* **2** famous, distinguished, celebrated. *Opposite words* are insignificant, unknown.

promise VERB give your word, swear, vow, agree, pledge, undertake.

promote VERB publicize, advertise, sell, market, support, sponsor.

prompt ADJECTIVE punctual, on time, ready, alert.

prone ADJECTIVE **1** face down, horizontal. **2** inclined, disposed to, liable, likely.

pronounce VERB **1** say, speak, utter, express. **2** declare, proclaim, decree.

prop VERB lean, rest, stand, support, uphold.

propel VERB thrust, push, drive, shove, launch, shoot.

proper ADJECTIVE **1** correct, fit, appropriate, suitable. **2** decent, respectable.

prophesy VERB foretell, augur. *See also* **predict**.

proposal NOUN scheme, suggestion, project, offer, proposition.

propose VERB **1** recommend, suggest, offer, put forward. **2** mean to, intend.

prosaic ADJECTIVE ordinary, commonplace, everyday, uninspiring, unimaginative.

prosecute VERB sue, accuse, summon, put on trial, try. An *opposite word* is defend.

prospect NOUN hope, expectation, chance, likelihood, future, outlook.

prosperous ADJECTIVE, thriving, booming, successful, rich, wealthy.

protect VERB **1** defend, guard, look after, preserve. **2** screen, shield, shelter.

protective ADJECTIVE shielding, sheltering, defensive.

protest VERB object, complain, oppose, dispute, disagree.

prototype NOUN model, original, pattern.

proud ADJECTIVE **1** happy, pleased, honoured/honored (US). **2** boastful, arrogant.

prove VERB show, demonstrate, verify, justify, confirm. An *opposite word* is disprove.

provide VERB supply, give, procure, furnish, equip.

provoke VERB **1** anger, upset, worry, irritate, annoy. **2** cause, give rise to, incite.

prowl VERB lurk, roam, rove, stalk.

pry VERB interfere, meddle, peep, snoop.

public ADJECTIVE general, national, common, communal, open, unrestricted, well-known.

pull VERB **1** drag, tug, haul, tow, draw, heave. **2** stretch. **3** hitch. *Pull up your socks.*

pull down VERB destroy, demolish.

pull through VERB recover, survive.

pull up VERB stop, halt.

punch VERB **1** hit, strike, bash, beat, rap, thump. **2** perforate, bore, puncture. *The machine punched the ticket.*

punctual ADJECTIVE prompt, on time, exact.

punish VERB scold, penalize, discipline, correct.

puny ADJECTIVE weak, feeble, frail, stunted, insignificant. *Opposite words* are strong, sturdy.

pupil NOUN student, scholar, learner, beginner, schoolboy, schoolgirl.

purchase VERB buy, obtain, get, earn, procure.

pure ADJECTIVE **1** clean, clear, natural, unpolluted. An *opposite word* is dirty. **2** real, undiluted, unmixed, neat. **3** chaste, blameless, innocent.

purge VERB **1** purify, cleanse. **2** eliminate, exterminate, kill, get rid of.

purpose NOUN **1** plan, reason, intent, object. **2** use, application, function. **3** determination, will.

purify VERB clear, clean, wash, cleanse, refine.

pursue VERB **1** follow, chase after, hunt, harry. **2** carry on, continue, conduct. *Pursue an occupation.*

pursuit NOUN **1** hunt, chase, search, race. **2** occupation, vocation.

push VERB **1** shove, press, force, crush, propel. **2** poke, prod, nudge.

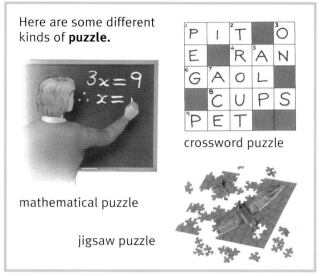

Here are some different kinds of **puzzle.**

mathematical puzzle

crossword puzzle

jigsaw puzzle

push off VERB go away.

push on VERB go on, continue.

push over VERB cause to fall, topple.

put VERB place, deposit, store, position, set out, lay, rest. An *opposite word* is remove.

put aside VERB save, preserve.

put away VERB replace, return.

put down VERB **1** note, record. **2** defeat, crush, humiliate.

put on VERB **1** dress. **2** present, display.

put off VERB postpone, delay.

put on VERB **1** dress. **2** present, display.

put out VERB **1** stretch. **2** extinguish. **3** dislocate.

put through VERB connect by telephone.

put together VERB assemble, construct.

put up VERB erect.

put up with VERB endure, bear, tolerate, stomach.

putrid ADJECTIVE rotten, stinking, decayed, rancid.

puzzle NOUN problem, riddle, question, enigma. VERB confuse, mystify, perplex.

quagmire NOUN bog, marsh, swamp, mire.

quail VERB tremble, quake, back away, cower, tremble.

quaint ADJECTIVE unusual, curious, strange, picturesque, old-fashioned.

quake VERB shake, shudder, quail, tremble, quiver.

qualification NOUN **1** competence, suitability, ability, fitness. **2** condition, limitation, stipulation.

quality NOUN **1** peculiarity, characteristic, attribute. **2** grade, standard, value, worth.

quandary NOUN dilemma, difficulty, predicament.

quantity NOUN amount, volume, portion, sum.

quarrel VERB argue, disagree, fall out, fight, squabble, bicker. An *opposite word* is agree.

quaver VERB shake, tremble, oscillate, vibrate, shudder, sway.

quay NOUN jetty, pier, landing-stage, harbour/harbor (US).

queasy ADJECTIVE sick, nauseous, groggy.

queer ADJECTIVE **1** strange, unusual, odd, funny, weird, peculiar. **2** suspicious, dubious.

quell VERB quash, crush, suppress, overcome, extinguish.

quench VERB **1** satisfy, slake, cool. **2** put out, extinguish, douse. *Quench the flames.*

query VERB question, ask, enquire, dispute, doubt.

quest NOUN search, hunt, chase, adventure.

question VERB inquire, ask, demand, query, interrogate, quiz. An *opposite word* is answer.

quibble VERB argue, carp, bicker.

quick ADJECTIVE **1** fast, rapid, speedy, swift, express. **2** instant, prompt, immediate. **3** nimble, sprightly, brisk, lively, agile. **4** sharp, shrewd, quick-witted.

quiet ADJECTIVE **1** noiseless, still, peaceful, calm, tranquil, restful, hushed. **2** shy, meek, mild.

quilt NOUN eiderdown, duvet, blanket, bedspread.

quip NOUN joke, wisecrack, witticism.

quirk NOUN whim, fancy, oddity, idiosyncrasy.

quit VERB leave, go, abandon, stop, cease, give up, surrender, renounce.

quite ADVERB **1** totally, wholly, absolutely, utterly. *Quite certain.* **2** rather, fairly, moderately.

quiver VERB tremble, shake, quake, shudder.

quiz NOUN test, puzzle, riddle, questionnaire.

quota NOUN share, portion, allowance, ration.

quote VERB **1** cite, mention, recite, name, repeat. **2** suggest, estimate. *He quoted a price for the car.*

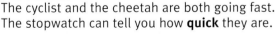
The cyclist and the cheetah are both going fast. The stopwatch can tell you how **quick** they are.

cheetah

cyclist

stopwatch

rabble NOUN crowd, mob, riff-raff.

race NOUN **1** nation, clan, tribe, people, ancestry. **2** chase, match, contest, sprint, steeplechase.

race VERB dash, run, sprint, speed, scamper.

racket NOUN noise, row, tumult, din, uproar.

radiant ADJECTIVE bright, beaming, brilliant, shining, splendid. An *opposite word* is dull.

radiate VERB emit, shine, beam, glow, spread, diffuse.

rage NOUN **1** anger, fury, wrath. **2** fad, fashion, vogue.

rail NOUN bar, railing, fence.

railway/railroad (US) NOUN Some different kinds of train: diesel, electric, steam, goods or freight.

rain NOUN shower, drizzle, downpour, squall, precipitation.

rainbow NOUN The colours/colors (US) of the rainbow are: red, orange, yellow, green, blue, indigo, violet.

raise VERB **1** lift, heave, hoist, pick up. **2** collect, obtain, make, get. **3** rear, bring up, grow.

rake VERB scrape, scour, collect, assemble.

rally VERB **1** meet, gather, convene, congregate. **2** recover, get better.

ramble VERB stroll, wander, hike, trek, amble. **2** ramble, digress. *His mind is rambling.*

ramshackle ADJECTIVE rickety, tumbledown, unstable, decrepit. An *opposite word* is stable.

rancid ADJECTIVE sour, bad, off, rank, fetid, rotten.

random ADJECTIVE haphazard, chance, accidental.

range NOUN **1** scale, gamut, scope, extent. **2** variety, class, sort. *There is a wide range to choose from.*

ransack VERB plunder, rife, sack, pillage.

rapid ADJECTIVE fast, quick, speedy, swift.

rare ADJECTIVE **1** scarce, uncommon, sparse. **2** excellent, choice, incomparable.

rash ADJECTIVE hasty, reckless, headstrong, impetuous, impulsive, hot-headed.

rate NOUN **1** speed, velocity. **2** charge, cost, tariff, tax, duty. **3** proportion, ratio, degree.

rather ADVERB **1** fairly, quite, moderately. **2** preferably, more.

ration NOUN portion, allowance, share, helping.

raucous ADJECTIVE, hoarse, rasping, rough, grating.

rave VERB **1** rage, storm, fume, rant. **2** enthuse, favour/favor (US). *They raved about the book.*

ravenous ADJECTIVE starving, hungry, voracious, famished.

raw ADJECTIVE **1** uncooked, fresh. **2** green, immature. **3** cold, freezing, biting.

ray NOUN beam, flash, shaft, glimmer.

raze VERB obliterate, destroy, level, flatten.

reach VERB **1** stretch, extend. **2** arrive, get to, attain.

read VERB study, interpret, peruse, decipher.

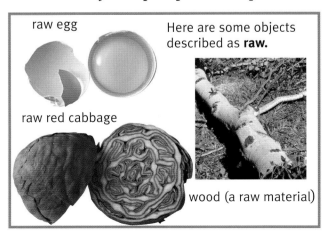

raw egg

Here are some objects described as **raw.**

raw red cabbage

wood (a raw material)

ready ADJECTIVE **1** prepared, waiting, willing, prompt. **2** available, convenient handy.

realistic ADJECTIVE **1** life-like, natural. **2** practical, sensible, down-to-earth, pragmatic. *Realistic plans.*

realm NOUN kingdom, empire, state, territory, land, sphere, domain.

rear ADJECTIVE back, end, bottom, tail. VERB raise, bring up, look after, cultivate.

reason NOUN **1** explanation, motive, cause, excuse. **2** intellect, sense, mind, brain, understanding.

reasonable ADJECTIVE **1** fair, moderate, average. **2** sensible, intelligent, wise, practical.

rebel VERB disobey, revolt, rise, mutiny.

rebellion NOUN uprising, mutiny, insurrection, rising.

rebuke VERB scold, blame, reprimand, tell off.

recall VERB remember, recollect.

receive VERB **1** get, earn, obtain, acquire. **2** welcome, greet, let in.

recent ADJECTIVE new, up-to-date, latest, modern.
recite VERB relate, tell, narrate, describe, repeat, perform, declaim.

reckless ADJECTIVE careless, thoughtless, rash.

reckon VERB **1** add up, calculate, count, estimate. **2** think, consider, suppose, feel sure, believe.

reclaim VERB recover, rescue, retrieve, regain, salvage.

recline VERB lean back, rest, repose.

recognize VERB know, remember, identify.

recollect VERB recall. *See also* **remember.**

recommend VERB **1** approve of, praise. **2** advise, suggest.

record NOUN diary, account, description, journal, log, minutes.

recover VERB **1** get better, improve. **2** get back, retrieve, find.

recreation NOUN enjoyment, fun, relaxation, amusement, pastime.

recuperate VERB get better, convalesce, mend.

recur VERB reoccur, return, repeat.

reduce VERB lessen, cut, decrease, shrink.

redundant ADJECTIVE **1** out of work, unemployed. **2** surplus, unnecessary, excess.

reel VERB totter, sway, stagger, spin.

refer VERB **1** consult, look up. *Refer to a dictionary.* **2** comment on, mention. **3** concern, relate, pertain. **4** direct, transfer. *The child was referred to a specialist.*

reform VERB **1** improve, correct, better. **2** remodel, reconstruct, reorganize, revamp.

refuge NOUN asylum, shelter, protection, sanctuary.

refuse NOUN rubbish, junk, waste, litter, trash.

Here are some different kinds of **recreation.**
reading
playing football
sun bathing
walking

buddha

There are many sacred objects that are part of **religion.**

mosque

Hindu shrine

Star of David

refuse VERB decline, reject, spurn, turn down, exclude. *Refuse entry.*

regal ADJECTIVE royal, majestic, noble, stately, kingly, queenly.

regard VERB think of, consider, notice, value, respect. An *opposite word* is disregard.

region NOUN district, area, territory, place, province, zone.

register VERB and NOUN record.

regret VERB repent, be sad about, grieve, mourn.

regular ADJECTIVE **1** even, steady, unchanging, uniform. **2** usual, normal, customary.

regulate VERB adjust, correct, control, arrange, manage, govern.

rehearse VERB practise, prepare, repeat, run through, go over, train.

reinforce VERB strengthen, support, fortify, toughen.

reject VERB turn down, decline, refuse, scrap, throw out. An *opposite word* is accept.

rejoice VERB celebrate, exult, revel.

relapse VERB get worse, weaken, deteriorate, fall back, regress. An *opposite word* is improve.

relate VERB **1** describe, narrate, tell, report, mention. **2** connect, link, concern. *There was an unresolved matter relating to her death.*

relation NOUN **1** relative, kinsman, kinswoman, family. **2** link, connection, bearing.

relax VERB **1** rest, unwind. **2** weaken, slacken.

release VERB **1** free, let loose, liberate, unfasten. **2** publish, circulate.

relentless ADJECTIVE remorseless, persistent, ruthless, cruel, unremitting.

reliable ADJECTIVE loyal, dependable, trustworthy, faithful, honest, staunch.

relief NOUN help, ease, aid, support, assistance, comfort, release.

relieve VERB comfort, ease, smooth, alleviate, lessen.

religion NOUN creed, belief, faith.

religious ADJECTIVE holy, devout, pious, godly, faithful, saintly, sacred.

reluctant ADJECTIVE unwilling, disinclined, hesitant, loath. *Opposite words* are willing, ready.

rely VERB depend on, count on, trust, swear by, believe in.

remain VERB **1** stay, stop, wait. **2** continue, last, persist, endure.

remainder NOUN balance, surplus, rest, remnant, residue.

remains NOUN remainders, relics, remnants, leftovers, dregs, ashes.

remark VERB **1** say, observe, mention, utter. **2** notice, regard, note.

remarkable ADJECTIVE unusual, amazing, extraordinary, outstanding, striking.

remember VERB recall, recollect, memorize.

remind VERB jog the memory, prompt, nudge.

remorse NOUN sorrow, regret, guilt, shame.

remove VERB **1** get rid of, take away. **2** extract, take out, wash off.

renew VERB restore, rebuild, renovate, mend, repair, rejuvenate.

renown ADJECTIVE fame, glory, celebrity, repute.

repair VERB mend, fix, put right, renovate, restore, make good, sew, darn, patch.

repay VERB **1** reimburse, refund. *Repay a debt.* **2** revenge, avenge, retaliate.

repel VERB **1** drive off, repulse, push back, oppose, withstand. *The two magnets repelled each other.* **2** revolt, disgust, nauseate.

replace VERB **1** substitute, supplant, succeed. **2** put back, restore, reinstate.

replica NOUN reproduction, facsimile, copy, likeness. An *opposite word* is original.

reply VERB answer, respond to, acknowledge.

report VERB announce, declare, state, tell, notify, publish.

repose VERB rest, sleep, recline.

represent VERB stand for, symbolize, depict, portray.

repress VERB control, curb, suppress, subdue, crush, overpower, hold back, bottle up.

reprieve VERB pardon, let off, acquit.

reprimand VERB rebuke, blame, scold, tell off, chide, admonish.

reproduce VERB **1** imitate, mimic, copy, duplicate. **2** breed, multiply, generate.

reptile NOUN Some different kinds of reptile: alligator, crocodile, lizard, snake, tortoise, turtle.

repugnant ADJECTIVE repellent, revolting, repulsive, sickening, distasteful, horrible, hideous.

reputation NOUN name, character, fame, renown, standing, good name, regard, repute.

request VERB ask for, beg for, appeal for, beseech.

require VERB need, desire, lack, want.

rescue VERB save, salvage, deliver, release, set free.

research VERB examine, study, explore, scrutinize, investigate.

resemble VERB look like, be similar to, take after.

reserve VERB **1** keep, save, hold, hoard. **2** book, order, secure. *Let's reserve some tickets.*

reserved ADJECTIVE shy, withdrawn, secretive, aloof, distant. *Opposite words* are friendly, open.

reside VERB live, inhabit, dwell, occupy, lodge.

resign VERB leave, quit, abandon, give up, step down, surrender, renounce, abdicate.

resist VERB oppose, confront, defy, fight. An *opposite word* is submit.

resolve VERB **1** decide, determine, make up one's mind. **2** decipher, unravel, solve.

respect NOUN consideration, admiration.

respond VERB reply, answer, retort.

responsible ADJECTIVE answerable, guilty.

Here are some different kinds of **reptile.**

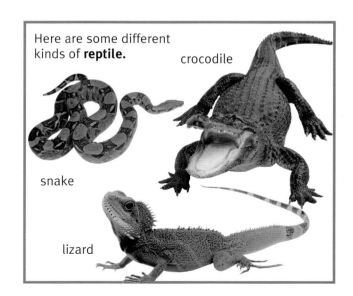

crocodile

snake

lizard

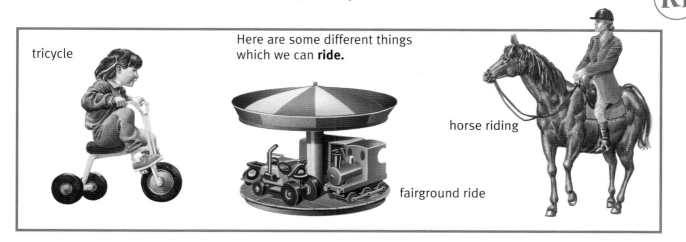

tricycle

Here are some different things which we can **ride**.

horse riding

fairground ride

responsibility NOUN duty, obligation, burden, fault, blame.

rest NOUN **1** remainder, remnant. **2** break, pause, breather, repose, siesta, sleep.

rest VERB **1** relax, lie down, sleep, repose. **2** lean, prop.

restful ADJECTIVE relaxing, peaceful, quiet, calm.

restore VERB **1** mend, repair, renovate, renew, rebuild. **2** replace, reinstate. **3** refresh.

restrain VERB curb, repress, hold back, check, prevent, stop. *Opposite words* are encourage, impel.

restrict VERB limit, confine, control, restrain.

result NOUN effect, consequence, outcome, upshot, product. An *opposite word* is cause.

retain VERB keep, hold on to, withhold, save.

retreat VERB run away, go back, depart, shrink.

return VERB **1** come back. **2** repay, give back.

reveal VERB show, disclose, make known, divulge, tell, uncover.

revenge NOUN get one's own back, avenge, retaliate.

reverse VERB **1** go backwards, turn, retreat. **2** change, alter. *Reverse the usual order.*

review VERB examine, assess, criticize, survey, judge, reconsider.

revise VERB alter, amend, correct.

revolution NOUN **1** rotation, orbit, circle. **2** rebellion, uprising, revolt, riot, rising.

revolve VERB spin, rotate, circle, orbit, turn, swivel.

reward VERB prize, award, bonus, payment, honour/honor (US).

rich ADJECTIVE wealthy, prosperous.

ride VERB travel, journey, move, trot, pedal.

ridiculous ADJECTIVE absurd, funny, laughable, comic, ludicrous, silly.

rigid ADJECTIVE **1** stiff, unbending, firm. **2** austere, stern.

right ADJECTIVE **1** correct, accurate, true, exact. **2** fair, honest, good, just. **3** appropriate, suitable.

rim NOUN border, edge, lip, brim, flange.

ring VERB **1** chime, jingle, tinkle, peal. **2** call, telephone, phone.

rinse VERB wash, clean, swill, bathe.

riot NOUN disturbance. *See also* **revolution**.

rip VERB tear, split, slit, slash.

ripe ADJECTIVE mature, grown, mellow, developed, ready. An *opposite word* is immature.

rise VERB **1** climb, go up, ascend, lift, soar, take off, tower. **2** increase, escalate, jump. *Prices have risen since the last election.* **3** get up, stand up.

risk NOUN chance, danger, peril, jeopardy.

rival ADJECTIVE opposing, competing.

rival NOUN opponent, competitor.

river NOUN brook, stream, waterway, torrent.

road NOUN Some different kinds of roads and paths: alley, avenue, boulevard, bridleway, bypass, drive, lane, motorway/freeway (US), expressway (US.

roam VERB wander, stroll, meander, range, rove.

roar VERB blare, bellow, cry, yell, boom.

robust ADJECTIVE strong, sturdy, stout, muscular, vigorous.

rock NOUN stone, boulder.

rock VERB **1** sway, swing, roll, soothe, lull. **2** stun, astonish.

rod NOUN pole, stick, staff, cane, baton, wand.

rodent NOUN gerbil, hamster, mouse, rat, squirrel.

rogue NOUN rascal, scoundrel, con, scamp, scallywag.

role NOUN **1** character, part. **2** duty, function.

roll VERB **1** rotate, revolve, turn, spin. **2** wrap, bind, enfold. **3** press, flatten, smooth. **4** roar, rumble, thunder. **5** swing, toss, pitch.

room NOUN **1** chamber, bathroom, bedroom, kitchen, sitting room, lounge, dining room, study, toilet. **2** space.

roomy ADJECTIVE large, spacious.

rotten ADJECTIVE **1** bad, mouldy/ moldy (US), putrid, decomposed, decayed. **2** useless, hopeless, nasty.

rough ADJECTIVE **1** coarse, harsh, scratchy. **2** bumpy, lumpy, uneven. **3** wild, violent, stormy. **4** severe, harsh, rude, impolite.

round ADJECTIVE circular, spherical, disc/disk (US), ball. *The skating rink was round.*

rout NOUN defeat, conquest, overthrow, thrashing.

routine NOUN method, system, procedure, pattern.

row NOUN (rhymes with now) **1** quarrel, fight, squabble, disagreement. **2** uproar, din, noise, racket, commotion. NOUN (rhymes with go) file, line.

rowdy ADJECTIVE noisy, unruly, boisterous.

rub VERB wipe, polish, stroke, caress, massage.

rubbish NOUN scrap, waste, refuse, junk, garbage.

rude ADJECTIVE bad-mannered, impolite, coarse, curt, vulgar (UK). An *opposite word* is polite.

rugged ADJECTIVE **1** robust, sturdy, strong. **2** rough, uneven, craggy.

ruin VERB destroy, wreck, spoil, damage.

rule NOUN command, law, regulation, order. VERB **1** govern, control, run, manage, command, reign. **2** judge.

ruler NOUN king, queen, monarch, emperor, empress, president, sovereign, sultan, tsar, rajah, dictator, tyrant, pharaoh.

rumour/rumor (US) NOUN gossip, hearsay, scandal.

run VERB **1** race, jog, sprint, scamper, dash, trot, canter, gallop. **2** work, operate. *It runs on diesel.* **3** manage, control. *She runs a business.* **4** flow, pour. *Water running down the hill.*

rush VERB dash, hurry, run, speed, hasten.

rusty ADJECTIVE **1** corroded, blighted, tarnished, rusted. **2** out of practice, unprepared.

ruthless ADJECTIVE pitiless, merciless, cruel, harsh, brutal, savage. *Opposite words* are merciful, kind.

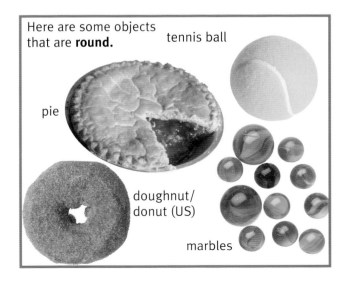

Here are some objects that are **round**.

tennis ball

pie

doughnut/ donut (US)

marbles

sack NOUN bag, pouch, container.

sack VERB **1** dismiss, fire, make redundant, lay off (UK). **2** pillage, plunder, despoil.

sacrifice VERB give up, offer, surrender, renounce, forgo.

sad ADJECTIVE gloomy, miserable, depressed, melancholy, unhappy, upset, wretched.

safe ADJECTIVE **1** secure, unharmed, protected. **2** harmless, tame, trustworthy.

safeguard VERB defend, protect, shield, guard.

sag VERB droop, dangle, hang, bend.

sail VERB cruise, float, put to sea, voyage, navigate, steer. *A word that sounds similar is sale.*

sailor NOUN mariner, seafarer, yachtsman, yachtswoman.

salad NOUN Some things we eat in a salad: carrot, celery, cucumber, lettuce, onion, pepper, tomato.

salary NOUN pay, wages, earnings, income, remuneration.

sale NOUN trade, transaction, selling, marketing, auction. *A word that sounds similar is sail.*

salute VERB greet, hail, acknowledge, wave.

salvage VERB save, rescue, retrieve, reclaim, repair.

same ADJECTIVE similar, alike, equivalent, matching, changeless.

sample NOUN specimen, example, illustration.

sane ADJECTIVE normal, intelligent, sound, sober, rational, all-there. *Opposite words are insane, mad.*

sanitary ADJECTIVE clean, hygienic, pure, germ-free.

sap NOUN weaken, undermine, tire out, exhaust.

sardonic ADJECTIVE bitter, jeering, mocking, biting, sarcastic.

satire NOUN ridicule, sarcasm, parody, burlesque.

satisfy VERB **1** please, gratify, delight. *The teacher is never satisfied.* **2** meet, pay, fulfil, convince, assure.

saturate VERB soak, drench, steep, impregnate.

saucy ADJECTIVE cheeky, impudent, rude.

savage ADJECTIVE cruel, brutal, ruthless, ferocious, heartless, violent, rough, uncivilized.

save VERB **1** keep, preserve, conserve, put aside, salvage, economize. **2** liberate, free, rescue, guard.

savour/savor (US) VERB taste, smell, relish, enjoy.

say VERB **1** talk, remark, speak, utter, declare, express, reply, retort. **2** tell, announce, order.

saying NOUN remark, proverb, axiom, adage, slogan, phrase, saw.

scale NOUN **1** measure, degree, range, gamut. **2** gradation, balance, calibration. VERB ascend, clamber up. *See also* **climb**.

scamper VERB scuttle, scoot, run, hasten, scurry.

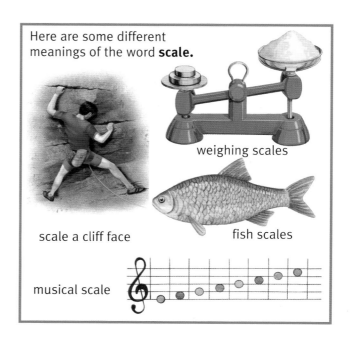

Here are some different meanings of the word **scale.**

scale a cliff face

weighing scales

fish scales

musical scale

227

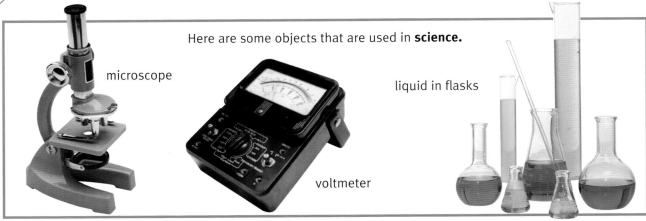

Here are some objects that are used in **science.**

microscope

voltmeter

liquid in flasks

scan VERB **1** inspect, scrutinize, examine, check. **2** glance at, dip into, skim.

scandal NOUN disgrace, infamy, outcry, smear dishonour/dishonor (US), shame, ignominy.

scanty ADJECTIVE scant, little, meagre/meager (US), small, insufficient, skimpy.

scar NOUN and VERB mark, wound, blemish.

scarce ADJECTIVE rare, few, scanty, in short supply.

scarcely ADVERB hardly, only, barely.

scared ADJECTIVE frightened, alarmed, terrified.

scatter VERB spread, sprinkle, sow, disperse.

scavenge VERB rummage, scrounge.

scene NOUN **1** view, landscape, location, setting, background, sight, spectacle, show, exhibition. **2** division, episode. *Act 2, Scene 3.*

scent NOUN smell, perfume, aroma, fragrance, odour/odor (US).

schedule NOUN agenda, plan, catalogue/catalog (US)programme/program (US), timetable.

scheme NOUN **1** plan, system, suggestion, arrangement. *A new scheme to make money.* **2** plot, intrigue, conspiracy, ruse, stratagem.

scholar NOUN student, pupil, academic, professor, highbrow, intellectual.

school NOUN college, academy, seminary, institute, kindergarten, comprehensive school (UK), boarding school.

science NOUN knowledge, technology.

scientific ADJECTIVE systematic, analytical, methodical, precise.

scoff VERB mock, make fun of, sneer, scorn, deride, ridicule, taunt.

scold VERB rebuke, tell off, reprimand, punish, blame. An *opposite word* is praise.

scope NOUN range, extent, field, room.

score VERB gain, earn, win, achieve, tally.

scorn NOUN despise, disdain, spurn, reject.

scrap NOUN bit, crumb, morsel. *See also* **fragment.** VERB abandon, discard, drop, throw away, dump.

scrape VERB scratch, grate, scour, graze.

scratch VERB scrape, mark, score, scuff, engrave, scrawl.

scream NOUN AND VERB shout, yell, bawl, shriek.

screw NOUN fasten, twist, turn, tighten, force.

scribble VERB scrawl, scratch, write.

scrounge VERB cadge, beg.

scrub VERB clean, scour, wash, mop.

scruffy ADJECTIVE messy, unkempt, untidy, shabby.

sculpt VERB carve, chisel, cut.

sea NOUN **1** ocean, main. **2** lost, adrift, puzzled, bewildered. *I'm all at sea, I don't understand at all.*

Ss

seam NOUN **1** join, stitching, weld. **2** layer, stratum, vein. *A rich seam of ore.*

search VERB **1** hunt for, look for, seek. **2** examine, explore, frisk.

seaside NOUN beach, coast, shore.

season NOUN spring, summer, autumn, fall, winter, period, time. VERB flavour/flavor (US), spice, salt. *Season the vegetables.*

seat NOUN chair, stool, bench, armchair, sofa.

secondary ADJECTIVE minor, inferior, lesser, supporting. *Opposite words* are primary, main.

secret ADJECTIVE **1** personal, private, hush-hush, confidential. **2** concealed, hidden, unknown, mysterious, undercover, camouflaged.

sect NOUN faction, cult, group, party.

section NOUN portion, piece, part, segment, division, department. An *opposite word* is whole.

secular ADJECTIVE lay, worldly, non-religious.

secure ADJECTIVE safe, fixed, firm, stable, certain.

sedate ADJECTIVE serious, calm, thoughtful, grave.

sediment NOUN dregs, grounds, residue.

Here are some different things used to **season** food.

pepper

spices

herbs

see VERB **1** look at, view, watch, behold. **2** notice, recognize, spot. **3** understand, know, follow, comprehend. *I see what you mean.*

seedy ADJECTIVE shabby, worn, sleazy, tatty, grubby.

seek VERB search, look for, hunt, ask, want.

seem VERB appear, look, feel, pretend.

seep VERB trickle, ooze, leak.

seethe VERB simmer, boil, froth, bubble.

segment NOUN bit, piece, portion.

segregate VERB separate, isolate, keep apart.

seize VERB grab, snatch, arrest, capture.

seldom ADVERB, not often, rarely, occasionally.

select VERB pick, choose, opt for, prefer.

selfish ADJECTIVE greedy, mean, thoughtless.

self-satisfied ADJECTIVE smug.

self-supporting ADJECTIVE independent, self-reliant.

sell VERB trade, vend, retail.

send VERB post, dispatch, forward, transmit.

senile ADJECTIVE old, aged, geriatric, decrepit.

senior ADJECTIVE elder, superior, high-ranking.

sensation NOUN **1** excitement, surprise. **2** feeling, impression, sense, awareness.

sensational ADJECTIVE spectacular, staggering, astounding, shocking, scandalous.

sense NOUN **1** hearing, sight, smell, taste, touch, faculty. **2** intelligence, wisdom, understanding. **3** meaning, significance.

sensible ADJECTIVE wise, thoughtful, reasonable.

separate ADJECTIVE apart, divided, isolated, segregated, detached, different.

serious ADJECTIVE careful, sincere, thoughtful, grave, sad, solemn, bad, terrible, severe.

servant NOUN domestic, employee, maid.

serve VERB help, assist, aid, wait on.

set VERB **1** harden, solidify, stiffen. *The concrete has set.* **2** arrange, place, lay out.

set off VERB depart, start.

settle VERB **1** colonize, populate, occupy. **2** fix, decide, agree, solve. *Settle an argument.* **3** pay. **4** fall, sink.

severe ADJECTIVE **1** serious, bad. **2** strict, rigid, stern, harsh. *A severe discipline.*

sew VERB stitch, darn, hem, tack, baste.

shabby ADJECTIVE old, faded, shoddy, ragged, frayed, scruffy, threadbare.

shade NOUN **1** colour/color (US), hue, tinge. **2** shadow, darkness, gloom. **3** blind, screen, awning, umbrella, sunshade, parasol.

shadow NOUN shade, darkness, dimness.

shady ADJECTIVE **1** shaded, cool, shadowy. **2** crooked, suspicious, fishy. *A shady character.*

shaggy ADJECTIVE hairy, woolly, rough, rugged, tousled. *Opposite words* are smooth, shorn.

sham ADJECTIVE false, fake, imitation, bogus, mock, forged. An *opposite word* is genuine.

shame NOUN disgrace, disrepute, dishonour/dishonor (US), ignominy.

shape NOUN form, outline, pattern, model, silhouette.

share VERB distribute, divide, allot, allocate, split, cooperate.

sharp ADJECTIVE **1** pointed, keen, cutting. **2** bright, quick, clever. **3** clear, distinct, bright.

shatter VERB smash, destroy, break, shock, wreck.

shelter NOUN cover, protection, safety, refuge, sanctuary.

shelter VERB guard, shield, protect, screen.

shield NOUN guard, protection, screen, buckler.

shifty ADJECTIVE sly, deceitful,

shimmer VERB glisten, gleam, sparkle.

shine VERB **1** glitter, gleam, sparkle, glisten, glow, twinkle. **2** polish.

shiny ADJECTIVE gleaming, glossy, polished, shining.

ship NOUN vessel, liner, craft. *See* **boat**.

shirk VERB avoid, shun, dodge.

shiver VERB tremble, shake, shudder, quiver.

shock VERB **1** startle, alarm, surprise, stun, scare, frighten. **2** disgust, upset, offend.

shocking ADJECTIVE horrible, scandalous, disgusting, repulsive, outrageous, disgraceful.

shoddy ADJECTIVE cheap, inferior, tawdry.

shoe NOUN Some of the things we wear on our feet: boots, clogs, pumps, slippers, sandals, sneakers (US), trainers (UK).

shoot VERB **1** aim, fire, discharge, explode. **2** bud, sprout.

shop NOUN store, departmental store, market stall, supermarket, hypermarket, emporium.

Shoes can be made out of leather, cloth or even plastic and come in many different styles and colours.

cowboy boots

brown leather lace-up shoe

buckle shoes

Here are some scenes of the **shore.**

seabirds

beachball

rockpool

shoreline

shore NOUN beach, seaside, sands, coast, waterfront, lakeside.

short ADJECTIVE **1** little, small, slight, dumpy.
2 brief, concise, compact. An *opposite word* is long.

shortage NOUN lack, deficiency, need, scarcity.

shorten VERB reduce, abridge, abbreviate.

shortly ADVERB soon, presently, quickly, briefly.

shout VERB scream, yell, shriek, call, cry out.

shove VERB push, thrust, prod, jostle.

show NOUN exhibition, display, spectacle, performance.

show VERB **1** exhibit, display. **2** point out, indicate, explain, show, tell. **3** reveal, disclose. **4** illustrate, portray, represent.

showy ADJECTIVE flashy, garish, loud, ostentatious, flash.

shred NOUN scrap, fragment.

shred VERB mince, chop, dice, tear.

shrewd ADJECTIVE clever, smart, astute, sharp, artful, cunning, sly.

shrink VERB **1** shrivel, wither, diminish, shorten. *Clothes that have shrunk in the wash.* **2** draw back, recoil, flinch.

shrivel VERB shrink, wither, dry up, wilt.

shudder VERB quiver, tremble, shiver, quake, shake.

shuffle VERB **1** trudge, limp. *Shuffle through the snow.* **2** mix, jumble. *Shuffle the cards.*

shun VERB avoid, evade, steer clear of.

shut VERB close, lock, fasten, bar.

shy ADJECTIVE timid, bashful, nervous, diffident.

sick ADJECTIVE ill, unwell, unhealthy, poorly.

sickness NOUN **1** illness, malady, disease. **2** queasy, vomiting.

side NOUN **1** face, surface, margin, edge, bank. *The other side of the river.* **2** team, party, sect.

sieve VERB strain, sift, riddle.

sift VERB strain, filter, separate, sort, examine.

sigh VERB grieve, moan, groan, lament.

sight NOUN **1** view, scene, appearance, spectacle. **2** vision, eyesight.

sign NOUN **1** indication, symptom, signal, symbol. **2** notice, poster.

signal NOUN sign, mark, beacon, gesture.

significant ADJECTIVE meaningful, important, weighty, indicative, defining, historic.

silence NOUN calm, peace, quiet.

silent ADJECTIVE quiet, still, noiseless, hushed, dumb.

silhouette NOUN outline, shape, form.

silky ADJECTIVE smooth, fine, sleek.

silly ADJECTIVE stupid, ridiculous, foolish, simple, weak, pointless.

silt NOUN mud, ooze, sediment, alluvium.

simmer VERB seethe, bubble, stew, boil.

simple ADJECTIVE **1** easy, clear, straightforward. **2** natural, unaffected, artless, naive, stupid, backward.

simper VERB smirk, giggle.

simply ADVERB **1** merely, solely, only. **2** easily, openly.

sincere ADJECTIVE honest, genuine, real, truthful, straightforward.

sing VERB chant, hum, croon.

singe VERB scorch, char, burn.

singer NOUN vocalist, chorister, baritone, bass, tenor, countertenor, alto, treble, contralto, soprano, choir, chorus.

single ADJECTIVE **1** solitary, alone, sole. **2** unmarried, bachelor, spinster, celibate.

sinister ADJECTIVE evil, bad, unlucky, menacing, threatening.

sink VERB **1** immerse, submerge, drown. **2** lower, drop, descend, disappear. **3** lower, dwindle, decrease.

sip VERB drink, taste.

sit VERB settle, rest, squat, perch.

site NOUN position, situation, spot, location.

situation NOUN **1** position, spot, locality. **2** plight, predicament.

size NOUN volume, extent, bulk, dimensions, width, breadth, length. *See also* **measurement**.

sizzle VERB sputter, fry.

sketch VERB outline, draw, design, trace, portray.

skid VERB slide, slip, slither, glide, skate.

skilful/skillful (US) ADJECTIVE clever, talented, skilled, able, expert, adept.

skill NOUN talent, ability, knack.

skim VERB **1** float, glide, plane, touch. **2** glance, scan, look through. *Skim the newspapers.*

skinny ADJECTIVE thin, scrawny, lean, weedy.

skip VERB **1** hop, leap, jump. **2** pass over, omit, disregard.

slack ADJECTIVE **1** loose, limp, hanging, flabby, baggy. **2** lazy, idle, slow.

slam VERB close, bang. *She slammed the door shut.*

slander VERB abuse, malign, discredit, backbite.

slant VERB lean, slope, incline, tilt, list.

slap VERB smack, spank, hit.

slash VERB slit, cut, hack, rip.

slave VERB toil, work, slog, drudge, labour/labor (US).

sledge NOUN sled, sleigh, toboggan.

sleek ADJECTIVE smooth, glossy, silky, slick.

sleep VERB snooze, nap, nod off, slumber, doze.

slender ADJECTIVE slim, slight, thin, lean.

slice NOUN piece, slab, wedge, section. VERB cut, split, sever, shred. *Slice the bread.*

slick ADJECTIVE shiny, smooth, suave, polished.

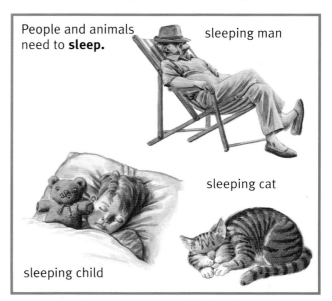

People and animals need to **sleep.**

sleeping man

sleeping cat

sleeping child

slide VERB glide, skate, skid, skim, slip, slither.

slight ADJECTIVE small, minor, unimportant, trivial. An *opposite word* is serious.

slim ADJECTIVE slender, thin, slim, thin, narrow.

slime NOUN mud, mire, ooze.

sling VERB hurl, throw, chuck, fling, toss.

slip VERB **1** slide, skid, slither.
2 err, blunder.

slippery ADJECTIVE smooth, icy, slimy, greasy, oily.

slipshod ADJECTIVE slapdash, slovenly, lax.

slit VERB cut, slash, rip, tear, gash.

slither VERB creep, slide, glide.

slog VERB toil, work.

slogan NOUN motto, catchphrase, saying, jingle.

slope VERB slant, lean, tilt, incline.

sloppy ADJECTIVE **1** slovenly, unkempt, careless. *Sloppy work.* **2** wet, watery, runny slimy. *The stew was very sloppy.*

slot NOUN opening, slit, hole, aperture, place.

slouch VERB slump, stoop, lounge.

slovenly ADJECTIVE lazy, slipshod, untidy, dowdy.

slow ADJECTIVE gradual, plodding, unhurried.

sly ADJECTIVE cunning, crafty, wily, artful, sneaky.

smack VERB hit, slap, strike, tap.

small ADJECTIVE **1** little, compact, tiny, minute.
2 minor, slight, unimportant, trifling.

smart ADJECTIVE **1** neat, spruce, tidy. *A smart suit.*
2 clever, alert, intelligent.

smart VERB sting. *See also* **hurt**.

smash VERB break, shatter, destroy, crash, collide.

smear VERB rub spread, daub, wipe, plaster.

smell NOUN odour/odor (US), scent, perfume, aroma, fragrance, stink, stench, whiff, tang.

Here are some things that have a distinctive **smell.**

rose

pot pourri

coffee beans

smelly ADJECTIVE stinking, fetid.

smile VERB grin, beam, smirk.

smirk VERB simper, smile.

smooth ADJECTIVE flat, even, level, sleek, shiny.

smother VERB stifle, suffocate.

smoulder/smolder (US) VERB burn, smoke, seethe.

smudge VERB smear, streak, stain, blot.

smug ADJECTIVE conceited, self-satisfied, complacent.

snack NOUN titbit, morsel, nibble, bite to eat.

snag NOUN problem, handicap, catch, handicap, difficulty.

snap VERB **1** break, crack, split. **2** snarl, growl.

snare NOUN trap, net.

snarl VERB **1** growl. **2** entangle, knot.

snatch VERB seize, grab, clutch, grasp, take.

sneak VERB creep, prowl, lurk, snoop, slink.

sneer VERB ridicule, scoff, jeer, taunt.

snigger VERB titter, sneer.

snoop VERB sneak, pry, spy, eavesdrop.

snug ADJECTIVE comfortable, cosy, warm, secure.

so ADVERB therefore, likewise.

soak VERB drench, wet, moisten, steep, saturate.

soar VERB rise, hover, fly, glide, tower.

social ADJECTIVE sociable, convivial, neighbourly/neighborly (US).

society NOUN **1** people, human beings, community. **2** group, club, association.

soft ADJECTIVE **1** limp, spongy, squashy, flexible. **2** smooth, silky, fluffy. **3** low, quiet, gentle, restful.

soften VERB **1** lessen, ease, alleviate, calm. **2** melt, dissolve.

soggy ADJECTIVE wet, sodden, saturated, spongy.

soldier NOUN cavalry, infantry, army, troops.

sole ADJECTIVE single, only, unique.

solemn ADJECTIVE serious, grave, sedate, formal.

solid ADJECTIVE firm, hard, dense, compact.

solitary ADJECTIVE sole, alone, only, lone, remote.

solution NOUN **1** explanation, answer. **2** mixture, blend, liquid.

solve VERB explain, answer, work out, decipher.

sombre/somber (US) ADJECTIVE serious, dull, dark, sad, dim, dismal.

song NOUN air, tune. Some different types of song: anthem, ballad, carol, folksong, hit, hymn.

soon ADVERB shortly, before long, presently.

soothe VERB calm, relax, pacify, comfort, relieve.

soppy ADJECTIVE sloppy, sentimental, slushy.

sordid ADJECTIVE slovenly, squalid, dirty, filthy, seedy, base, corrupt.

sore ADJECTIVE painful, tender, aching, inflamed.

sorrow NOUN sadness, unhappiness, misery, grief, remorse.

sorry ADJECTIVE apologetic, repentant, regretful, grieved.

sort NOUN type, kind, variety, breed, species, class, genre.

sort VERB classify, organize, arrange, catalogue, order.

sound ADJECTIVE **1** healthy, fit, well, strong, good. **2** valid, trustworthy, reliable.

sound NOUN noise, din, racket, tone.

sour ADJECTIVE sharp, acid, tart, bitter.

source NOUN origin, beginning, starting point, fount, spring, wellhead.

sow VERB scatter, strew, plant.

space NOUN room, gap, area, expanse, hole, opening, blank.

span VERB stretch, reach, bridge, cross.

spank VERB smack, slap, thrash.

spare ADJECTIVE extra, superfluous, additional, over, remaining.

sparkle VERB **1** flash, glitter, glisten, scintillate. **2** fizz, bubble.

Here are some different types of **soldier.**

American cavalry officer

Roman soldier

contemporary soldier

sparse ADJECTIVE scanty, thin, meagre/meager (US). An *opposite word* is dense.

speak VERB talk, say, express, state, utter.

spear NOUN javelin, lance, harpoon, pike.

special ADJECTIVE important, distinct, unusual, particular, different, personal, individual.

species NOUN kind, type, group, sort, breed.

specimen NOUN example, sample, copy, illustration.

speck NOUN dot, bit, grain, spot, particle.

spectacle NOUN show, exhibition, display, scene, sight.

spectacular ADJECTIVE impressive, exciting, big, striking, stunning.

spectator NOUN onlooker, bystander, witness, observer, watcher.

speed NOUN pace, haste, swiftness, velocity, tempo, rate.

spell VERB **1** charm, enchantment, sorcery, magic power. **2** time, period, term.

spend VERB **1** pay, use up, fritter. **2** pass, use, employ.

sphere NOUN **1** globe, ball, orb. **2** field, area, domain.

spice NOUN seasoning, zest. *See also* **herb**.

spill VERB upset, overturn, tip, topple, shed, drop.

spin VERB turn, revolve, rotate, whirl, twirl, gyrate.

spite NOUN malice, ill-will, venom, hatred.

splash VERB spatter, sprinkle, slop.

splendid ADJECTIVE impressive, superb, grand, brilliant, magnificent, gorgeous.

split VERB chop, crack, cleave, splinter, divide, cut.

spoil VERB **1** damage, ruin, injure, wreck, mar. **2** pamper, indulge. *A spoiled child.*

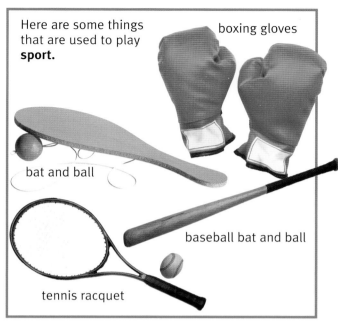

Here are some things that are used to play **sport.**

boxing gloves

bat and ball

baseball bat and ball

tennis racquet

spooky ADJECTIVE frightening, eerie.

sport NOUN recreation, play, fun, activity, pastime.

spot NOUN **1** mark, stain, blot, dot, speck, blemish. **2** pimple, boil. **3** place, position, situation. **4** plight, predicament. *In a bit of a spot.* VERB recognize, identify, see, spy.

spotless ADJECTIVE unstained, immaculate, pure.

sprawl VERB lounge, loll, stretch out, spread.

spray VERB splash, sprinkle, shower, scatter.

spread VERB unfold, open, lay out, expand.

sprightly ADJECTIVE brisk, agile, lively, nimble.

spring VERB **1** jump, leap, bound, hop, pounce. **2** grow, shoot up.

sprinkle VERB scatter, rain, strew, pepper.

sprint VERB race, run, dash.

spruce ADJECTIVE smart, tidy, neat. An *opposite word* is scruffy.

spurn VERB reject, turn down, despise, scorn.

spurt VERB gush, spew, stream, erupt.

spy VERB see, discover, detect, pry.

Here are some different kinds of **stamp.**

Stamp is also a verb. You can stamp in a puddle.

postage stamp

seal

official mark

squabble VERB quarrel, fight, clash.

squalid ADJECTIVE filthy, foul, dirty, seedy, sordid.

squander VERB spend, waste, fritter.

squash VERB crush, press, push, shove, squeeze, flatten.

squat ADJECTIVE stubby, stocky, crouching.

squeal VERB squeak, cry, squawk, screech.

squeeze VERB pinch, nip. *See also* **squash.**

squirt VERB spurt, spray, spout, gush.

stab VERB pierce, jab, wound, spear.

stable ADJECTIVE firm, steady, staunch, fixed, secure, steadfast.

stack NOUN and VERB pile, heap, load, mount.

stage NOUN **1** period, phase, point, juncture. *The next stage in your career.* **2** platform, scaffold, podium.

stagger VERB **1** reel, totter, lurch. **2** shock, astonish. **3** alternate, vary. *Staggered working hours.*

stain NOUN mark, smudge, spot, blemish, soil.

stale ADJECTIVE **1** dry, old, decayed. *Stale bread.* **2** flat, uninteresting, trite. *Stale ideas.*

stalk NOUN stem, twig, shank.

stalk VERB follow, pursue, track, trail, shadow.

stamina NOUN endurance, power, energy.

stamp NOUN mark, seal, label.

stamp VERB **1** mark, print, impress. **2** trample, pound, crush.

stand VERB **1** get up, rise. **2** arrange, place, put, position. **3** endure, tolerate, bear, put up with, abide. *She can't stand noise.*

stand down VERB resign, give up, quit, withdraw.

stand over VERB oversee.

stand up to VERB defy resist.

standard ADJECTIVE normal, consistent, regular.

standard NOUN **1** quality, level. **2** flag, banner, ensign, pennant.

staple ADJECTIVE basic, main, principal, chief.

stare VERB gape, gawk. *See also* **look.**

start VERB **1** begin, commence, open. **2** create, set up, found, establish.

startle VERB frighten, alarm, surprise, shock, scare.

starve VERB famish, be hungry, die, perish.

state NOUN **1** country, nation. **2** situation, condition.

state VERB say, declare, affirm, express, announce.

stately ADJECTIVE impressive, imposing, grand.

stationary ADJECTIVE motionless, unmoving, immobile, at rest, stable, fixed.

stay VERB **1** remain, wait, abide, stop, dwell. **2** keep, carry on. *Opposite words* are go, stray.

steady ADJECTIVE **1** stable, solid, secure, firm. **2** constant, continuous, regular.

steal VERB pinch, take, thieve, burgle, pickpocket.

steep ADJECTIVE sheer, precipitous, sharp.

steep VERB soak, submerge, souse.

steer VERB guide, pilot, direct.

stem VERB **1** arise, originate. *It stems from a Latin word.* **2** stop, oppose, check.

stench NOUN stink. *See also* **smell**.

step NOUN **1** pace, stride, tread. **2** stair, rung. **3** measure, action, deed. *The city is taking steps to reduce crime.*

stern ADJECTIVE strict, severe, hard, harsh, grim.

stick NOUN pole, cane, walking stick, club, staff, wand, baton, stalk, twig. VERB **1** glue, paste, attach, adhere. **2** pierce, thrust, stab.

stiff ADJECTIVE **1** rigid, hard, unbending. **2** hard, tough, difficult. *It's a stiff exam.*

still ADJECTIVE quiet, calm, tranquil, peaceful.

still ADVERB **1** always, even now, continually, ever. **2** yet, even.

stimulate VERB excite, interest, encourage, arouse, inspire, motivate.

sting VERB wound, pain, prick.

stingy ADJECTIVE mean, miserly, niggardly, close.

stink NOUN reek, whiff. *See also* **smell**.

stint NOUN job, task, work, shift, share.

stir VERB **1** mix, whisk, churn, shake. **2** arouse, stimulate, excite.

stoop VERB bend, crouch, squat, hunch, bow. **2** descend, sink. *Stoop to their level.*

stop VERB **1** end, cease, finish, pause, halt. **2** check, prevent, hinder. **3** stay.

store VERB save, put away, keep, reserve, accumulate. *An opposite word is use.*

storm NOUN **1** blizzard, hurricane, gale, tornado, rainstorm, squall, tempest, upheaval, thunderstorm. **2** uproar, commotion.

stormy ADJECTIVE wild, tempestuous, squally.

story NOUN tale, narrative, fairy-tale, fable, legend, myth, parable, yarn, anecdote, newspaper article.

stout ADJECTIVE plump, overweight, fat, tubby, big, chubby. *An opposite word is thin.*

straight ADJECTIVE **1** direct, undeviating, upright, vertical. **2** honest, fair, upright, frank.

straighten VERB disentangle, unbend, tidy, adjust.

strain VERB **1** struggle, try hard. **2** damage, injure, hurt, wrench. **3** exhaust, weaken, tire out. **4** filter.

strange ADJECTIVE **1** unfamiliar, foreign, alien, unknown, novel. **2** extraordinary, unusual, queer, odd, peculiar, weird, bizarre, funny.

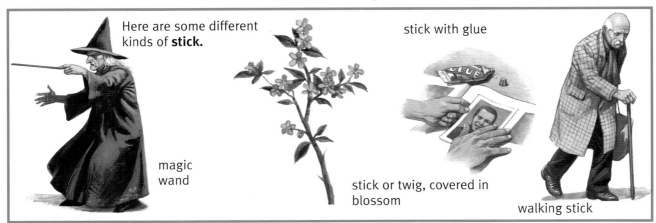

Here are some different kinds of **stick.**

magic wand

stick or twig, covered in blossom

stick with glue

walking stick

stranger NOUN foreigner, newcomer, outsider.

strap VERB **1** fasten, tie. **2** beat, belt.

strategy NOUN plan, scheme, tactics, design.

stray VERB wander, get lost, roam, digress.

stream NOUN brook, rivulet, beck, course, race.

street NOUN lane, avenue. *See also* **road**.

strength NOUN **1** might, power, toughness, force, vigour/vigor (US), stamina. **2** sturdiness.

strengthen VERB reinforce, support, fortify.

strenuous ADJECTIVE energetic, vigorous, tough, demanding, exhausting.

stress NOUN strain, pressure, worry, tension. VERB emphasize, underline, highlight, accentuate.

stretch VERB lengthen, elongate, expand, reach.

strict ADJECTIVE **1** harsh, stern, austere, severe, rigorous. *It's a very strict diet.* **2** exact, precise.

stride NOUN walk, march, step.

strike VERB **1** hit, knock, beat, thump, smite, pound. **2** stop work, walk out, down tools.

string NOUN cord, rope, lace, twine, wire.

strip VERB remove, take off, peel, undress, expose, clear, plunder, loot.

strive VERB struggle, try, endeavour/endeavor (US).

stroke VERB fondle, caress, rub, massage.

stroll VERB saunter, amble, promenade, ramble.

strong ADJECTIVE **1** tough, sturdy, muscular, powerful, robust, tough, unbreakable. *A strong personality.* **2** deep, eager, ardent.

stronghold NOUN castle, keep, citadel, fort.

structure NOUN **1** building, edifice. **2** form, design, framework, construction, composition.

struggle VERB wrestle, strive, try, grapple, fight.

stubborn ADJECTIVE obstinate, wilful/willful (US).

student NOUN scholar, pupil, learner, apprentice.

study VERB **1** learn, revise, swot. **2** analyze, consider, investigate, think about, examine.

stuff NOUN **1** substance. **2** cloth, fabric, material, textile. **3** belongings.

stuff VERB **1** cram, pack, fill, compress. **2** gorge.

stumble VERB trip, stagger, fall.

stun VERB daze, amaze, astonish, astound.

stunning ADJECTIVE amazing, gorgeous, beautiful.

stunt NOUN feat, exploit, performance.

stupid ADJECTIVE foolish, silly, idiotic, slow, thick.

sturdy ADJECTIVE strong, robust, solid, well-built.

style NOUN **1** fashion, chic, vogue. **2** way, method.

subject NOUN theme, topic, point. ADJECTIVE liable, prone, susceptible. *Subject to delays.*

submit VERB **1** present, put forward, tender, hand in. **2** give in, surrender, yield.

subsequent ADJECTIVE following, succeeding, later, after.

subside VERB diminish, sink, decrease, lessen.

subtract VERB take away, deduct.

succeed VERB **1** do well, prosper, work well, thrive, triumph. **2** follow, come after, replace, ensue.

success NOUN luck, good fortune, triumph, achievement, victory.

succulent ADJECTIVE juicy, moist.

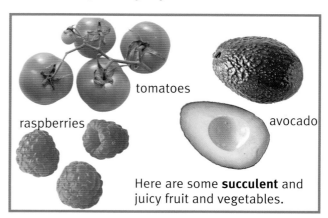

tomatoes

raspberries

avocado

Here are some **succulent** and juicy fruit and vegetables.

a mother supports her child

stilts support this building

a person supported by crutches

Here are some different kinds of **support.**

sudden ADJECTIVE quick, hasty, abrupt, unexpected. An *opposite word* is gradual.

suffer VERB endure, bear, go through, undergo, stand, tolerate, allow.

sufficient ADJECTIVE enough, adequate, ample.

suffocate VERB smother, stifle, strangle, choke.

suggest VERB propose, advise, recommend, put forward, intimate.

suitable ADJECTIVE appropriate, apt, fitting.

sulk VERB mope, glower, brood, grouch.

sullen ADJECTIVE morose, gloomy, glum, moody.

sum NOUN total, whole, amount, aggregate.

summary NOUN resume, outline, digest, synopsis, precis, abridgment.

summit NOUN peak, top, apex, acme, pinnacle.

summon VERB send for, call invite, beckon, rally.

sunny ADJECTIVE bright, clear, fine, cloudless, cheerful, radiant. *A sunny smile.*

sunrise NOUN dawn, daybreak, daylight, morning.

superb ADJECTIVE excellent, splendid, first-rate, magnificent, exquisite.

superficial ADJECTIVE surface, exterior, skin-deep.

superior ADJECTIVE better, greater, higher, excellent, first-class. *Superior quality.*

superlative ADJECTIVE best, greatest, finest, outstanding.

supersede VERB replace, supplant, displace, replace.

superstitious ADJECTIVE illusory, false, credulous.

supervise VERB oversee, manage, control, direct, oversee, superintend, administer.

supple ADJECTIVE flexible, lithe, pliable, bending.

supply VERB give, provide, contribute, sell.

support VERB **1** aid, help, assist, encourage, back, defend. **2** hold up, bear, bolster, prop up. **3** feed, nourish, provide for, maintain.

supporter NOUN fan, follower, defender, ally.

suppose VERB imagine, believe, pretend, guess, deduce, assume, conclude.

suppress VERB quell, put down, crush, subdue, stifle, stop. *The protests were suppressed.*

supreme ADJECTIVE highest, chief, best, greatest, foremost, leading, paramount.

sure ADJECTIVE certain, positive, confident, convinced.

surly ADJECTIVE morose, crusty, testy, bad-tempered.

surplus NOUN excess, remainder, residue.

surprise VERB astonish, amaze, shock, startle, dumbfound, stagger.

surrender VERB give in, yield, concede, renounce, capitulate, forego.

surround VERB encircle, ring, enclose, besiege.

surroundings NOUN environment, background, locality.

survey VERB investigate, study, inspect, scan, scrutinize.

survive VERB live, outlive, last, outlast, keep going.

suspect ADJECTIVE dubious, suspicious. VERB **1** think, fancy, guess. **2** mistrust, doubt.

suspense NOUN uncertainty, anxiety, anticipation, tension, excitement.

suspension NOUN break, stoppage, delay, postponement.

suspicion NOUN mistrust, doubt, misgiving.

swallow VERB **1** eat, drink, devour, gobble. **2** swallow up, absorb, accept, believe. *He swallowed the story.*

swamp NOUN bog, marsh, quagmire, fen.

swap VERB exchange, switch.

swarm VERB crowd, collect, cluster, amass, teem.

swat VERB hit, clout, crush.

sway VERB **1** swing, wave, rock. **2** influence, convince, guide. *She was swayed by his promises.*

swear VERB **1** promise, declare, vow, pledge. **2** curse, damn.

sweep VERB brush, clean, clear.

sweet ADJECTIVE **1** sugary, honeyed, syrupy. **2** charming, agreeable, lovable. *The kittens are sweet.* **3** melodious, dulcet, mellow, tuneful.

swell VERB bulge, get bigger, grow, dilate, expand, puff up. *Opposite words* shrink, contract.

swelling NOUN bump, lump, bulge, boil, protuberance.

swerve VERB veer, turn, bend, dodge, deviate, lurch.

swift ADJECTIVE quick, fast, rapid, speedy, nimble.

swill NOUN **1** rinse, wash. **2** swig, drink, tipple.

swindle VERB cheat, deceive, trick, defraud.

swing VERB sway, dangle, hang, vibrate, rock.

swipe VERB **1** hit, slap. **2** steal.

swirl VERB spin, whirl, churn, eddy.

switch VERB change, swap, replace, transpose, substitute.

swivel VERB spin, revolve, rotate, pivot, turn.

swoop VERB dive, pounce, plunge, pounce.

sword NOUN steel, brand, rapier, foil, cutlass, sabre, scimitar, claymore.

swot (UK) ADJECTIVE study, work hard, revise, cram.

symbol NOUN emblem, sign, token, mark, representation.

symbolize VERB signify, stand for, represent.

sympathy NOUN feeling, pity, compassion, understanding, condolence, harmony.

symptom NOUN sign, indication, mark, evidence, warning.

synthetic ADJECTIVE artificial, manufactured, sham, mock.

system NOUN method, procedure, mode, process, scheme.

systematic ADJECTIVE logical, orderly, efficient, thorough.

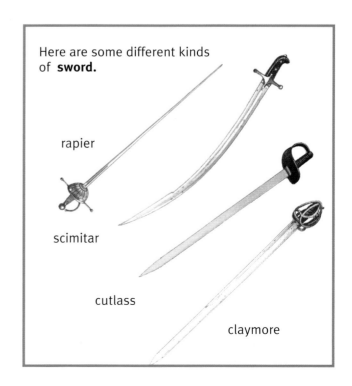

Here are some different kinds of **sword.**

rapier

scimitar

cutlass

claymore

tab NOUN label, sticker, tag.

table NOUN **1** list, index. **2** board, slab, counter.

taboo ADJECTIVE banned, prohibited, unmentionable. *A taboo subject.*

tackle VERB try, attempt, take on, undertake, deal with.

tact NOUN discrimination, delicacy, skill, discretion.

tactics NOUN strategy, plan, policy, method.

tactless ADJECTIVE indiscreet, clumsy, blundering, inept.

tag NOUN label, ticket, docket.

tail NOUN rear, end, extremity.

take VERB **1** grasp, grab, snatch, clasp, hold, seize, pick, choose. capture, catch. **3** carry, convey, deliver, transport. **4** steal, snatch, remove, pinch. **5** bear, tolerate, put up with.

take in VERB understand, realize, grasp.

take after VERB resemble, be like.

take away VERB subtract.

take place VERB occur, happen.

tale NOUN yarn. *See also* **story**.

talent NOUN skill, gift, ability, knack, flair, genius.

talk VERB say, discuss, converse, speak, utter, chat, gossip, natter, prattle, shout, interview.

tall ADJECTIVE high, lofty, lanky, towering.

tame ADJECTIVE obedient, domesticated, trained, gentle. *Opposite words* are wild, savage, dangerous.

tamper VERB interfere, tinker, meddle.

tangle VERB knot, twist, coil, muddle.

tantrum NOUN outburst, temper, hysterics, fury.

tap VERB knock, strike, hit, rap.

target NOUN ambition, objective, aim, goal.

task NOUN job, chore, undertaking, stint, errand.

taste NOUN **1** flavour/flavor (US), tang, salty, sweet, sour, bitter. **2** lick, nibble, mouthful, piece. *Have a taste of this ice cream.* **3** discernment, judgement.

tasty ADJECTIVE delicious, appetising, mouth-watering.

taunt VERB jeer, scoff, tease, sneer, make fun of, torment.

taut ADJECTIVE tight, stiff, tense, stretched.

tawdry ADJECTIVE gaudy, loud, flashy, vulgar.

teach VERB educate, instruct, train, drill, coach, lecture. An *opposite word* is learn.

teacher NOUN instructor, trainer, tutor, lecturer, professor, coach.

team NOUN side, group, company, crew.

tear VERB **1** rip, slit, slash, shred. **2** rush, dash.

tease VERB taunt, pester, badger, bait, make fun of, annoy, laugh at.

tedious ADJECTIVE boring, dreary, humdrum.

Here are some things that are **tall.**

a giraffe is very tall

a tall skyscraper

a tall cactus

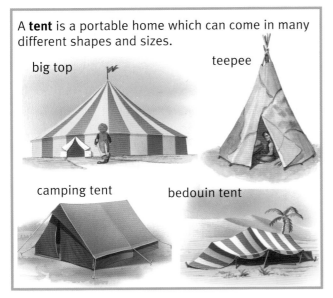

A **tent** is a portable home which can come in many different shapes and sizes.

big top

teepee

camping tent

bedouin tent

teem VERB swarm, crawl with, abound.

telephone VERB call, ring, phone.

tell VERB **1** inform, notify, reveal, admit, state. **2** narrate, relate, describe, recount. **3** order, command, instruct. **4** distinguish. *Can you tell butter from margarine?* **5** work out, figure out.

tell off VERB tick off, scold, rebuke.

temper NOUN mood, rage, anger.

temperamental ADJECTIVE sensitive, moody, touchy, emotional. An *opposite word* is calm.

temple NOUN sanctuary. *See also* **church**.

temporary ADJECTIVE transient, momentary, impermanent, makeshift.

tempt VERB lure, entice, persuade, coax, seduce.

tend VERB **1** be liable to, incline. **2** look after, protect, care for, mind, manage.

tender ADJECTIVE **1** kind, gentle, loving, caring. **2** delicate, soft. **3** sore, sensitive.

tense ADJECTIVE tight, stretched, strained, edgy, nervous. An *opposite word* is relaxed.

tent NOUN wigwam, teepee, big top, marquee.

tepid ADJECTIVE cool, lukewarm, unenthusiastic.

term NOUN **1** time, period, semester. **2** expression, phrase.

terminate VERB end, stop, finish, conclude, close, complete. *Opposite words* are begin, start.

terrible ADJECTIVE awful, dreadful, horrible, vile, frightful, frightening, bad.

terrific ADJECTIVE **1** good, great, excellent. *We had a terrific time.* **2** huge, enormous.

terrify VERB frighten, scare, upset, alarm, horrify, petrify.

territory NOUN region, district, area, domain, country, land, estate.

terror NOUN fear, dread, alarm, panic, horror.

test VERB **1** examine, investigate, study, question. **2** try, check. *Test the light switch.*

tether VERB tie up, chain, fasten, secure, fetter.

texture NOUN grain, surface, pattern, feel.

thaw VERB melt, unfreeze, defrost, soften.

theatrical ADJECTIVE dramatic, affected, ostentatious, showy.

theme NOUN topic, subject, matter, thesis, keynote.

theory NOUN idea, conjecture, hypothesis, opinion.

therefore ADVERB **1** so, thus, consequently, hence. **2** for that reason.

thick ADJECTIVE broad, wide, chunky, dense, sticky, stodgy. *Thick porridge.*

thicken VERB congeal, clot.

thief NOUN robber, burglar, mugger, shoplifter, pickpocket, pilferer.

thin ADJECTIVE **1** slender, lean, skinny. **2** fine, flimsy, delicate, sheer. **3** narrow.

think VERB **1** believe, consider, fancy, reckon, feel, hold. **2** expect, guess, imagine, suppose. **3** concentrate, pay attention. **4** judge, conclude. **5** know, realize.

thirsty ADJECTIVE parched, dry, arid, desiccated.

though ADVERB however, all the same, even so, nevertheless. *The work is hard. I enjoy it though.*

though CONJUNCTION although, while, notwithstanding, and yet, in spite of.

thought NOUN idea, concept, notion, opinion.

thoughtful ADJECTIVE **1** kind, friendly, attentive, considerate. **2** serious, solemn, pensive, reflective.

thoughtless ADJECTIVE unthinking, inconsiderate.

threadbare ADJECTIVE frayed, ragged, shabby.

threat NOUN menace, danger.

threaten VERB menace, loom, bully, intimidate.

thrifty ADJECTIVE frugal, economical, careful, sparing. *Opposite words* are spendthrift, wasteful.

thrilling ADJECTIVE exciting, exhilarating, rousing, stirring. *A thrilling experience.*

thrive VERB flourish, boom, grow, thrive, bloom, succeed. *Opposite words* are fail, die.

throb VERB beat, pulsate, thump, pound.

throng NOUN crowd, mob.

throw VERB hurl, lob, chuck, toss, bowl, fling, sling.

thrust VERB shove, ram, stab, push, poke, jab.

thump VERB hit, punch, clout, batter.

tick VERB mark, indicate.

tide NOUN stream, flow, ebb, trend.

tidy ADJECTIVE neat, smart, orderly, shipshape.

tie VERB fasten, fix, moor, tether, anchor, knot, secure.

tight ADJECTIVE small, close-fitting, fixed, secure.

tilt VERB lean, slope, incline, slant.

time NOUN age, era, period, interval, season.

timid ADJECTIVE nervous, shy, coy, timorous, diffident, fearful. An *opposite word* is confident.

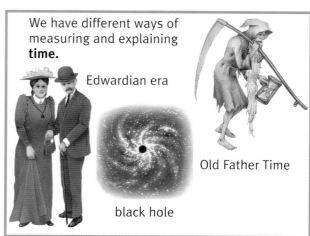

We have different ways of measuring and explaining **time**.

Edwardian era

black hole

Old Father Time

tinge NOUN colour/color (US), shade, tint, tincture, hue, tone.

tingle VERB vibrate, thrill, throb, sting.

tiny ADJECTIVE little, minute, small, microscopic.

tip NOUN **1** end, point, top, head. **2** advice, clue, tip-off. **3** reward, gratuity.

tipsy ADJECTIVE drunk, inebriated.

tire VERB exhaust, fatigue, bore.

tiresome ADJECTIVE boring, annoying, irritating.

tired ADJECTIVE weary, sleepy, exhausted.

tiring ADJECTIVE exhausting, hard.

title NOUN name, designation, rank, status.

titter VERB giggle, snigger, laugh.

toil NOUN work, labour/labor (US), struggle, slave, grind.

token NOUN coupon, voucher, symbol, memento, souvenir.

tolerant ADJECTIVE easy-going, lenient, patient, open-minded.

tolerate VERB put up with, bear, endure, suffer, permit.

too ADVERB **1** as well, besides, in addition. *Can I come too?* **2** very, over, excessively. *Don't drive too fast.*

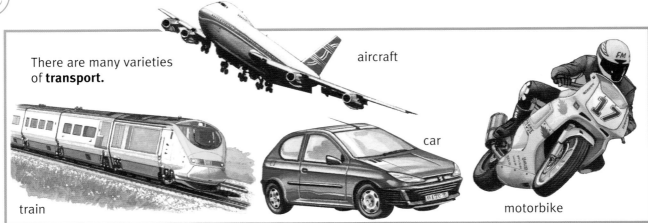

There are many varieties of **transport.**

aircraft

car

train

motorbike

tool NOUN implement, gadget, instrument, utensil, device, contraption.

top NOUN **1** peak, summit. **2** cap, cover, lid.

topic NOUN theme, subject, matter.

torment VERB annoy, bully, tease, pester, provoke.

torture VERB hurt, be cruel to, torment, rack.

toss VERB throw, fling, hurl, chuck.

totter VERB stagger, reel.

touch VERB **1** handle, feel, finger, fiddle with, caress, fondle, hug, stroke, rub, contact, grope. **2** impress, stir.

tough ADJECTIVE **1** strong, firm, rugged, hard, leathery. *Tough meat.* **2** severe, harsh, rigid. **3** arduous, difficult. *A tough exam.*

tour NOUN visit, trip, excursion, ride.

tourist NOUN traveller/traveler (US), sightseer, tripper.

tow VERB haul, pull, drag, tug. A word with a similar sound is toe. *Tow the car away.*

toxic ADJECTIVE poisonous, dangerous, noxious.

trace VERB **1** track, hunt, follow, detect. **2** sketch, draw, copy.

track NOUN road, path, way, footprint.

track VERB follow, hunt, chase, trace, pursue.

tragedy NOUN disaster, calamity, catastrophe.

tragic ADJECTIVE sad, dreadful, unfortunate, disastrous.

train VERB teach, instruct, coach, exercise, practise/practice (US).

tranquil ADJECTIVE peaceful, quiet, placid, calm.

transfer VERB switch, change, move, transmit.

transform VERB turn, change, alter, adapt.

transmit VERB send, dispatch, relay, forward, communicate.

transparent ADJECTIVE clear, translucent, see-through, obvious, plain, lucid.

transport VERB carry, convey, move.

trap VERB capture, catch, ensnare, ambush.

travel VERB journey, voyage, tour, trek, cycle, drive, fly, hitchhike, ride, sail, walk.

treachery NOUN disloyalty, unfaithfulness, betrayal. An *opposite word* is loyalty.

tread VERB walk, trample, plod, trudge.

treasure NOUN wealth, riches, booty, hoard.

treat VERB care for, look after, handle, nurse, doctor.

treaty NOUN agreement, pact.

tree NOUN evergreen, conifer, shrub. Some different kinds of tree: alder, ash, beech, birch, cedar, chestnut, elm, fir, holly, horse chestnut, larch, lime, maple, mulberry, oak, palm.

tremble VERB quake, quiver, shake, shudder, shiver, vibrate.

tremor NOUN shaking, vibration, trembling, quake.

trend NOUN inclination, tendency, fashion, style, vogue.

tribe NOUN race, clan, family, dynasty, sect.

trick NOUN **1** fraud, deception, hoax. **2** prank, practical joke, jape.

trickle VERB drip, leak, dribble, seep.

tricky ADJECTIVE difficult, delicate, awkward.

trim VERB **1** decorate, ornament. **2** *See* **cut**.

trip NOUN outing, excursion, visit, tour, jaunt, spin, drive. *Take a trip to the seaside.* VERB stumble, slip, stagger.

triumph NOUN victory, achievement, success, conquest. An *opposite word* is defeat.

trivial ADJECTIVE unimportant, trifling, petty, paltry.

trouble NOUN **1** misfortune, distress, hardship, difficulty, worry. **2** unrest, row, bother, disturbance, disorder. **3** care, effort.

trouble VERB annoy, upset, bother, pester, worry.

truce NOUN peace, armistice.

trudge VERB plod, tramp, trek, march.

true ADJECTIVE **1** correct, right, factual, real, genuine, authentic. **2** loyal, reliable, honest, sincere, constant.

trust VERB count on, depend on, rely on, be sure of, believe in. *Opposite words* are distrust, doubt.

trusting ADJECTIVE trustful, innocent, unquestioning.

truth NOUN honesty, fact, reality.

try VERB **1** attempt, strive, aim, endeavour/endeavor (US). **2** test, sample, try out, taste. *Try this coat for size.*

trying ADJECTIVE troublesome, annoying, irksome.

tuck VERB fold, insert, push.

tumble VERB fall, topple, drop.

tune NOUN melody, song, air.

turmoil NOUN trouble, disorder, chaos, confusion.

turn VERB **1** spin, rotate, revolve, twirl, twist. **2** become, change into. **3** curve, twist, bend. **4** convert, transform.

turret NOUN tower, spire, steeple, minaret.

tussle VERB struggle, fight, scuffle.

twaddle NOUN nonsense, prattle, drivel, bunkum, gossip.

twinkle VERB sparkle, shine, flash.

twirl VERB whirl, turn, spin.

twist VERB **1** writhe, distort. **2** interweave, intertwine, wind, wreathe.

type NOUN kind, sort, variety, species, breed, style.

typical ADJECTIVE usual, normal, common, characteristic.

tyrant NOUN dictator, despot, autocrat.

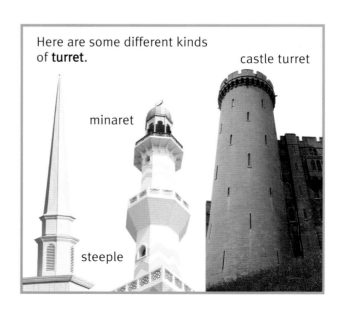

Here are some different kinds of **turret**.

castle turret

minaret

steeple

ugly ADJECTIVE unattractive, unsightly, hideous, repulsive. An *opposite word* is beautiful.

ultimate ADJECTIVE last, eventual, final.

umpire NOUN referee, judge, arbiter.

unable ADJECTIVE incapable, helpless, ineffective.

unanimous ADJECTIVE agreeing, consenting, uniform, united. An *opposite word* is disunited.

unbiased ADJECTIVE fair, unbiased, impartial, disinterested. An *opposite word* is biased.

unbroken ADJECTIVE **1** whole, complete. **2** continuous, endless. **3** unbeaten.

uncanny ADJECTIVE strange, weird, unearthly, eerie, bizarre.

uncertain ADJECTIVE unsure, doubtful, unconvinced.

uncommon ADJECTIVE rare, infrequent, unusual, odd, scarce. An *opposite word* is common.

unconscious ADJECTIVE **1** insensible, stunned, knocked out. **2** unaware, ignorant, oblivious.

uncouth ADJECTIVE clumsy, loutish, boorish, crude, coarse.

uncover VERB reveal, expose, show, unveil.

undecided ADJECTIVE unsure, hesitant, dubious, wavering, in two minds.

undergo VERB bear, suffer, tolerate, endure, go through, weather.

underhand ADJECTIVE sly, deceitful, stealthy, sneaky, dishonest. *Opposite words* are honest, open.

underline VERB emphasize, highlight, underscore.

undermine VERB **1** excavate, tunnel. **2** weaken.

understand VERB **1** comprehend, see, grasp, realize, twig, sympathize. **2** hear, learn, believe.

undertaking NOUN venture, attempt, enterprise.

undo VERB untie, unfasten, open, free, unravel.

undue ADJECTIVE excessive, unnecessary, undeserved. *Undue praise and attention.*

unearth VERB uncover, dig up, find.

unearthly ADJECTIVE strange, weird, uncanny, eerie, supernatural.

uneasy ADJECTIVE worried, anxious, restless, edgy.

unemployed ADJECTIVE out of work, unoccupied, jobless, redundant. An *opposite word* is employed.

unequal ADJECTIVE uneven, disproportionate, varying. An *opposite word* is equal.

uneven ADJECTIVE **1** bumpy, rough. **2** irregular.

unexpected ADJECTIVE sudden, surprising, unforeseen, chance. An *opposite word* is expected.

All these animals are **uncommon**.

leopard

tiger

white rhino

orang utan

unfair ADJECTIVE unjust, wrong, prejudiced, biased, one-sided. *Opposite words* are fair, impartial.

unfasten VERB undo, detach, open, release, untie.

unfit ADJECTIVE **1** incompetent, unable, unqualified, incapable. **2** unhealthy.

unfold VERB open, unroll, unwrap, spread, reveal.

unfortunate ADJECTIVE unlucky, unhappy, deplorable. An *opposite word* is fortunate.

unfriendly ADJECTIVE cold, unkind, hostile, aloof.

ungainly ADJECTIVE awkward, clumsy, lumbering.

unhappy ADJECTIVE sad, gloomy, miserable, depressed. An *opposite word* is happy.

uniform ADJECTIVE unchanging, constant, steady, regular.

unify VERB combine, unite, amalgamate.

unimportant ADJECTIVE petty, trivial, trifling, irrelevant.

uninteresting ADJECTIVE boring, dull, tedious, monotonous, prosaic.

union NOUN **1** alliance, association, combination, amalgamation, blend, mixture, fusion. **2** agreement, harmony.

unique ADJECTIVE single, only, exceptional, sole.

unison NOUN harmony, agreement, unity.

unit NOUN one, individual, component, part, element.

unite VERB combine, join, connect, link, merge, marry. An *opposite word* is separate.

universal ADJECTIVE world-wide, general, whole, entire, total, unlimited.

unkempt ADJECTIVE dishevelled/disheveled (US), scruffy, tousled. An *opposite word* is neat.

unkind ADJECTIVE cruel, callous, pitiless, heartless, unfriendly. An *opposite word* is kind.

unlikely ADJECTIVE improbable, incredible, dubious, far-fetched, remote. An *opposite word* is likely.

To **unite** is to join together.

The United States of America

The United Kingdom

united businesses

unite in matrimony

unlock VERB open, release, unbolt.

unlucky ADJECTIVE unfortunate, ill-fated, unsuccessful. An *opposite word* is lucky.

unnatural ADJECTIVE **1** unusual, uncommon, abnormal. **2** artificial, affected, forced, false, stilted.

unoccupied ADJECTIVE empty, vacant, open, uninhabited. An *opposite word* is occupied.

unpleasant ADJECTIVE **1** dreadful, frightening, terrible, upsetting. **2** rude, unfriendly. **3** nasty, disgusting, obnoxious. An *opposite word* is pleasant.

unpopular ADJECTIVE disliked, friendless, shunned.

unravel VERB disentangle, unwind, sort out, solve.

unreasonable ADJECTIVE irrational, immoderate, unwise, excessive.

unreliable ADJECTIVE untrustworthy, unsound, undependable, fickle.

unrest NOUN disturbance, turmoil, upset, agitation.

unruly ADJECTIVE disobedient, uncontrollable, rebellious, riotous, rowdy, disorderly.

unscathed ADJECTIVE unharmed, undamaged.

unscrupulous ADJECTIVE dishonest, unprincipled.

unseemly ADJECTIVE shocking, indecent, improper.

unsightly ADJECTIVE ugly, hideous, unattractive.

unskilled ADJECTIVE inexpert, inexperienced.

unsound ADJECTIVE **1** imperfect, impaired, unhealthy, feeble. **2** wrong, incorrect, false.

unstable ADJECTIVE shaky, unsteady, wobbly, fickle, changeable, variable.

unsuitable ADJECTIVE unacceptable, inappropriate.

untidy ADJECTIVE disorderly, jumbled, muddled, scruffy, disorganized, cluttered.

untie VERB undo, unfasten, release, free.

untold ADJECTIVE countless, measureless, undreamed of.

unusual ADJECTIVE uncommon, odd, strange, curious, surprising.

unwell ADJECTIVE sick, ill, ailing, poorly.

unwelcome ADJECTIVE uninvited, rejected, not wanted, upsetting, disagreeable, distasteful.

unwieldy ADJECTIVE heavy, unmanageable, cumbersome. An *opposite word* is manageable.

unwilling ADJECTIVE averse, reluctant, opposed.

unwrap VERB open, unfold, undo.

update VERB modernize, revise, revamp, improve.

upheaval NOUN disruption, turmoil, confusion.

uphold VERB support, keep up, back, defend.

upkeep NOUN support, maintenance, care.

upright ADJECTIVE **1** perpendicular, vertical. **2** honest, good, just, honourable/honorable (US).

uproar NOUN disorder, turmoil, noise, tumult.

uproot VERB pull up, eradicate, destroy, remove.

upset VERB **1** spill, knock over, topple. **2** frighten, trouble, worry, bother.

uptight ADJECTIVE angry, nervous.

urge NOUN wish, desire, compulsion, impulse, drive. VERB entreat, encourage, beg, goad, plead.

urgent ADJECTIVE important, vital, pressing, immediate, crucial, priority.

usage NOUN **1** tradition, custom, habit, routine, practice, fashion. **2** handling, use, treatment.

use VERB **1** employ, utilize, apply. **2** consume, finish.

useful ADJECTIVE helpful, valuable, handy, practical, convenient.

useless ADJECTIVE unusable, incompetent, worthless, futile.

usual ADJECTIVE ordinary, regular common, expected, habitual, customary.

utensil NOUN *See* **tool**.

utilize VERB employ, use, exploit.

utmost ADJECTIVE greatest, extreme, last, distant, farthest.

utter VERB speak, say, pronounce, express.

utterly ADVERB completely, entirely, wholly.

U-turn NOUN about-face, reversal, turn about.

Here are some different kinds of **utensil.**

frying pan

rolling pin

mop

dustpan and brush

Vv

vacant ADJECTIVE unoccupied, free, not in use, void. *Opposite words* are occupied, full.

vacation NOUN holiday, rest, recreation.

vacuum NOUN emptiness, space, void.

vague ADJECTIVE **1** forgetful, absent-minded. **2** indefinite, imprecise, uncertain, undetermined.

vain ADJECTIVE proud, conceited, arrogant. Words that sound similar are vane, vein.

valiant ADJECTIVE brave, gallant, courageous, intrepid, heroic, stout, staunch.

valley NOUN dale, vale, dell, glen.

valuable ADJECTIVE **1** precious, priceless, expensive. **2** helpful, worthwhile, constructive.

value NOUN cost, price, worth, use. VERB prize, treasure.

vanish VERB disappear, go away, fade, depart, go.

vanity NOUN pride, conceit, big-headed.

vanquish VERB beat, conquer, subdue, overcome.

vapour/vapor (US) NOUN steam, fog, haze, smoke.

varied ADJECTIVE mixed, diverse, assorted.

variety NOUN **1** difference, assortment, mixture. *A variety of ice cream.* **2** kind, type, sort, class.

various ADJECTIVE mixed, different, numerous, varied, several. *She has various names.*

vary VERB change, alter, differ, diverge.

vast ADJECTIVE enormous, immense, colossal, huge, wide.

vault VERB *See* **jump**.

veer VERB shift, change, swerve.

vegetable NOUN. Some different kinds of vegetable: artichoke, asparagus, broad bean, broccoli, Brussels sprouts, cabbage, carrot, cauliflower, celery, French bean, kale, kohlrabi, lentil, okra, onion, parsnip, pea, potato, radish, shallot, soybean, spinach, squash, sweet potato, tomatoes, turnip, yam.

vehicle NOUN conveyance, transport carriage, car.

veil VERB cover, hide, mask, conceal.

velocity NOUN speed, swiftness, rate.

vengeance NOUN revenge, retaliation.

ventilate VERB air, freshen.

venture NOUN chance, risk, undertaking.

verbal ADJECTIVE spoken, oral, said, unwritten.

verbose ADJECTIVE wordy, long-winded, loquacious.

verdict NOUN decision, judgement, conclusion, sentence. *The jury reached their verdict.*

verge NOUN edge, margin, rim, border.

verge VERB incline, lean, come close to.

verify VERB authenticate, confirm, bear out, testify.

versatile ADJECTIVE adaptable, flexible, capable, skilled.

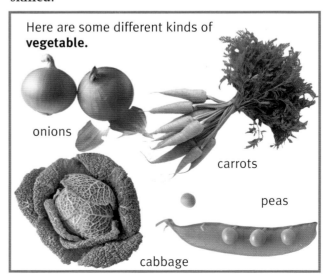

Here are some different kinds of **vegetable.**

onions

carrots

peas

cabbage

Vv

verse NOUN rhyme, poem, jingle.

vertical ADJECTIVE perpendicular, upright, erect.

vessel NOUN **1** craft. **2** bowl. *See also* **boat, container**.

veto VERB forbid, prohibit, reject, turn down.

viable ADJECTIVE workable, practicable, feasible.

vibrate VERB shake, quiver, shudder, tremble.

vicinity NOUN surroundings, proximity.

vicious ADJECTIVE savage, cruel, ruthless, malicious, wicked, depraved.

victim NOUN prey, dupe, sufferer, casualty.

victory NOUN triumph, win, success, conquest, achievement. *Opposite words* are defeat, loss.

view NOUN **1** scene, spectacle, vista. **2** opinion, belief, impression.

view VERB watch. *See* **see, observe, survey**.

vigilant ADJECTIVE watchful, wary, alert, on the look out.

vigorous ADJECTIVE **1** active, energetic, dynamic. **2** healthy, strong, robust.

vile ADJECTIVE wicked, mean, nasty, disgusting, foul, revolting.

vindictive ADJECTIVE spiteful, unforgiving.

violent ADJECTIVE **1** strong, severe, destructive, rough. **2** fierce, fiery, cruel, brutal, ferocious.

virile ADJECTIVE manly, strong, vigorous, robust.

virtual ADJECTIVE essential, substantial.

virtue NOUN goodness, excellence, honesty.

visible ADJECTIVE clear, plain, obvious, evident, noticeable, observable.

vision NOUN **1** seeing, sight. **2** perception, foresight. **3** ghost, spectre/specter (US), apparition.

visit VERB call, drop in, stay at, stop.

visitor NOUN caller, guest, tourist.

visualize VERB imagine, picture.

vital ADJECTIVE essential, necessary, indispensable, fundamental.

vivacious ADJECTIVE lively, sprightly, animated, high-spirited.

vivid ADJECTIVE colourful/colorful (US), bright, lucid, clear, striking. *A vivid sunset.*

vocation NOUN calling, career, profession, occupation, business, pursuit.

vogue NOUN style, fashion, mode, trend, fad.

void ADJECTIVE **1** empty, unoccupied. **2** null, invalid, annulled.

volume NOUN **1** amount, mass, size, capacity, quantity. **2** book, tome.

vote VERB elect, choose, select, ballot, opt.

vow VERB promise, pledge, swear, give your word.

voyage NOUN journey, cruise, passage, crossing.

vulgar ADJECTIVE rude, coarse, common, bad-mannered, impolite, indecent.

vulnerable ADJECTIVE unprotected, exposed, sensitive, defenceless/defenseless (US).

A **vessel** is any kind of container.

vase of flowers

FIRE

bucket

boat

tumbler and carafe

wad NOUN pack, packet, bundle. *A wad of money.*

waddle VERB shuffle, wobble, toddle.

wag VERB flap, wave, shake, wiggle.

wage NOUN earnings, pay, salary, fee.

wage VERB undertake, conduct, carry on. *Wage war.*

wait VERB stay, remain, stop, halt, linger, pause, delay, hesitate.

waive VERB forego, renounce, yield.

wake VERB rouse, awaken, call.

wakeful ADJECTIVE alert, vigilant, observant, wary.

walk VERB march, step, tread, stroll, amble, hike, trek, tramp, trudge, saunter, plod, creep, stride, shuffle, strut, tiptoe.

wall NOUN screen, partition, barrier.

wallow VERB **1** roll, flounder, loll, wade. *Wallowing in a bath.* **2** enjoy, revel, indulge. *Wallowing in wealth.*

wander VERB stray, roam, rove, meander, drift.

wane VERB decrease, decline, lessen, recede, ebb, sink, shrink.

want VERB wish for, desire, crave, long for, need, require.

war NOUN battle, fighting, combat, hostilities, invasion, siege. An *opposite word* is peace.

warden NOUN custodian, guardian, keeper, protector, supervisor, caretaker.

warehouse NOUN depot, store, repository.

warm ADJECTIVE **1** tepid, luke-warm, sultry. **2** enthusiastic, kind, friendly. *A warm welcome.*

warn VERB give notice, caution, alert, notify, admonish.

warrior NOUN hero, champion, soldier.

wary ADJECTIVE careful, cautious, watchful, prudent, vigilant.

wash VERB clean, cleanse, bath, scrub, rinse, shampoo, mop.

washing NOUN laundry, cleaning.

wasteful ADJECTIVE extravagant, lavish, spendthrift, prodigal. An *opposite word* is thrifty.

watch VERB **1** *See* **gaze at**, **observe**, **view**. **2** look after, mind, guard, oversee.

watchful ADJECTIVE attentive, vigilant, wakeful, alert. An *opposite word* is inattentive.

water VERB dampen, moisten, wet, sprinkle, spray.

A **warrior** is someone who fights.

Maori warrior

Greek footsoldier

Samurai warrior

David killed Goliath with a slingshot

251

watery ADJECTIVE **1** damp, wet. **2** diluted, watered-down, weak.

wave VERB flutter, flap, flourish, shake, signal, gesticulate. *She waved goodbye.*

waver VERB hesitate, dither, swither, vacillate, falter.

wax VERB increase, grow, enlarge. An *opposite word* is wane.

way NOUN **1** method, system, technique. **2** style, manner. *The way she walks.* **3** route, direction, path, road. *Do you know the way to my house?*

way-out NOUN exit, outlet, exodus, departure, farewell. An *opposite word* is entrance.

weak ADJECTIVE delicate, faint, feeble, frail, fragile, puny, flimsy, watery. *A weak excuse.*

wealthy ADJECTIVE rich, prosperous, affluent, prosperous. An *opposite word* is poor.

weapon NOUN dagger, dirk, bomb, mine, bow and arrow, longbow, crossbow, catapult, boomerang, torpedo, tomahawk, truncheon.

wear VERB **1** have on, dress in, carry, bear. **2** rub, use, scrape, corrode, consume, deteriorate. *Your soles have worn thin.*

Here are some different types of **weapon.**
axe
bow and arrow
rapier

weary ADJECTIVE tired, exhausted, worn out, dead beat, whacked. An *opposite word* is fresh.

weather NOUN climate, condition, temperature.

weather VERB **1** last, endure, survive, resist, withstand. **2** ill, depressed. *Under the weather.* Some different kinds of weather: **1** chilly, cold, cool, freezing, frosty, icy, snowy, wintry. **2** close, fair, fine, hot, mild, sunny, warm. **3** damp, drizzly, rainy, showery, wet. **4** cloudy, foggy, hazy, misty. **5** blustery, breezy, stormy, windy.

weave VERB plait, braid, knit, entwine, unite.

wedding NOUN marriage, wedlock, matrimony, nuptials. An *opposite word* is divorce.

wedge NOUN chock, block, chunk.

wedge VERB force, push, jam, thrust, ram.

weedy ADJECTIVE skinny, thin, weak, wimpish/wimpy (US).

week NOUN The seven days of the week are: Monday, Tuesday, Wednesday, Thursday, Friday, Saturday, Sunday.

weigh VERB balance, gauge, evaluate, consider, think. A word that sounds similar is way.

weird ADJECTIVE strange, odd, peculiar, scary, creepy, uncanny, unearthly.

well ADJECTIVE healthy, fit, hale, sound.

well ADVERB properly, adequately, properly, correctly, ably, greatly. *She swims well.*

wet ADJECTIVE **1** damp, dank, moist, soaking, drenched, wringing-wet, soggy. **2** rainy, showery, drizzly. *Opposite words are* dry, arid, parched. **3** feeble (UK). *See also* **weedy.**

wet VERB moisten, dampen, soak, water, sprinkle, spray, drench, drown.

whet VERB **1** sharpen, grind, strop. **2** stimulate, excite. *Whet the appetite.*

whiff NOUN a whiff of scandal. hint, breath, trace. **2** See **scent, smell.**

whim NOUN fancy, notion, impulse, humour/humor (US).

Here are some different kinds of **wind instrument.**

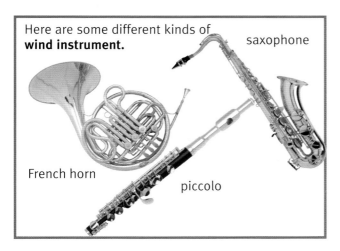

saxophone

French horn

piccolo

whimper VERB whine, moan, cry, wail, complain.

whip VERB flog, thrash. *See also* **hit**.

whirl VERB *See* **spin**.

whisper VERB murmur, mutter, hint, disclose.

whistle VERB cheep, chirp, tweet.

whole ADJECTIVE complete, entire, undamaged, sound.

wicked ADJECTIVE evil, bad, wrong, depraved, immoral. An *opposite word* is good, virtuous.

wide ADJECTIVE broad, large, extensive, vast.

widespread ADJECTIVE far-flung, universal, general.

width NOUN breadth, wideness, thickness, range.

wield VERB use, handle, brandish, control.

wild ADJECTIVE **1** untamed, savage, undomesticated. **2** stormy, violent, rough. **3** noisy, rowdy, turbulent, unruly. *A wild party.* **4** uncultivated. *A wild forest.*

wilderness NOUN wasteland, desert, outback.

will NOUN **1** choice, preference, wish, order, command. **2** determination, decision. **3** legacy, testament.

willing ADJECTIVE ready, eager, disposed, agreeable, helpful.

wilt VERB wither, shrivel, sag, droop, dry up. An *opposite word* is thrive.

wily ADJECTIVE sly, sneaky, cunning, scheming, designing, crafty.

win VERB **1** earn, gain, acquire, receive. **2** succeed, triumph. An *opposite word* is lose.

wince VERB flinch, blench, shrink, start.

wind NOUN draught, air, gust, gale, breeze, hurricane, cyclone, typhoon, whirlwind.

wind VERB curl, twist, coil, twine, curve, meander. *The road winds up the hill.*

wind instruments NOUN oboe, clarinet, flute, piccolo, bassoon, saxophone.

wink VERB blink, squint, flicker, flash.

winner NOUN victor, champion.

wipe VERB clean, dust, polish, dry, mop, swab, take away.

wise ADJECTIVE sensible, intelligent, thoughtful, astute, sage. An *opposite word* is silly.

wish VERB **1** want, desire, long for. **2** require, order.

wit NOUN humour/humor (US), sparkle, intelligence, wisdom, cleverness, discernment. *He had a very sharp wit.*

withdraw VERB **1** retreat, retire, pull back, depart, flee. **2** recant, retract, revoke.

withdrawn ADJECTIVE aloof, shy, unsociable.

wither VERB pine, languish. *See also* **wilt**.

withhold VERB retain, keep back, reserve. *Opposite words* are give, grant.

witness VERB observe, notice, see, watch, bear out.

witty ADJECTIVE funny, humorous, droll, amusing, clever, facetious.

wobble VERB shake, tremble, sway.

woe NOUN sorrow, grief, anguish, misery, unhappiness. An *opposite word* is joy.

wonder VERB ask yourself, question, ponder, conjecture, marvel at.

wonderful ADJECTIVE amazing, fabulous, superb, astonishing. An *opposite word* is dreadful.

won't VERB the short form of 'will not'.

wood NOUN **1** copse, grove, thicket, forest. **2** timber, boards, planks, logs.

word NOUN **1** term, expression, statement. **2** news, information. *We sent word of the president's arrival.* **3** command, order, instruction. *Stop, when I give the word.* **4** promise, pledge. *Always keep your word.* Some different kinds of word:**nouns** names of people, things or ideas for example John, men, hope. **pronouns** words used in place of a noun as in he (for John), they (for men), it (for hope). **adjectives** words that describe a noun or adjective for example **white** houses, **dark green** shirt. **adverbs** words that tell how or when something happens for example talk **loudly. verbs** words that describe action, experience or state for example 'Jim **worked** hard.'

work NOUN **1** labour/labor (US), effort, toil, chore, drudgery. **2** employment, job, career, profession, occupation, business, trade.

work VERB **1** toil, labour/labor (US), struggle. **2** go, function, operate, act, play. *The TV doesn't work.* **3** use, operate. *Can you work a computer?*

worn-out ADJECTIVE **1** exhausted, weary, whacked, dead beat. **2** used, ragged, shabby.

worry VERB be anxious, be concerned, fret. **2** upset, irritate. *See also* **annoy**.

worsen VERB deteriorate, get worse, decline, aggravate. An *opposite word* is improve.

worship VERB adore, venerate, idolize, exalt, love.

worth VERB value, merit, cost, usefulness.

worthless ADJECTIVE useless, valueless, cheap. An *opposite word* is valuable.

worthy ADJECTIVE honest, admirable, fine, praiseworthy, deserving.

wound VERB **1** hurt, injure, harm, cut, damage, bruise. **2** is upset, distress, insult. *Wounded pride.* An *opposite word* is **1** heal.

wrap VERB cover, enclose, pack, envelop, enfold.

wrath NOUN anger, fury, rage, indignation.

wreck VERB destroy, break, smash, shatter, ruin, ravage. *Opposite words* are reconstruct, rebuild.

wreckage NOUN remains, rubble, flotsam and jetsam.

wrench VERB twist, strain, sprain, pull, yank, rick.

wrestle VERB fight, battle, contest, struggle.

wretched ADJECTIVE **1** unhappy, miserable, forlorn. **2** pitiable, pathetic.

wriggle VERB writhe, twist, squirm, worm.

wring VERB twist, squeeze, force, mangle.

write VERB **1** scribble, pen, scrawl, jot down, type. **2** compose. *She writes music.*

writer NOUN author, novelist, journalist, poet, playwright, hack, scribe.

wrong ADJECTIVE **1** evil, wicked, criminal, sinful, immoral. **2** incorrect, false, untrue, mistaken. **3** unfair, unjust.

wry ADJECTIVE twisted, distorted, crooked, ironic, sardonic. *She has a wry smile.*

There are many different types of **writer.**

novelist

playwright

journalist

yank VERB jerk, snatch, pull.

yap VERB bark, yelp, prattle.

yard NOUN court, enclosure, quadrangle, garden.

yardstick NOUN measure, criterion, standard.

yarn NOUN **1** tale, story, anecdote. **2** thread, fibre/fiber (US).

yawn VERB gape, open.

year NOUN The months of the year: January, February, March, April, May, June, July, August, September, October, November, December.

yearly ADJECTIVE and ADVERB annually, once a year, per annum.

yearn VERB long for, hanker after, desire, want.

yell VERB shout, call out, cry, shriek, scream.

yield VERB **1** surrender, give in, succumb. **2** produce, provide, bring in.

yoke NOUN harness, link, chain, bond, burden, oppression. A word with a similar sound is yolk.

yonder ADJECTIVE and ADVERB over there, in the distance.

young ADJECTIVE youthful, juvenile, junior, little, immature. *Opposite words* are adult, old, mature.

youth NOUN **1** lad, youngster, young man, boy. **2** adolescence, childhood.

zany ADJECTIVE funny, clownish, comical, goofy, daft. An *opposite word* is serious.

zap VERB **1** attack, shoot, destroy. **2** switch suddenly. **3** delete data.

zeal NOUN enthusiasm, fervour/fervor (US), passion, devotion, dedication. An *opposite word* is indifference.

zenith NOUN peak, apex, summit, climax, high point, pinnacle. An *opposite word* is nadir.

zero NOUN nil, nought, nothing, duck, zilch.

zest NOUN relish, gusto, zeal, enthusiasm.

zigzag VERB twist and turn, wind, snake.

zodiac NOUN The signs of the zodiac: Aries (The Ram), Taurus (The Bull), Gemini (The Twins), Cancer (The Crab), Leo (The Lion), Virgo (The Virgin), Libra (The Scales), Scorpio (The Scorpion), Sagittarius (The Archer), Capricorn (The Goat), Aquarius (The Water-carrier), Pisces (The Fishes).

zone NOUN area, district, region, sector, territory.

zoo NOUN zoological gardens, menagerie, aquarium, aviary.

zoom VERB flash, streak, whizz, shoot.

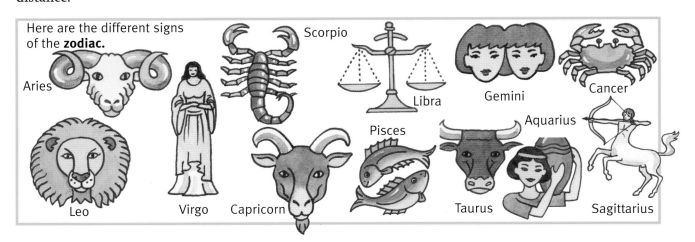

Here are the different signs of the **zodiac.**

Aries Scorpio Libra Gemini Cancer Pisces Aquarius Leo Virgo Capricorn Taurus Sagittarius